The Art of
Bolivian Highland
Weaving

The Art of Bolivian Highland Weaving

by Marjorie Cason and Adele Cahlander

WATSON-GUPTILL PUBLICATIONS, NEW YORK

To the weaver-craftsmen of Bolivia
whose artistry has delighted us,
and whose craftsmanship is both
a challenge and an inspiration.

Copyright © 1976 by Watson-Guptill Publications
First published 1976 in New York by Watson-Guptill Publications
a division of Billboard Publications, Inc.,
1515 Broadway, New York, N.Y. 10036

Manufactured in U.S.A.

Library of Congress Cataloging in Publication Data
Cason, Marjorie.
    The art of Bolivian Highland weaving.
    Bibliography: p.
    Includes index.
    1. Hand weaving—Bolivia.   I.   Cahlander, Adele,
joint author.   II.   Title.
TT848.C3   746.1′4   76-41703
ISBN 0-8230-0264-0

First Printing, 1976

Acknowledgments

It has been a joy for us to gather together all the material for this book. We hope to share not only what we have learned, but also some of the excitement and wonder. We are indebted to many for their various helpful contributions along the way. Our sincere thanks:

● First, to our husbands, Wallace Cason and Loren Cahlander, who encouraged and understood us.

● To Suzanne Gaston, who taught us both and gave initial encouragement to Margie on the project.

● To Grace Goodell, whose article in *Natural History* magazine deepened our insight, and who later helped us personally.

● To Felipa Paucara, who was willing to teach Margie the beginning techniques on narrow pattern bands, in spite of their language barrier, and to Juana, her sister-in-law, who showed Margie how the awayo is woven.

● To many others in Bolivia, who made our research there possible: students at Ancoraimes; Sr. Jaime Urioste Arana and Srta. Maria Elizabeth Rojas Toro at the University Museums, Sucre; Sra. Rojas and her Quechua neighbors; Rev. Kenneth Fowler, various students, and the director at the Seminaria at Carachipampa; Dr. Jaime Ampuero in Sucre; Sra. Flora de Mendoza at the Bazar Kantuta, Sucre; Mrs. Bruce Anderson, Mlle. Micheline Beauchemin, Mrs. Ruth McFarren, and Mrs. Ann Smith, whose personal collections we were permitted to photograph; Sr. Freddie Javier Flores and his wife Martha, our interpreters among the Quechuas; and Sandy Harrison who helped us in Bolivia and also later in the States.

● To those who have generously shared their fabrics and/or photos for us to study since our return from Bolivia: Harriet Adams, Steve Berger, Judy Conger, Phil Druker, Jim Drum, Merry Elg, Ann Houston, Charlie Jirousek, Ruth McFarren, Jacquetta Nisbet, Michael O'Neal, Bill Schulze, Bill Siegal, Alice Snow, Craig Springer, Carole Toreano, Ann Wynia, and most especially, Lynn Meisch, who has shared her many treasures so generously across the country, and from which we have learned so much.

● To the museums that granted us permission to reproduce photographs of items from their collections: The American Museum of Natural History, Department of Anthropology, New York; The International Folk Art Collections in the Museum of International Folk Art, a division of the Museum of New Mexico, Santa Fe, New Mexico; The Museum of the American Indian, Heye Foundation, New York; The Musée de l'Homme, Paris, France; and The Museo Colonial Charcas, Museo Antropológico, Sucre, Bolivia.

● To various museum staff members who shared some of their expertise and made it possible for us to study items in the museum collections: Dr. Junius B. Bird, curator of South American Archaeology at the American Museum of Natural History, and his assistant, Mrs. Milica Skinner; Nora Fisher, curator of textiles, and Jim Drum, head of exhibitions, at the Museum of International Folk Art, Museum of New Mexico; Phyllis Dillon, conservator, Anna Roosevelt, curator of

Middle and South American collections, and Lynette Miller, registrar, at the Museum of the American Indian; and Sr. Jaime Urioste Arana, supervisor de Museo Colonial Charcas, Sucre, Bolivia.

● To Irene Emery, curator of technical studies, and Anne P. Rowe, assistant curator, western hemisphere textiles, at the Washington, D.C., Textile Museum, and to Nobuko Kajitani, associate textile conservator at the Metropolitan Museum of Art, for stimulating discussions and communications regarding various aspects of the weave structure of Bolivian fabrics.

● To Irene Emery's book, *The Primary Structures of Fabrics,* whose classification and terminology we tried to follow to the extent that they seemed adaptable to our purposes.

● To David Cahlander and Mel Jacobsen, who advised and encouraged Adele in her photo work, and to Byron Bennett, Mel's assistant, who not only photographed all the sample bands and some other items, but gave special attention to the many enlargements he made from Adele's photos and various slides she gathered together.

● To Nancy Jacobsen, who came to our rescue and typed the last part of our manuscript.

● To Jacquetta Nisbet and Esther Warner Dendel for their enthusiasm, counsel and encouragement.

● To the Handweavers Guild of America, who published our magazine article in *Shuttle, Spindle & Dyepot,* and to Ruth Holroyd and her slide library committee, for preparing a rental slide kit, combining some of our slides with Ann Houston's collection.

● To the Weavers Guild of Minnesota, who gave us valuable experience by asking us to present programs and to teach classes and workshops.

● To members of our Bolivian study group, who have shared our excitement and helped with the latter part of the book, especially to Sue Baizerman, who has given counsel and helped in many ways to motivate us all.

● To Adele's daughters, Lorraine Anderson and Marianne Borgeson, who helped in various ways.

● And, lastly, a special note of thanks to all those who graciously offered to care for Yaska, Margie's son, at times of special need from his birth through toddlerhood.

May this book open some new vistas for you!

Marjorie Cason
Adele Cahlander
1976

Contents

Preface

First contact with the fascinating color and designs of highland Bolivian weaving came to Margie Cason in 1970, when she and her husband spent a year in a missionary school in the village of Ancoraimes near Lake Titicaca, the legendary birthplace of the Incas. While walking in the streets and markets, she could not keep her eyes off the beautiful *awayos*—large squares of homespun wool fabric in which the women carried their babies or other burdens on their backs. She found the colors were in exciting shades and the designs of the bands intriguing.

Margie had an art background and soon began sketching the designs she had seen in the street. Not daring to offend by staring, she later sketched what she had slyly glimpsed. After some months she gained rapport with Felipa, the cook at the dormitory, and secured her willingness to impart some of the secrets of the ancient weaving traditions.

Looms have a minimum of wood in the almost treeless *altiplano*. Although larger fabrics are woven on a primitive horizontal loom similar to the backstrap loom, much of the weaving was done merely with the wool yarns and string heddles manipulated by skilled fingers. At last she learned how these traditional motifs were woven and mastered several techniques in spite of the language barrier.

After returning to Minnesota, she began teaching various pupils and classes what she had learned. She searched for a book on these Bolivian techniques, but was informed that there was none. Feeling that such a folk art should not be entirely lost, she dreamed of writing a book and decided to save money for a return to Bolivia to learn more.

As a pupil in one of Margie's classes, I also became intrigued, and began developing ways to diagram various types of patterns. With the aid of a magnifying lens, I studied the fabrics Margie had brought back with her and succeeded in making replicas of some kinds that Margie had not been taught. However, the question remained, "How do the Bolivians do this?"

Margie returned to Bolivia to research their methods in the summer of 1973, and I was invited along as her technical collaborator and photographer. Together, we went to a variety of highland weaving communities, where various types of traditional designs and techniques could still be found on the streets, in the markets, in museums, and in far-off villages.

In some Central and South American countries, one may find weavers who demonstrate their craft publicly. In Bolivia, on the contrary, it is very difficult to find the weavers. Customarily they weave in the privacy of their homes or courtyards. In an area where the loom is staked out on the ground, the weaver will probably disappear as you approach.

Because of this, the opportunities for us to observe the weaving in process needed to be arranged, chiefly through personal contacts. Usually the places were remote and reached in adventurous ways. Our first trip was an all-night ride in a crowded bus. The route went through some of the very high mountain passes with hairpin curves that look as if they had been carved out by a berserk roller coaster. Many of the passengers slept on the floor, while we were lucky enough to have seats; but it was so cold that we slid into our sleeping bags to keep warm. At one point the male passengers were called upon to get out and push the bus.

Riding on the back of an open truck is one of the commonest forms of transportation. After waiting five hours while a tire was repaired, we rode a couple of hours on the back of a truck, as gringos among the Indian and Spanish co-passengers, accompanied by large truck tires and cement dust. Our interpreter made hats out of newspaper to protect us from the glaring sun. The trucks to the village of Ancoraimes depart only at 4 AM. Passengers huddle together to keep from freezing in the icy morning chill. Some remote areas can be reached only by long trips on foot. For these and many other reasons, the experiences we had in learning the techniques are particularly precious.

When we returned to the States, we began to sort out what we had learned and to put it into practice. On the basis of what we had observed, we found it easier to also replicate some of the pattern weaves we had not been able to watch being done. We began classifying all the various techniques, analyzing the structure, and making replicas. This was challenging and very time-consuming.

Several times when we thought we had finally completed our analysis, we were surprised to find yet another technique represented in a specimen loaned to us for examination. The crossed warp band was one of those surprises. As complete as our listing now appears to us, we are aware there may yet be other specialties to add. We invite our readers to contact us about such findings. My address is given below rather than Margie's because it is more permanent. We would also like to know about your Bolivian-inspired creations.

May you discover some of the joy and excitement we have found in becoming involved with the warps, in these very special ways of color patterning!

Adele Cahlander
3522 Knox Avenue North
Minneapolis, Minnesota 55412

The continent of South America   Bolivia

This ancient pre-Incan warp-pattern chuspa, or coca bag, was excavated near Arica, Chile. A definite relationship to present-day Bolivian weaving is evident in pattern and weave structure. Weaving started against the heading at the ends and terminated at the center along the bag bottom. Courtesy of the American Museum of Natural History, New York.

Chapter One

The Weaver of Highland Bolivia

From Incan and pre-Incan times, highland Bolivia has had a heritage of weaving excellence. Spinning and weaving were important to the Indians, not only as a means of survival against the cold at the high altitude and as payment of taxes, but also as a means of creative expression that related to their ceremonial rituals and to their legends. Today weaving is still important in the lives of many Bolivian Indians, and its purpose is still primarily personal rather than commercial.

CULTURAL HERITAGE

The Andean region has long been famous for its textiles. On the Paracas peninsula, south of present-day Lima, the first great textile-oriented culture appeared around 700–200 B.C. A profusion of textile structures that are still unequalled developed during this period. Finely decorated textiles have been excavated from coastal burial mounds, marvelously preserved due to the aridity of the coastal area.

As early as 600 A.D., Colla Indians lived at the southern end of Lake Titicaca near Tiahuanaco, one of South America's most important archeological sites. Contact with the Nazca culture of the Late Paracas period stimulated and enriched Colla life. The Collas often used fabrics as a part of their ceremonial rituals. This powerful and populous group spread its influence as far south as modern Chile and westward into Peru, at a time when the Incas were yet a small tribe of mountain dwellers.

While the Inca culture was maturing, the Colla empire, though still powerful, was declining. Realizing that the Colla confederacy was a con-siderable threat to the Inca empire, Sinchi Rocca (1062–1091), the second Inca, launched the first campaign against the Collas. Later Incas completed the conquest of Colla territory.

As the Incas rose in power they conquered numerous small tribes and incorporated them into their social, economic, political, and cultural systems. This included imposing their own language—Quechua—on the conquered peoples. Textile production was a finely developed art in the Inca culture. When the Spaniards arrived, they found such beautifully woven fabrics that they were unable to comprehend how such intricate fabrics could be produced on such simple, primitive looms.

The Collas belonged to the linguistic group which, in modern times, is called *Aymara*, the name by which the majority of the Indians of the Bolivian *altiplano*—a barren plateau fenced in by the Andes—are known today. The Collas were never completely subjugated by the Incas and managed to maintain their own language and much of their native culture, which still persists to the present day.

During the conquest, those people who accepted the official Inca language came to be known as *Quechuas* throughout the Andean region. Thus began the transformation of the Inca culture into the modern Quechua community. Both of these historic groups of Indians are present in Bolivia today, and they still differ in language and in culture.

Bolivia has inherited a rich cultural legacy from the Colla and Inca civilizations. Elements of these pre-Columbian cultures can be seen in

Numerous polleras, worn one over the other at fiestas and dances, is considered an indication of wealth. Photo by Marjorie Cason.

Bolivian textiles today, clearly illustrating the continuation of the strong Andean textile traditions.

CLOTHING AND ACCESSORIES

The characteristic clothing is distinct for each of many rural regions in Bolivia. The wide and rich variety of colors and styles makes it one of the more picturesque regions in Latin America. Although the native dress may vary strikingly from village to village, there are certain items that are nearly universal throughout the Bolivian highlands. The costumes reflect the traditions of Incan textiles and also show Spanish influence in the use of materials and styles. The male garments have been strongly influenced by Spanish colonial fashions. On the other hand, most female items of apparel are shaped in the pre-Columbian tradition.

Aymara Woman's Costume.   The bright dress of the Aymara woman appears miles away on the horizon of the altiplano as a vivid spot of color. As she walks along, the Aymara wife simultaneously performs several of her many chores. On most days she can be seen driving her sheep home from the pasture, invariably busy with spindle in hand, while carrying her baby on her back.

Her baby is carried in an *awayo,* probably the most universal and versatile item of the Indian costume. This square of brightly colored material is twisted into a pouch that hangs on the back by means of two diagonal corners tied in front of the shoulders. Vendors in the marketplace squat on the ground with their goods spread before them on their awayos. Buyers open their awayos to display goods in exchange.

The awayo is woven in the tradition peculiar to its region. Fascinating patterns are produced both by color combinations and designs. This beautiful textile usually consists of two rectangles joined together to form a square. Sometimes it is slightly smaller and is all of one piece. To wear a beautiful awayo is a matter of pride, especially if woven by its owner.

Beneath her awayo the Aymara woman wears a *manta,* or shawl, that is fastened with a large pin. The manta may be patterned or plain, in bright or subdued colors, or it may be solid golden brown or black. Sometimes an awayo is worn across the shoulders in place of a manta.

The manta covers an overblouse and part of the brightly colorful and distinctive skirt called a *pollera.* This very full skirt has numerous tiny accordion pleats at the waist and a series of narrow horizontal tucks near the hem. For fiestas and dances, a woman may wear five or six, or even ten polleras one over the other, their number and richness being a sign of wealth.

Important accessories to the costume are the belt, bag, and *incuña.* The intricately designed belt, or *waka,* can be either very narrow or quite wide depending on village custom. The pear-shaped bag is customarily knit instead of woven. The incuña is a small carrying cloth, about fifteen inches square, used to carry small objects. When filled with eggs and some grain to keep them from breaking it serves as an egg carton. The costume is completed with a felt derby hat, sandals made from old tires, and a *tula,* a band especially designed to hold the woman's braids behind her back.

The Aymara wife is invariably busy with her spindle while carrying her baby on her back.

The incuña,
a brightly colored square,
is tied into a pouch
to carry small bundles.

Warm knit caps
called lluchus are
needed for warmth
in the cold climate.

Aymara Man's Costume. The red, striped fiesta poncho of the Aymara man also lends color to the drab altiplano landscape. For everyday wear he puts on a beautiful plain golden brown poncho. These simple yet extremely durable and versatile garments are among the Indian's most prized possessions. During the day the poncho serves as an overcoat and raincoat, protecting the wearer from the stinging cold winds. At night it becomes a mattress and a blanket. It may take the weaver several months of steady weaving to produce a high-quality poncho, but it will then last the owner half of his lifetime.

A homemade felt hat worn over a knit cap with ear flaps is the traditional male headgear. This cap is often called a *lluchu* or a *chullo.* It is multicolored, has a variety of figures, and sometimes has numbers indicating the year in which it was knit. In the cold highland climate, the lluchu is necessary for warmth.

Other items in the male wardrobe include a shirt and trousers of obviously Spanish origin, to which have been added a vest and a belt. Neck scarves are a soft, natural brown, often made of alpaca, but occasionally of vicuña. The altiplano male also wears sandals and uses a coca bag and a *capacho,* a bag that holds what would otherwise be carried in his pockets. Sometimes a *tari*—a small square cloth with multicolored stripes used for carrying coca leaves—is tucked under the belt instead of the coca bag. Though the designs differ from one tari to another, in one community two are made exactly alike for a newly married couple. Elsewhere, if a boy's parents want to ask for someone's daughter to be his wife, they have a third party deliver a tari filled with coca leaves

to the girl's home. If the tari is not accepted, the son has been rejected as a possibility. If accepted, the boy, his parents, and the third party go together to the girl's house with gifts and drinks, then the girl leaves with them.

The universal awayo invariably completes the costume, but the male awayo is worn differently from its female counterpart. It is slung over one shoulder, brought underneath the other arm, and then tied in front of the chest.

Quechua Woman's Costume. The small bright areas of extremely intricate and complicated designs set against a dark background catch the eye in the Quechua woman's costume. These extraordinary designs are most noticeable in the *aksu,* an overskirt that is worn somewhat like an apron put on backwards. It is held in place by a belt that is equally intricate in design. It is about a yard square and is usually black or brown with a colored border. A beautifully patterned narrow tubular edging, called a *ribete,* goes around three sides of the aksu.

The *urk'u,* a dark tunic worn under the aksu, is another traditional female garment. Over the urk'u is a manta that is fastened in the front at the throat and hangs down to the knees, covering only the back and not circling around to the front. In some areas, mantas are fastened with large silver spoon-shaped pins called *tupus.* The Quechua woman's carrying cloth—called a *lliklla*—is less brightly colored but has finer designs than the Aymara awayo.

The most varied feature of the female costume is the hat, which has many regional differences. In Cochabamba the woman wears a high, wide-

The altiplano male is seldom seen without his poncho and awayo.

13

North of Lake Titicaca, the women retain the ancient Incan tradition of wearing winchas, or headbands. The bands are woven of fine handspun wool in one-weft double cloth.

The exquisitely patterned aksu, an over-skirt, is the crowning glory of the Quechua woman's costume. Her manta is fastened with large spoon-shaped pins called tupus. Courtesy of the Museo Antropológico, Sucre, Bolivia.

Uncus, fringed squares with pleasing color variations in warp-faced plain weave, are worn over the shoulders and also around the hips.

brimmed white hat with a black ribbon design on one side. To the south, the hat is similar in shape but is black or dark green felt. Elsewhere, one finds a flat-topped hat decorated with sequins and rick-rack. In one area a headband of Incan origin, called a *wincha,* replaces the hat.

Quechua Man's Costume. The poncho is the most noticeable feature of the Quechua man's outfit. Poncho styles vary greatly from area to area. In one particular region, the Indians wear a brilliant fringed poncho with stripes of mostly maroon and red, accented by other brightly colored stripes. The seam on this particular poncho goes over the shoulders and down the arms instead of down the front and back as in most ponchos.

Underneath this brilliant fringed poncho, men often wear a smaller brilliant poncho called an *uncu.* The men in this region may also wear an additional small poncho folded in half diagonally to form a triangle that hangs down in back over the seat and is held in place by a leather money belt.

Other items in the male wardrobe can include a sack-like textured shirt, a sleeveless jacket, and knee-length pants. A belt, or *chumpi,* may be wrapped around the top of the pants in classical matador style.

In ancient times, only the Inca and other important officials were allowed the privilege of wearing a coca bag. Today however, the coca bag, or *chuspa,* is a universal and important male accessory. Nearly every Indian chews coca leaves from which cocaine is extracted. It is believed that the

plant has magical properties. The chewing of coca is understandable in light of its ability to make the Indian indifferent to hunger, pain, cold, and fatigue. The chuspa is hung around the neck by its strap or is tucked under the belt. In addition, a *capacho* may be worn over the shoulder outside the poncho.

There is as much variation in the male headgear as there is in the female. There are various shapes and colors of felt hats. Brown, and especially white, are popular colors for these hats. Perhaps the most unusual male hat is a black suede helmet with a sequinned brim that is modeled after those of the conquistadores. This hat is also worn by many women of the area.

CUSTOMS IN WEAVING

Traditions whose origins have long been forgotten govern the work of the Bolivian weaver. While it is possible that the weaving craft could be the victim of such strenuous traditions, the creativity of the Bolivian seems to flourish under the discipline of such a strict code.

Although the loom used by the Indians is extremely simple, the fabrics produced are of the finest quality. What the Indian weaver lacks in mechanical equipment is more than compensated for by his familiarity with the weave structures and by his artistry with color and design.

Designing the Fabric. Most Bolivian pattern weaves are warp-faced, hand-picked, and reversible. Woven from either a two- or three-color warp, the design area is the same on both sides of the fabric but the colors are reversed.

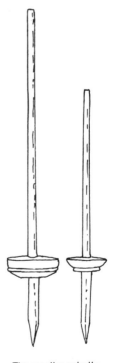

In a capacho, (above), the Indian man carries items that would otherwise go in pockets. Collection of Judy Conger. The chuspa, (left), used to carry coca leaves, is an important accessory to the male costume. Collection of Lynn Meisch.

Many of the textiles are woven as specific shapes and sizes to form garments or garment parts. Wide fabrics are customarily woven with four finished or selvedge edges. End selvedges are possible because the warps are wound continuously and because the string heddles are easily removed. Two well-matched rectangles are often joined with hand stitches to make a larger square. Often a narrow tubular edging is woven around the edges of the piece for decoration and to prevent fraying.

Each geographical area has its traditional color combinations, motifs, and finishing touches. In the Sucre area bright-colored pattern bands are enhanced by larger black areas. Near Lake Titicaca a rainbow of stripes in blended shades and narrow pattern bands accent solid-colored areas. Fanciful animals predominate in some places, while others specialize in geometric patterns. In many areas, fancy braids, tassels, and other embellishments adorn headbands, coca bags, and ends of belts. The characteristic features of a woven piece often make it possible to identify the geographical area in which it was produced.

In addition to the hand-picked pattern weaves, there are also loom-controlled weaves. Several items, such as ponchos and blankets, are made from a warp-faced, striped plain weave. Although these pieces have no picked pattern areas, great care is taken in choosing colors and planning their sequence within the fabric. Sometimes the warps are ikat dyed, and occasionally a name will be spelled out in the band where it is used, as in a blanket.

One of the more beautiful of the plain-weave items is the *costal*. It is a storage bag that comes in a variety of sizes, depending on its use. Large costales are used for agricultural products, especially for the numerous varieties of Andean potatoes. Loosely loaded with produce, these bags are slung over the back of a llama or burro like a saddle bag. Smaller costales are used to store a variety of items. As a part of her dowry, the Indian girl has a number of these bags for storing household necessities and occasional treasures. Made of beautiful natural-colored handspun wool, they are woven to last a lifetime.

Other loom-controlled fabrics are produced by the Indian men on treadle looms. *Bayeta,* a coarse woolen cloth, is used for basic plain-weave garments. This solid-color fabric may be unbleached white for use in pants or shirts, brightly dyed for use in making polleras, or dark-colored for pants, shirts, or an urk'u. For *jerga,* a heavy suiting material, natural black and white alpaca yarns are combined to form a twill, plaid, or shepherd's check.

Handspun Yarns. The Bolivian spinner works mainly with wool from sheep or hair from llama or alpaca. Wool is popular because it is easy to spin and dye and because it is readily available. Llama hair is valued for its strength because it produces an extremely durable fabric. Alpaca hair is softer and finer than llama hair and is valued for the soft quality it gives.

Those spinners who take most pride in their craft may prefer wool or hair from a certain part of the animal's body. *Koña,* the soft wool from

The smaller spindle is for making a oneply yarn from the wool; the larger spindle is used for the plying and then for the over-twisting.

A Quechua woman (above) is weaving a capacho, in which there are pattern bands of warp-faced double cloth. Photo by Ann Houston. The photo on the right shows the weaving tools and yarn that are stored and carried in a small costal.

the front of the sheep, is used for awayos. *Costillas,* the wool from the middle of the body, is used for bayeta. The coarse wool used for blankets comes from the hind part.

The Indians produce yarn with a very hard twist, or overspin, which gives it three valuable qualities. Most important is its strength, which gives it the capability to withstand much friction during the weaving process. A second quality of overspun yarn is its elasticity. Bolivian weaving yarn looks very kinky and may spring back to as little as half its length when not under tension. This gives the weaver considerable freedom to subordinate the structure of his weave to the needs of the design without creating tension problems, and also allows for other subtleties in the weaving process. A third characteristic is the hard, smooth surface of the yarn. This, along with the elasticity of the yarn, makes it possible to obtain a shed that would otherwise be almost impossible. Ordinarily the Indians spin the wool themselves with a drop spindle called a *puska,* ply it with a heavier drop spindle called a *c'anti,* and then dye it. A vigorous third spinning is needed to give it the characteristic hard twist. Some spinners now purchase already-dyed industrial wool yarn and re-ply it to give it the hard twist.

Dyes. The bright and fast colors of former times were prepared with natural dyes. The techniques used to make fast colors were especially important when a garment was designed to last a lifetime, being constantly exposed to the intense Andean sun. But the ingenious methods for ob-

taining these permanent colors have become almost completely forgotten due to the availability of analine dyes that are now commonly sold.

However, there are three natural dyes that are still in common use. *Carbon de casa,* or soot, is used for black and brown. The walnut tree leaf, *nogal,* is used for browns and yellows. Red shades are produced by using *cochinilla,* or powdered cochineal insects.

Llama and alpaca hair comes in a pleasing range of deep rich shades that are woven without dying. Certain items, such as costales, are customarily woven from such natural-colored yarns. Shades of llama hair are also used in making strong ropes.

Looms and Equipment. Although a crude Spanish-type treadle loom is used to make cloth for some basic garments, most all the beautiful textiles are woven by methods in use long before the Spaniards arrived. Flexibility in design and weave structure is achieved by hand-picking from a simple two-shed arrangement of a string heddle and a shed rod or loop. Additional string heddles are needed to produce some of the weaves. For narrow bands, an off-loom technique is used with just a finger inserted in the shed to provide tension. The far end of this narrow warp might be attached to a post, a spike in the ground, or even a toe! For wider bands, a backstrap is used to control tension.

Most wider pieces are woven on either a horizontal loom or an oblique loom. The difference in the looms is the position in which the loom is placed and consequently the weaver's position at

The pattern for the strap on this suede bag (left) was found in a tiny ancient Peruvian fragment. Pebble weave, wool rug yarn, inkle loom. The photo above shows how the Aymara color schemes are reminiscent of Gaugin's paintings. Photo by Marjorie Cason.

Finely-spun yarns, vegetable-dyed in traditional Bolivian colors, were used in this fine old Iliklla. An air of refinement is imparted by the simple repetition of motifs in the double cloth band and in the narrow pebble band. Tube 5 embellishes the edge. Photo by Byron Bennett.

The awayo above is a versatile backpack used by young and old alike. Photo by Jim Drum.

This small chuspa (right) in complementary-warp uneven twill has a special strap, woven with crossed warps. The color of the diamond outline is changed at intervals.

This aksu has fantastic birds that fill the space of a wide pattern band in complementary-warp uneven twill. Collection of Ruth McFarren. Photo by Byron Bennett.

Margie wove this tie (left) for her husband, who also enjoys wearing it with the opposite side showing. The front end was woven in a modification of doubled pebble, then the rest was narrowed and woven without a design. Single-ply weaving wool, inkle loom.

An Aymara woman (above) weaves her awayo, or carrying cloth, one half at a time, on a horizontal, 4-stake loom. Narrow pattern bands with different structures enliven larger areas of plain weave in graduated shades. Photo by Marjorie Cason.

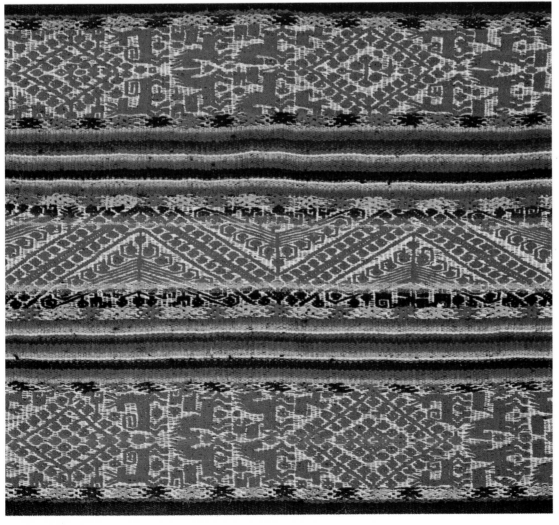

Bright wool yarns are alternated with thinner white cotton yarns and woven in modified intermesh to form llamas, horses, and geometric flower designs in the bands of an aksu. The bands are brightened further by the three-color companion bands at their edges. Photo by Byron Bennett.

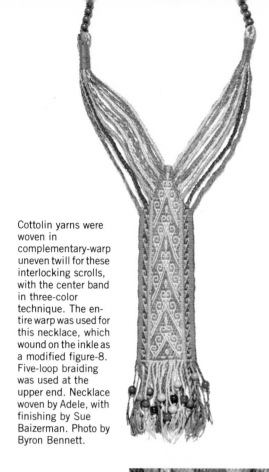

Cottolin yarns were woven in complementary-warp uneven twill for these interlocking scrolls, with the center band in three-color technique. The entire warp was used for this necklace, which wound on the inkle as a modified figure-8. Five-loop braiding was used at the upper end. Necklace woven by Adele, with finishing by Sue Baizerman. Photo by Byron Bennett.

Detail of an awayo. Balance is achieved by limiting the amount of pattern, so it does not compete with the multi-stripe plain-weave areas. The yarns are almost as fine as sewing thread. Courtesy of the *Museo Antropológico,* Sucre, Bolivia.

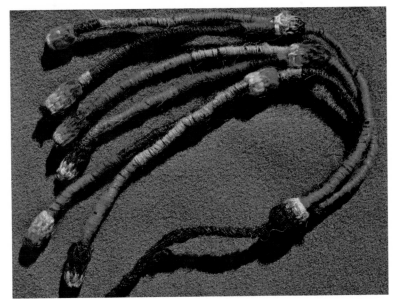

Small chuspas (left) like this unusual supplementary-weft bag are used to carry charms or other small treasures. Tasseled pendants add a note of grace. Collection of Lynn Meisch.

Wrappings and small pompoms (above) embellish the end of a tula, a hairband used to hold a woman's braids in place. Collection of Lynn Meisch.

Warm earthy colors are used for stylized birds and flowers in a geometric setting. These bands of modified intermesh, bordered with 3-color companion weave bands, are woven in the lower end of an aksu. Photo by Byron Bennett.

Detail of a manta (above) in complementary-warp uneven twill. The three-color band in the center has a horizontal color shift. Collection of Harriet Adams.

This comtemporary hanging by Sue Baizerman (right) was inspired by Bolivian textiles. The hanging uses pebble and plain weave, and carpet warp.

Detail of a chuspa (right). Horses and llamas are also popular motifs in modified intermesh. Flower and twill companion weaves are used here.

Horses and birds (far right) are favorite motifs for winchas, or headbands, woven in "one-weft" double cloth. Collection of Micheline Beauchemin, Quebec.

Marie Nodland wove and shaped this silk blouse (far left) on her floor loom. Where the pattern colors overlap, she wove in three-color non-reversible pebble.

Supplementary warp capachos, like this one at left, have unusually wide shoulder straps. Courtesy of the American Museum of Natural History.

Detail of an awayo with pattern bands in warp-faced double cloth. Courtesy of the International Folk Art Foundation Collection in the Museum of New Mexico.

23

Series of small tassels (above) are a popular embellishment for chuspas. Collection of Michael O'Neal.

Wide sections of 3-color non-reversible modified intermesh are a unique feature of this chuspa (right). The colorful pompoms and bottom trim are made by a wrapping technique. Collection of Ann Houston.

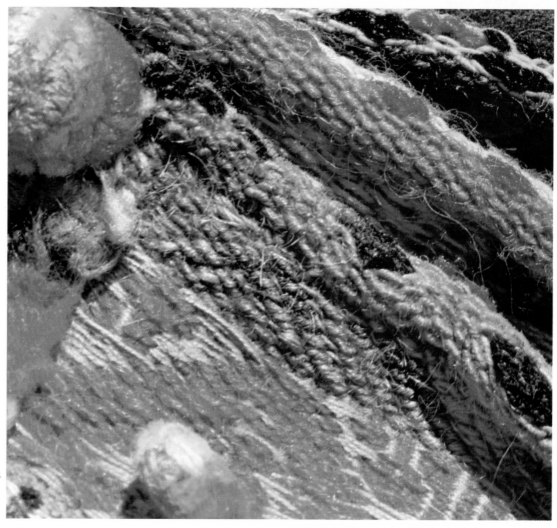

Tubular edge bindings called ribetes embellish the edges of weavings.

A Quechua woman is weaving a blanket on an oblique loom in the courtyard of her home. Photo by Marjorie Cason.

the loom. For the horizontal loom the warp and cloth beams are anchored to four wood or iron stakes in the ground. In the oblique loom the beams are lashed to two long poles leaning on a wall, doorway, or even a low roof. Other pieces of the loom are the graduated shed rods, the graduated swords, the heddle rod, shuttle, strummer, and bone beater.

Warping. The yarn is specially prepared for warping by being rolled into a very compact ball about the size of a baseball. This aids the weaver in maintaining even tension during warping. Often a ball is begun by tying the yarn to a small stone so tension may be maintained to the last inch of the yarn.

Warping is done on the loom after the beams have been lashed in place. The warp is wound in figure-8 fashion. In the pattern sections, two or three yarns of different colors are treated as a single yarn wound together during warping. A safety pin is sometimes used as a marker to enclose the counted warps for pattern sections. These groups of pattern warps are then rearranged according to the needs of the particular structure being woven, before the string heddle and shed rod are inserted.

Beating. One of the secrets of the Bolivian weaver is her forceful beating technique. Strong beating is necessary because of the closeness of the warps. For narrow bands such as belts, beating is done with a special sword. In wider pieces, a llama bone is used as a beater with a staccato motion, section by section. The result of such a strong beating motion is a very dense fabric with truly distinct patterns.

One of the secrets of the Bolivian weaver is her forceful beating technique. Photo by Elizabeth Barnard.

"The Cloth of The Quechuas"
by Grace Goodell

Reprinted, with permission, from *Natural History* Magazine, December, 1969.

"When Manco Capac, the legendary founder of the Inca Empire, and his sister-wife, Mama Ocllo, emerged from the ground near Cuzco and crossed the Andean highland with their entourage, the poets tell us that it was their resplendent garments, above all else, that measured their nobility. "They went forth clothed in dresses of fine wool delicately worked with fine gold thread, and from these they took out purses, also of wool and gold, skillfully woven. . . ."

"To understand the significance of textiles to the Incas, the ancient craft of weaving has to be seen as a major art medium, for long before the Spanish conquest textiles had become a measure of national wealth. As techniques were perfected through time, remarkable artistry developed. Textiles were collected as taxes, used in ceremonial rituals, and distributed to officials and to armies. The peasant valued the works of the loom for himself as well because then, as often now, he depended on weaving for all his clothing, his containers for transportation and storage, his furnishings. Thus the importance of textile production pervaded the culture at every level and is naturally expressed in its myths.

"It is no wonder then that the high quality of weaving should have been the prime indicator of personal excellence in the Andes. In some areas even today the Quechuas, direct descendants of the Incas, still consider the skills of hand spinning, dyeing, and weaving to be the essential criteria of human dignity.

"But each year there are fewer and fewer people who wear the old garments, fewer who spin and weave. Soon it will be impossible to collect some of the textiles I saw on a recent survey of Indian weaving in Bolivia. Even now the best weavers are reluctant to sell their rare pieces, and just to see such craftwork requires traveling to the remotest regions. There, usually in an isolated valley, the geography itself has helped to preserve with little change the subtleties of the art as they were developed by pre-Columbian cultures. The land is rugged, men are isolated, and ancient techniques have not been compromised by proximity to large towns.

"In the Bolivian highlands, three major areas of special weaving interest are apparent. The greatest variety of weaving techniques is found in the central part of the country. Here it is not uncommon to see five or more distinct means of textile production being employed by different members of one family, all in one courtyard on the same afternoon. Their looms range from the indigenous and most ancient to a later type introduced by the Spaniards and often constructed with a twentieth-century touch—an axle from an old Ford, for example, or bolts from a Toyota truck.

"Nowhere else in the southern Andes have I seen a region so vitally concerned with weaving. The variety of weaving techniques and looms in this area reflects the extent and diversity of the Indians' weaving needs, and the significance of weaving to their daily lives. Furthermore, while in many parts of Bolivia (and southern Peru) only women spin yarn outside of the home, here it is commonplace for men and boys to spin outdoors as they gossip or tell stories in the winter sun. Even the more sophisticated Indian boys, who have just returned to their small hamlets from

Using a technique that requires strength, men in one area make thick belts on lap looms.

army service or cutting cane in the jungle, take up the spindle readily. And it is in this region that weaving is still the critical measure of material worth: a boy weaves a belt for a girl before proposing to her; he weaves a coca bag for him in consent. Farmers barter textiles for coffee, buttons, tin cups. At regional celebrations there is rivalry among communities to establish or preserve a collective reputation for weaving excellence.

"Of all the area's assortment of looms, the principal one is the backstrap, typical of primitive craftsmen throughout the Andes and elsewhere in the New World and parts of Asia. It consists essentially of two horizontal loom bars supported a foot or more above the ground, with the warp (lengthwise yarns) extended between them. One end of this loom is fastened around the waist of the weaver, who sits cross-legged on the ground; the other end is tied to a tree or post, which he faces. In Andean prisons where Indians weave all day, having nothing else to do but cook their own meals, one can see six or more such looms spread out like a Maypole from the jail yard's central loom post.

"Sometimes weavers tie what would otherwise be a backstrap loom to four pegs in the ground, rather than tire their backs with its constant support. Or they fasten the loom to two long vertical poles that lean against the wall of the house. However, neither of these adaptations allows for the same subtleties as the backstrap: with one end of the loom tied around the weaver's back, she has more control over the tension of the warps. She is able to slacken it merely by leaning forward, tightening it again by leaning back, a delicate nuance of control that cannot be achieved if both ends of the loom are fixed.

"The size of these looms can be modified in many ways, depending upon the product desired. The textile on a larger loom might become a poncho, a *lliclla,* or a *costal.* For a poncho, two woven pieces, usually two to three feet wide, are sewn together with part of the seam left open for the wearer's neck and head. A *lliclla* is similar but has no opening—a strong square cloth to be tied around the shoulders for carrying bundles on the back. A *costal* is a long sack used for storage or for transporting heavy burdens by llama. *Costales* around the house tend to look lean and hungry toward summertime, but they are filled to bulging after harvest.

"A smaller backstrap loom produces belts, straps, and coca bags, as well as small *costales,* in which a family keeps household luxuries and necessities—thread, a spoon, sugar, a spare candle. Village medicine men display their remedies in these *costales* on market day—bits of yellow pods, dried starfish, crushed sulfur, cactus thorns, or withered herbs, each sold from its own little sack. Headbands, saddlebags, capes, and purses are other common products of the backstrap loom.

"In addition to the backstrap, the Indians of the

Oruro region use a crudely made lap loom, on which they create belts using a Soumak-type technique, in which the wefts encircle the warps instead of interweaving with them. Often patterned with a bold, zigzag design of striking colors, such belts are only made by men and boys for their wives and girl friends. Making them is indeed a man's task, for they are exceedingly thick and must be firmly bound and interlaced. This type of loom was also used by pre-Spanish weavers in Peru. Today it has a specialized and highly appreciated place in the weaving repertoire of this area.

"In this region also Indians weave rugs and blankets, mainly for commercial use, on upright frame looms. This enormous loom fills the weaver's hut from the rafters to the floor. Beautiful Spanish designs in a tapestry weave have characterized these rugs, but more recently, contemporary patterns have been suggested by Peace Corps volunteers. Also ubiquitous in the Oruro region is the treadle loom introduced by the Spaniards. Most remote communities here possess several treadle looms; it is on these looms that the men weave *bayeta* (a coarse woolen cloth for pants, vests, shirts, and women's skirts), as well as gay plaid sashes. Young boys in particular sport these sashes tied low below the waist with studied casualness. And because they are also used for weaving blankets, three or four treadle looms—one for each member of the family—may be going at one time in an Indian home.

"In addition to these, there are smaller looms and methods of off-the-loom weaving and braiding that these Indians have at their disposal. The younger children sit on the ground, legs outstretched, working on a toe loom that may have as many as five or six heddles. They make straps and hat bands, often with elaborate designs. Using still other techniques they make *ribete,* the narrow edging along a poncho that protects it from fraying. Boys braid numerous strands into complex "snakeback" slingshots, which broaden out into a short woven strap where the stone will be held; they also produce splendid llama-hair rope. Finally there are the soft alpaca *tulas* with their colorful pom-poms—a kind of ribbon specially made to hold a woman's long braids together behind her back while she stirs the soup or bends over the baby.

"In this area of Bolivia, where textiles are so important in daily life, even the spirits of the mountains value the yarn and the loom. In some communities Saint Isidore, the patron of farmers and a peasant himself, must also have a poncho; so a local weaver is commissioned to keep his statue well attired with a bright new garment on his feast day every year. Furthermore, at planting and harvesttime the earth goddess may demand her annual tribute wrapped in a specially woven cloth. To ward off evil spirits, magical *lloq'e,* a yarn spun in the reverse direction from the normal spinner's twist, is tied around the ankle or wrist. This is worn by travelers, pregnant women, the

With one bar of the small backstrap loom tied around her body, the weaver controls the warp tension by leaning forward or back.

ill—by anyone hoping for good luck. Even the statues of saints in the churches sometimes find it advisable to wear *lloq'e* on their wrists. No one can survive without the loom.

"In northern Bolivia beyond La Paz, weaving takes on a different mood. This region is a series of deep valleys set among magnificent, soaring mountains; the communities own fewer llamas and alpaca, so most of the weaving is done with sheep's wool. Because of its nature, that is, its scale structure and kinkiness, sheep's wool is usually easier to spin than alpaca or llama hair. With it the spinners produce some of the finest of present-day highland yarns.

"With all fibers like wool or hair, spinning is indispensable for weaving, and a high level of weaving can hardly flourish without good spinning. Throughout Bolivia the Indians spin with a drop spindle similar to that used elsewhere in the world: a slender stick nine or ten inches long with a round whorl toward the bottom for balance. Because it can be used even while the spinner walks or runs, it is not unusual to see heavily loaded Indian porters from the mountains industriously working the spindle, which dangles and swings by their legs as new yarn is formed.

"Children learn to spin at an early age. Lying on the ground near many an Indian hut are toy spindles with bits of wool; some of the finest yarn is spun by young girls under ten.

"A good spinner controls the diameter of his yarn by a sensitive fiber-selecting process, which he performs almost unconsciously with his fingers, thinning out the fiber bundles as he feeds them into the yarn he is twisting. All careful spinners aim for an even yarn without noticeable variation in its diameter. Only in areas where craftsmanship has declined and the spinners have become indifferent—often they are embarrassed by this when questioned—does one find yarn spun with considerable irregularity. In a few regions, spinners may deliberately produce such crude yarn to suit the tourist market. Tourists often cannot believe that the skillfully spun yarn is indeed hand-spun, and will pay more for proof in irregularities. Generally these "lumpy" yarns are more frequently found in knitted wear, especially sweaters, as it would be difficult to use them extensively on a native loom.

"After the wool is spun into yarn, it is plied; that is, two or more yarns are twisted together to make a stronger yarn. This is usually a man's work, although I have never known an idle woman who would not pick up the plying when the need arose. The men ply the yarn at home or while working, using a larger and heavier spindle than that used in the original spinning of wool. When all the wool has been spun and plied, it is ready for dyeing.

"In a few areas of the southern Andes, and especially in the isolated north of Bolivia, vegetable, animal or mineral dyes are still used, but in very little time the recipes and processes will be forgotten, replaced by commercial dyes. And

Although the toe loom is simply constructed, children can weave elaborately designed straps and hat bands on it.

sooner still, no one will any longer know on which hill to pick the brightest *cher'chi,* or exactly on which day its dye will be the subtle shade desired. Dyeing is a lore and a science unto itself, and requires a thorough knowledge of local geography, botany, and geology, as well as expertise in mixing mordants (which fix the dye to assure permanence); in timing the boiling, steeping, and cooling; and in anticipating color modifications that may take place with temperature change or variations in wool composition.

"An interesting feature of weaving in some of these northern valleys is its extremely local character. In this region—perhaps here alone of all the regions in Bolivia—each community has its own distinctive motif variation or color rendering. Thus a person familiar with these local characteristics can stand in the market on Sunday and identify the exact valley of each visiting Indian, even his particular hamlet in that valley. This is done by closely examining his *capacho,* a foot-long, flat bag carried by men.

"Many of the marks of differentiation are obvious; they are simply distinct patterns. However, there are others that may appear identical to the unpracticed observer. Nevertheless, the indications are consistent and are never omitted: a geometric form may be elongated, instead of rounded out; birds other than ducks may decorate a narrow band; a "rainbow" warp may be used in place of a solid shade. To the weavers these are as much a part of the design as are the major motifs.

"Despite such a seemingly compulsory code, the creativity of the craftsman is never inhibited. This artistic use of a local pattern can be compared to the development of a theme in a fugue: the theme clearly distinguishes one fugue from others but in no way limits the freedom of the composer. Rather, it provides him with challenge and form. The *capachos* from a single hamlet are never the same, but each manifests the local "theme" in a slightly new way, within its implicit local restrictions.

"Elsewhere in Bolivia weaving designs tend to characterize much larger geographic areas, a single theme extending at least across a wide pampa or a valley. That many of these tiny communities, perhaps only half an hour apart on foot, can preserve such individuality in their textiles is indicative of the Indians' attitudes toward weaving. Their handmade garments are part of their identity, sometimes even more so than their names, many of which are common throughout the entire region. This localization of weaving designs is also found in parts of Central America and in the Cuzco area of Peru. What will be the reaction of these people as the commercial clothing industry drives the hand loom from their valley in the near future, and they have to wear shirts identical to those worn over a vast geographical area by total strangers?

"In some respects the most exciting textile region in Bolivia is around Sucre, the original capital of the country. It is in this area that the anthropologist is most strongly challenged by questions of artistic creativity: How does a primitive artist conceive the idea of his work and then enter into its elaboration? Does a craftsman deep in a weaving tradition in any sense enjoy a spontaneity comparable to that of, say, a potter or watercolorist? Why make weaving difficult with designs? The region around Sucre lends itself well to the study of influences that foreign cultures, penetrating farther into the backlands, may bring to bear upon the primitive artist.

"Although it has been reported that weaving samplers are used in the central Andes, I have never seen anything that might serve as a sampler, and in fact the creative tradition communicated to me by weavers would have no room for such an aid. Most weavers of several years' experience are so thoroughly acquainted with the motifs used in their village or region, and with the manipulations possible on their looms, that weaving these motifs or transmitting them to a beginner needs no record or reminder. It is true that young weavers may often be seen using a finished product as a model, especially while warping the loom. But as soon as the first few rows of weft (the horizontal yarn) have been finished, they usually find picking out the design of one row to be a logical sequence based on what has been done in the row immediately preceding it.

"However, except in pieces requiring continual repetition of a single motif, there is considerable opportunity for creativity. Most weavers invent as they go along, sometimes carrying and developing in their minds numerous different design sequences across the width of the loom at one time.

"If the design sequences consist of geometric patterns, complex mathematical calculations are frequently required to work them out, especially on the backstrap loom. And if the designs are representations of men, plants, or animals, as many as five or six distinct figures in different stages may be emerging simultaneously across the loom. Yet no weaver has ever reported sketching out the over-all pattern beforehand, most do not even have the finished design firmly in mind from the start. This process does of course depend upon the creativity of the weaver, his experiences, perhaps his daring—and his humor.

"On several occasions I have been able to compare eight or ten weavings by the same craftsman, gathering them from neighbors and family in his village. Never did I find two pieces alike, although the diversity represented in the "portfolio" of any one craftsman depended upon his own creative energies, as is to be expected.

"The area around Sucre includes great extremes in style of weaving designs. East of the city lies hilly land with very few roads. One may walk three days or more hardly seeing a person; then, after a casual inquiry in a hut, suddenly find it to be a region of the most imaginative, bizarre weaving motifs. Here, with finely spun yarn,

hand-dyed in basic color combinations, weavers have set forth a fabulous parade. Red condor birds dive through purple backgrounds, scarlet bulls graze on a green field, cows have foxes inside their bellies. If you should laugh, the Indians will usually laugh with you at a comical spotted toad or a Wizard-of-Oz lion. After the bands of repeated geometric designs characteristic of weaving in much of the southern Andes, this burst of representational fantasy is startling.

"On the other hand, not far away the weaving is a complete contrast in color and spirit. There the designs are almost sinuous, highly baroque. In color harmonies that could never be achieved by natural dyes (and thus are subject to outside influence), intricate forms interlock abstractly. If any representational figures appear, they are likely to be stern horses and stiff riders, motifs derived from the Spanish tradition. Much of the yarn itself is commercially spun, which probably reflects outside contacts as a tourist community.

"In many other areas of the southern Andes I have observed a correlation between quality of handspinning and dyeing on the one hand and preservation of pre-Spanish designs on the other. This is not to say that such factors need always accompany one another. In Mexico, Indians who weave designs of motorcycles and political posters into their textiles maintain a very high spinning standard. However, it may be true that in Bolivia and southern Peru, a community that readily accepts the innovation of commerical yarn or dye, may also be a community with a more flexible attitude toward new, even foreign designs.

"But wherever one searches in such a study, one thing is constant: it is not difficult to distinguish the craftsman who weaves with an artist's love of expression and a passion for the mastery of his material, from the craftsman who works merely out of need. One woman I met near Sucre was typical of the former. Her husband, who shortly before our meeting had joined the work crew of a road being built near the community, was ashamed of his peasant clothes in his new job. Because a plain poncho devoid of all design indicates higher class 'among mestizos (the Spaniards never liked patterned ponchos, but instead considered solid black or gray to distinguish the true "caballero"), the Indian on a road crew is marked as a hillbilly by the brilliance and intricacy of his poncho. This man therefore demanded that his wife weave a solid gray poncho for him. He would no longer be seen in the garment it had taken her half a year to create. As she explained this, she wept. He had asked her to betray the very essence of her craftsmanship: for her, weaving without design was a contradiction.

"She, like many a weaver in Bolivia, is among the last to serve a historic tradition preserved from one generation to the next for more than two thousand years: the skills and craft of textile production recorded only in the minds and hands, yet for ages so critical for survival in the Andes.''

A boy weaves a sash on a Spanish treadle loom, which is also used to produce the coarse woolen homespun for his clothing. Line drawings reproduced by permission of Nicholas Amorosi, the American Museum of Natural History, New York.

The wide pattern bands in aksus are profusely decorated with numerous motifs. Collection of Ruth McFarren.

THE GLORY OF THE CRAFT

Bolivian weavers excel in their use of color and sense of composition. Color combinations are often lively and straightforward. Pattern areas frequently are abundantly decorated with diverse motifs. Many of the weave structures used to produce the various types of patterning are quite complicated. Fanciful finishing touches and embellishments enrich and unify the whole. A high standard of quality is maintained in producing each individual weaving. All these factors, added together, result in the production of truly remarkable textiles.

Color and Design. The Indian palette is very diversified and the variations of geometric, human, plant, and animal motifs are too numerous to record. The fabrics display elaborate composition and masterful color harmonies. In any single piece the coloring may be quite varied, reflecting the Indian spirit in its daring, brilliance, and liveliness. It is common to see bands of bright pink and grass green side by side in a fabric. By placing a narrow stripe of another color between these two bands, the weaver creates a diversion that causes the contrasting bands to complement each other rather than compete. In addition, balance is maintained by allotting different widths to the bands of each color: a band of high intensity will be narrower than one that is less intense.

The inspiration for the motifs comes from ancient traditions and from observations of the physical and social environment. The weaver creates animals such as bats or birds and various plants from memory. She also draws on the fiestas and

ceremonial rituals to create dancers, marriage figures, etc. To these are added both ancient and modern geometric motifs. The motifs are not placed in each pattern band in consistent orientation. A duck placed with his head in the direction of the length of the band may be followed by a dancer placed in the direction of the width. Other figures may be "upside-down" in comparison with previous motifs.

One of the more astonishing design achievements is apparent in larger fabrics, such as awayos, in which two pieces woven separately are joined to form a completed textile. The finished fabric gives the impression of perfect symmetry, but careful examination reveals that the two pieces are dissimilar. While designing the second width, the weaver does not merely copy the first piece. Instead she creates a new composition following the inspiration of the original part.

Aymara and Quechua weavers follow different traditions in creating their fabrics. The Aymara supersede the Quechuas in their artistry with color; the Quechuas excel in combining the decorative motifs for harmonious compositions. The Aymara readily turn to native plants for inspiration; Quechuas prefer the animal world for creating motifs.

The bright Aymara colors are a welcome relief from the dusty brown of the desolate altiplano. The extreme transparency of the high altitude atmosphere heightens the effect of the luminous color combinations. The Aymara use of color reminds one of the post-Impression painter Gauguin, whose style was inspired by folk art and medieval stained glass. In many pieces a wide

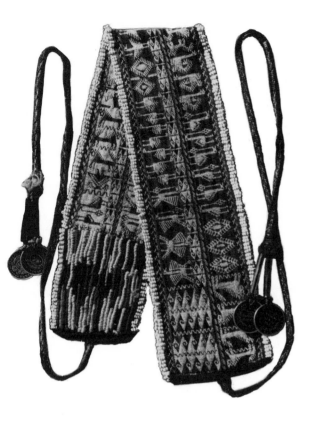

The coins that embellish this chuspa (above) add a special note of interest. Collection of Judy Conger. Winchas (left) are traditionally finished with a beaded edge. Collection of Micheline Beauchemin, Quebec, Canada.

stripe of a solid color is set off by narrow stripes of analogous shades in sharp contrast. Color schemes based on complementary color combinations are very popular, especially the red-green combination.

The pattern bands in Aymara pieces are usually narrow, not too numerous, and are filled with delicate animals and geometric or plant motifs. The Aymara weaver delights in taking a single motif and making as many variations as possible from it. It is customary for one or more of the pattern bands to contain words and numbers, perhaps the name of the weaver or the owner and the date the piece was woven. By limiting the amount of pattern in a piece, there is no competition between the effect of the pattern bands and the multistripe plain-weave areas. The result is always one of balance.

In contrast to the Aymara, there is great variation in the designs and color combinations used by the Quechua weavers. Quechua pattern bands are wide and are profusely decorated with numerous geometric or animal motifs. Each of the separate motifs is beautifully designed, especially each particular little animal. While it would be easy to end up with merely a ''busy'' appearance, the Quechua designer achieves a sense of harmony and balance. The total design of a piece is spontaneous, born and brought to completion as the weaver proceeds; it is not planned out in advance. The weaver, therefore, has to have a great storehouse of traditional motifs whose manipulations she has mastered, as well as the ability to put these designs together in a new way.

Quechua weavers favor muted colors and limit the number of colors in a single piece. Large areas of black, brown, or other dark colors are relieved by not too intense contrasting colors. Color combinations vary markedly from one locality to another. One area uses wine, gold, cherry red, and white against a black background. In another area, yellows, oranges, and dark green relieve the black.

Quality of Construction. The excellent and durable construction of the Bolivian fabrics and the infinite attention paid to finishing techniques and embellishments are related to a certain philosophy about weaving. The Indian weaver is not primarily concerned with how long it takes to produce her textile. One does not hurry to complete an item that is designed to last a lifetime. There is no questioning the great amount of time necessary to produce an item with an intricately designed, hand-picked pattern. It takes time to beat the weft securely into place, sometimes beating each shot, section by section, all across the fabric width many times. Fancy tassels, braids, and complicated tubular edgings or other embellishments are not produced in a hurry. But to the Bolivian weaver, such considerations as efficiency of time are of little importance.

Embellishments. The true charm of many of the smaller pieces lies in their finishing touches. Coca bags are especially noted for their embellishments. By means of coins, small pockets, ribetes (tubular edgings), fancy straps, wrappings, and tassels, or pompoms, the small rectangular piece of cloth destined to become a chuspa is transformed into a work of art. The wincha is

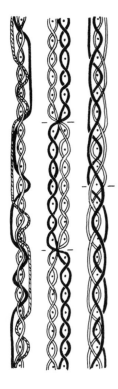

Weavers in an area near Lake Titicaca are master craftsmen in weaving patterns in warp-faced double cloth. Courtesy of the Musée de l'Homme, Paris, France.

Compound weave structures shown in vertical cross-section views are (left) two colors of supplementary warps added to a plain weave ground; (middle) "one-weft" double cloth, where two layers of warp-faced plain weave are interconnected at the color changes of the pattern; and (right) a complementary-warp structure in which 3-span warp floats are in alternate alignment (intermesh).

another item that is often abundantly embellished with beads and occasional coins as well as ornamental cords. Belts are often finished with handsome braids.

WEAVE STRUCTURES

It would be impossible to trace the origin and development of the numerous weave structures and variations used by the Bolivian Indians. Many of their structures are amazingly complex. In fact, it almost seems as if the Bolivian weaver delights in making the job as complex as possible.

Familiar Structures. To a weaver who has done some pick-up weaving, perhaps the most familiar of Bolivian patterning techniques would be the use of supplementary elements on a plain-weave ground. Fabrics with supplementary-warp patterning are more common in Europe and Peru. There seem to be two types woven in Bolivia, one with coarser yarns, and the other, even less prevalent, with finer yarns. For both, the plain-weave ground has paired warp yarns, with the supplementary warp lifted to the surface between the two yarns of a pair.

In the small area of northern Bolivia where the coarser type is woven, there seem always to be two colors, or sets, of the coarser supplementary yarns of the pattern, with each color brought to the surface as needed for the design. Even with some tie-down spots, this causes a mixture of longer floats on the 'wrong' side of the fabric. Motifs are usually geometric or human forms against a ground of light, natural-color wool. Not only are the yarns fairly coarse, but the embel-

lishments are also large in scale. The tassels are large, and the strap on a capacho, or man's bag, is several inches wide.

In the second type, another color such as red or gold might be used for the ground weave. Here there was only one set of supplementary warps wound for each band. However, in parts of the bands, a reversible float pattern in two colors was achieved in a unique manner. Alternate warps of the ground color were used to serve in the role of complementary warps, or "opposite partners," for the supplementary warps.

A few examples of supplementary-weft patterning were found in some very narrow hat bands, a bag strap, and a coca bag. Areas of very fine, white warp-faced plain weave form the pattern, surrounded by a colorful background of the supplementary-weft floats in blocks of different colors. Since the colored yarns are held in the shed of the ground weave when not used for the background, this fabric is two-faced.

Many handweavers are also familiar with some kind of double cloth. Some Bolivian women wear commercially woven *mantas*, or shawls, with patterns often composed simply of large squares in two colors. However, the fine handcrafted type is a warp-faced "one-weft" double cloth, with the hidden weft weaving first the upper layer, then the lower one, forming a flattened tube. Double-faced color patterning is effected by the interchange of warps between the faces. When woven as pattern bands in wider pieces, the weft for one layer continues from selvedge to selvedge, and a secondary weft is used for the other surface of the band.

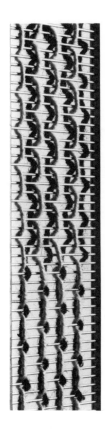

Three-span warp floats in alternate alignment (intermesh, light face). In the lower half, the L and D warps are shown as opposite partners. In the upper half, the floats slide over, tending to conceal the tie-downs.

a

c

In the lower half, three-span warp floats alternate in pairs ("pure" pebble, light face). In the upper half, two-span warp floats in diagonal alignment, with even twill order (2/2).

b

Two-span warp floats in diagonal alignment, with uneven twill order (2/1). The lower half shows light face; the upper half, dark face.

d

Weavers in an area near Lake Titicaca are master-craftsmen with this pattern weave. It is included in nearly every item of their everyday costume, in llikllas, capachos, coca bags, and belts, as well as for the distinctive Incan headband or wincha worn only in this area. In other parts of the country, warp-faced double cloth is used for belts, straps, and pattern bands.

Belts, purses, and large bags are commercially produced in a variation of the technique around Cochabamba, a tourist center. Instead of being either a balanced weave or warp-faced, it is "warp-predominant," since the weft is not completely covered. The yarns are much coarser than those used in other regions and larger-scaled traditional motifs are used.

Complementary-Warp Structures. More difficult for most weavers to comprehend are the varieties of warp-faced compound structures with complementary sets of warp, typical of much Bolivian double-faced patterning. This is sometimes referred to as "opposites patterning." Very little is written in this field, and it has been an exciting adventure to discover what is involved, not only in the basic structures, but also in the rich patterning and combinations of structures.

Since the term complementary warp (CWp) is unfamiliar to many experienced weavers, a short explanation will follow. When the weaver has a warp in which the yarns are alternately light and dark, a double-faced fabric may be woven if the warps are treated as complementary pairs, with a light warp and an adjacent dark one in each pair. When the complementary warps interlace the wefts on opposites, there are floats on both sides

of the fabric in opposite colors. These floats may be aligned diagonally or alternately.

To illustrate the basic Bolivian double-faced, warp-faced complementary-warp structures, a few light (L) and dark (D) yarns have been interlaced in a 6-dent floor loom reed. The wires of the reed represent the wefts, and the L and D complementary warps interlace them on opposites. A side-angle view is presented here (photos a–d) for a series of the basic weave structures. The floats are in alternate alignment in a and they alternate in pairs in b; whereas they are in diagonal alignment in c (even twill) and in d (uneven twill).

Patterning Versions. These structures are used in a variety of ways for the patterning of Bolivian fabrics, either alone or in many variations and combinations. The typical versions are outlined below, with letters to indicate the basic structures involved. Based mostly on their visual characteristics, the authors have adopted shorter names for some of the versions: *intermesh* ("ingrain" in a previous publication), *modified intermesh, pebble,* and *stepped diagonals.* These names aid in identifying the characteristic types, as well as in teaching the weaving techniques. In this book these shorter names are not intended to designate particular weave structures, but rather to denote traditional patterning versions that are often combinations of various complementary-warp structures. See the chart in the Appendix.

Alternate alignment, 3-span warp floats:
  intermesh (*a*)
  pebble, if "pure" (*b*)
  stepped diagonals (variation of *b*)

Three of the basic weave structures are represented in this small costal. The lion at the top is "pure" pebble, with diagonals of complementary-warp even twill. The animals at the bottom are complementary-warp uneven twill. Courtesy of the American Museum of Natural History, New York.

Diagonal alignment, 2-span warp floats:
  CWp (complementary-warp) *even twill,* 2/2 (*c*)
  (usually in combinations)
  CWp uneven twill, 2/1 (*d*)

Combinations of alternate and diagonal, 2-span & 3-span warp floats:
  pebble, patterned (*b* & *c*) (in broader sense)
  modified intermesh (*a* & *c*)

Diagonal Alignment. Since many simple twills are well-known, the patterns with diagonal alignment will be discussed first. The numbers 2/2, used here for denoting an even twill order, refer to the over-two, under-two interlacement of the warps with the weft. The weft is hidden in this warp-faced structure by the complementary warps interlacing on opposites. Note that it differs from the ordinary 2/2 twill of simple structure, in which there are two-span weft floats on the surface, as well as the two-span warp floats.

Although some Bolivian patterns may be mainly composed of this complementary-warp even twill, its chief use is to provide the diagonal lines, diamonds, and other variations in pebble or modified intermesh. CWp even twill may also be used for smaller areas of pattern with CWp uneven twill, but in only one instance have we seen it used in combination with intermesh, and then only for the wings and tail of one bird.

Patterning in complementary-warp uneven twill makes use of the light and dark faces, 1/2 and 2/1, of this weave. This patterning was developed to a high level of creativity in one Quechua area, where the dark and light faces of the weave are skillfully counterchanged to fill wide bands with fantastic animals and birds of many sizes and shapes. Other areas use finer-scale versions of the weave, with small geometric designs and different color characteristics. Variations such as interlocking scrolls are used whenever desired to achieve a special visual effect. This twill is also used at times to fill in small areas in pebble patterns.

Alternate Alignment. In intermesh, there are 3-span warp floats in alternate alignment as illustrated in the accompanying diagram. The L and D warps are shown spaced as opposite partners. In the upper part, the yarns have merely been slid on the "weft" wires of the reed to show that when the yarns are compacted as in the warp-faced fabric, the 3-span floats tend to conceal the tie-down yarns from the opposite face of the fabric. The alternation of floats on the surface then seems to resemble the alternation of yarns in warp-faced plain weave. However, the structure of this compound weave is more complex, as may be observed in the vertical cross-section view, which shows the manner in which the four consecutive warps in the basic unit interlace the weft. Its structure may be easily contrasted with that of double cloth.

In the four-heddle method commonly used to produce this weave, the odd-numbered rows are heddle-controlled tie-down rows, with the warps grouped as shown in the upper part of the diagram. There are two warps (a light one and an adjacent dark one) in each loop of the two tie-down heddles. The weft in these rows functions as a binding weft, going over two, under two, and if only these rows were woven, a plain weave

The basic complementary-warp structure having 3-span warp floats in alternate alignment (intermesh) is illustrated in this blanket border.

with paired warps would result. In the even-numbered rows the weft functions as an inner weft to separate the layers of light and dark complementary warps, so there are two faces, one light and one dark, each with 3-span floats in alternate alignment.

When these faces are counterchanged for the design, there is an effect of "intermeshing" on the pattern edges, with 2-span floats there instead of the 3-span floats. This is apparent at the lines of the horizontal color changes. The two faces of the fabric are not perfectly identical along the diagonal lines of the pattern because of a "feathering" that develops on one side or the other. Customarily intermesh is not combined with other complementary-warp pattern weaves within the pattern bands, but may be used immediately adjacent to pebble patterning.

Aymara Indians of the northern altiplano use intermesh pattern bands to incorporate words and designs into wider pieces. Some regions use it for wide border designs in heavy blankets. Other communities produce awayos, capachos, and belts in which the pattern areas are entirely composed of this weave. Sometimes a thinner cotton yarn is used for the light-colored warps of the pattern.

Modified intermesh is a variation developed in a community in central Bolivia. To the weavers there, the thinner white yarn is considered an essential for the light warps. It produces a lattice-effect background for the pattern figures of darker, coarser wool, which appear in relief. Since it is woven with two heddles and all hand-picked, it is far more varied than intermesh. The

tie-downs occur in the odd-numbered rows in the light background, but in the even rows for the dark pattern areas. This makes it possible to have neat horizontal lines. In the patterning, complementary-warp even twill is used very freely for diagonals, zigzags, and staircase effects. Animal and floral forms are often woven in a geometric setting.

In *pebble weave,* 3-span warp floats alternate in pairs. Note however that this differs from the paired warps of a simple structure, because of the complementary warps in between that are interlacing the wefts on opposites. In the photograph on page 34, the pebbled light area of the lion and the pebbled dark area of his background show the "pure" form of this pattern weave. The tie-down warps from the opposite surface appear as "pebbles" in the odd-numbered rows, where the weft functions as a binding weft. In the even-numbered rows, where it functions as an inner weft, it separates the warp layers so there are two identical faces, one light and one dark.

The color changes are sometimes made on horizontal lines, but most are made with the diagonal lines of CWp even twill. These diagonals are woven by continuing the same sequence for the tie-down rows and merely changing the pickup on the even, or design, rows. This results in the smooth diagonal lines of 2-span floats instead of the 3-span floats. In this book, the term *pebble weave* is used in the broadened sense, which includes all of these pattern combinations built on the system of the "pebble" tie-down rows.

The versatile pebble weave is widely used in

(Right) The wider bands in this awayo have patterns of doubled pebble weave. Collection of Lynn Meisch.

(Far right) This detail of an awayo with stepped diagonal pattern bands shows a 3-color example in the center. Courtesy of the American Museum of Natural History, New York.

the Andean highlands. Its truly reversible designs appear alone or in combination with other pattern weaves. More extensively used by the Aymaras than the Quechuas, pebble weave has many uses and a great variety of design possibilities.

Doubled pebble and *tripled pebble* are two variations of pebble weave produced by the Bolivians. The designs in these variations appear spread out because there are twice or three times as many warps per unit. A traditional diamond design favored by the Indian weavers is similar to weft-faced, loom-controlled rosepath "on opposites."

Stepped diagonals might also be considered a variation of pebble, since it basically has complementary-warp floats alternating in pairs. However in this case the tie-downs are not as regular and are not just in the odd-numbered rows, but shift to the even rows in the pattern areas. By this means the 3-span floats are retained at the color edges, with a "stepped" effect instead of the smooth even-twill lines created by the 2-span floats in the traditional pebble weave. In some stepped diagonal patterns there may be a few 5-span floats. This patterning version is not widespread in Bolivia, but has been observed more frequently in Peruvian textiles.

Three-Color Complementary-Warp Patterning. Weavers in some areas seem to delight in the play of color possible with an additional set of warps. More skill is needed for the manipulation, and sometimes there is a sacrifice in the clarity of the pattern. By skillfully varying the colors in the light and/or dark sets of warps, and by using cer-

tain color combinations, the weaver can create an optical illusion that leads the observer to conclude initially that the weaving has 3-color (3-set) warp patterning when there are only two sets.

Usually when there are three sets, one color is common to both surfaces of the fabric throughout. When the color change is in blocks, the common color may be the pattern in block A and the background in block B. In block A, the second color may be on the front, and the third color on the back, with these positions reversed in block B. Whenever warps of color two or three are replaced on their respective surfaces by the common color, they are hidden in the center of the warp-faced fabric by one of three ingenious methods, according to the nature of the pattern structure for double-faced patterns.

Three-Color Pattern Weaves with One Weft. When the pattern is composed of 3-span floats, the hidden third warp can interlace the wefts over one, under one. We have identified and named four such pattern weaves, although two of them actually are not complementary-warp structures like the others in this section, but rather, combinations of turned twill and horizontal herringbone.

Near Lake Titicaca, layered three-color weave is seen as a narrow pattern stripe in clothing and accessories. While two of the three colors interlace to form a layer of cloth (with an "H" pattern), the third color floats on the opposite side, producing a square "pillow." These float squares alternate with the "H" pattern on both sides of the fabric, with the surface color changed at in-

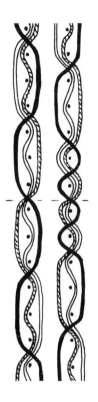

There are three general methods of weaving reversible 3-color complementary-warp weaves: (a) When there are 3-span floats, the hidden warp interlaces with the weft over-one, under-one. (b) For pebble weave, a secondary weft may be used in alternate rows. (c) A secondary weft is needed in every row for CWp twill weaves.

tervals. *Crinkle weave* is a heddle-controlled relative, used to produce firm but elastic belts near Sucre. Their patterns resemble checkerboards. When woven with overspun yarns, elasticity is provided in the float areas.

The other two in this group have complementary-warp structures. One was called *three-color companion weave* because it has only been seen used on both edges of modified intermesh pattern bands. The same thin white warp is used, but there are two sets of colored wool warps instead of one. Bolivian examples of the latter have been hard to find, but there are some in the collection of the American Museum of Natural History.

Three-Color Pattern Weaves with Two Wefts. The two pattern weaves in this category are more widely used in Bolivia. Sometimes, in three-color reversible pebble weave, the secondary weft is used in every row to separate the color layers, which seems best for designs with mostly diagonal lines. In most of the fabrics analyzed however, the secondary weft was used in alternate rows only, either in the pebble rows or in the design rows. Motifs are usually framed in blocks of alternating colors. Sometimes the third color is brought to the surface for a small area within the motif, such as the eye of a rooster.

For 3-color complementary-warp uneven twill, however, the secondary weft is needed in every row to separate the warp color layers. Sometimes the shift of color layers is done horizontally by blocks, but it may also be done diagonally or for smaller areas like hexagons. This weave is most frequently used for geometric patterns, though occasionally it is used for small animal or bird designs. According to locale, the color combinations and predominating motifs vary a great deal.

Two-Faced Complementary-Warp Pattern Weaves in Three Colors. We have never seen a Bolivian intermesh pattern done in three colors, but we have seen one coca bag in modified intermesh with a three-color warp. However, it was not double-faced, but had long floats on the back inside the bag. Only one weft is needed for this result.

A two-faced three-color pebble weave may be woven in a similar way, with one weft. Although it is the one technique in this book that apparently is not Bolivian, it is included because of its relationship to three-color reversible pebble.

Three- (and Four-) Color Warp-Faced Double Cloth. Even with a third (and more rarely a fourth) set of warps, only one weft is needed for a belt of warp-faced double cloth. The warps not used on either surface float between the two webs until needed, causing a padded effect. Sometimes the background on the front is the common color, forming the motifs on the back. The other two colors alternate in forming motifs on the face and appear in background blocks on the back. When a fourth set of warps is used, the motifs on the back become crowded. A few coca bags were found with three-color pattern bands having a mottling of the colors on the inside of the bag. This was due to the fact that warps had been allowed to remain paired instead of separated by color on the lower layer.

Crossed-Warp Structures. Two of the most unusual fabric structures encountered are used to embellish other weavings. Both have warps that cross and recross, and complex manipulations are required to produce them.

Occasionally, as a tie at the end of a wincha or as a strap for a chuspa, there is a narrow crossed-warp band whose pattern resembles a popular pebble-weave diamond motif. This band can best be described as a crossed-warp structure with groups of four interworking warps. Its surface resembles sculpture in relief, with shallow ridges and valleys. Although it appears reversible, upon examination it can be found that the diamonds on the back are not located directly behind the diamonds on the face, but between them.

The other embellishment is customarily woven as a tubular edging or as a round cord. It is a crossed-warp structure with diverted warps. When woven as an edge binding, the tube has a sinuous snake-back effect, with colorful diamond eyes alternately at the left or right. Some of the colors are diverted from side to side within the tube.

OTHER FABRIC STRUCTURES

There are a few other types of handwoven fabrics in the highlands that are beyond the scope of this book: pile rugs with Ghiordes knots, hangings with weft-loop designs (a more recent commercial product), chenille-like saddle pillows, soumak-type belts, saddle blankets woven with a soumak-like technique, and tapestry blankets. Slings and ropes are also not included.

Preserving the Craft. How much longer will there be weavers to carry on such a rich and varied craft? As fellow members of the craft, we need to be concerned with ways to encourage continuation of such folk art. Grace Goodell expressed concern and decided she did not want to name the better weaving villages in her section of this book. Consequently the authors also adopted this policy, although it might also be argued that such mention could be a matter of recognition and pride for the craftsmen of these areas, and could possibly be of help to them financially through by-passing the middleman. In answer to a query from the authors about how to protect the weavers from exploitation, Dr. Junius Bird of the American Museum of Natural History made the following suggestion:

"It is inevitably a losing proposition, as you point out but we should do what we can to minimize it. One thing of course is to point out that the quality cannot be maintained if the weavers are not adequately paid. Think of the Pisac-type poncho we analyzed for the labor involved—somewhere between 500 and 600-plus hours—for which the weaver received $15.00 U.S. (Textile Museum Journal, December 1968). If she had been paid the minimum wage in this country, she would have had between 1,200 and 1,500 dollars. If she could have had even a hundred, a not unreasonable figure, she would be making another good one now. Emphasize this type of information whenever you can."

The wide pattern bands in asksus of complementary-warp uneven twill are profusely decorated with numerous motifs in unusual ways. Collection of the International Folk Art Foundation Collection in the Museum of New Mexico.

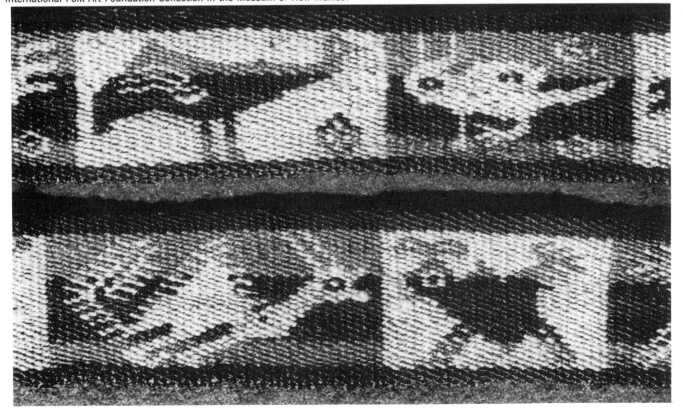

The weaver's sense of humor is evident in this narrow polychrome belt in 'one-weft' double cloth.

The popular interlocking scroll motif is often used in a variety of color combinations, as it is in this little chuspa.

Chapter Two

Learning the Craft

The Bolivian Indian learns as a child to weave on a simple primitive loom, stretching a narrow warp between his fingers and a toe. It is challenging and satisfying to weave bands this way, and no elaborate equipment is required. You can take your bundle of yarns out of your pocket almost anywhere—even in the car or by the lake—and begin to weave.

We have selected two types of narrow bands to introduce you to the basic techniques of warp-faced pick-up weaving. They are both double-faced, are woven with complementary warps, and are typical of bands from Bolivia. The techniques for weaving the bands shown in this chapter will be expanded in Chapter 3 where you will weave a series of more complicated bands.

YARNS AND EQUIPMENT

The warp-faced structure of this type of fabric necessitates using yarns that will not be too sticky to form a shed, and that can withstand a lot of friction without breaking. It is hard for us to find any wool of such quality as produced by the Bolivians.

Beginners should start with cotton yarns such as 8/4 carpet warp or Knit-Cro-Sheen crochet cotton. Perle cotton may be used, but it tends to "pill"; Double-Quick crochet cotton and Speed-Cro-Sheen are both usable, but are a bit stretchy. For coarser items, such as belts, you could use hard-twist rug yarn or jute cord.

Few supplies are needed, and you can easily improvise with what is available. Some options and desirable extras are indicated in the following list:

Carpet warp in three contrasting colors: light (L), medium (M), and dark (D)

Two warping posts or a set of C-clamps (Figure 1). You can also improvise with the back of a straight chair or the legs of an upside-down card-table

Something to hold the lease, such as: a safety pin, short lease sticks (made from tongue depressors or short lengths of screen molding with holes drilled near the ends), short shuttles held together with rubber bands, nylon stripping, or a rag strip or cord

Materials for the beginning end of the band: the first band: filler (rag strip, strips of paper towel, etc.); the second band: a safety pin

Desirable extras: scissors, light-colored Knit-Cro-Sheen for the heddle string, two bowls or coffee cans to hold your yarn during warping, and a yarn needle to help with unweaving and other corrections

WARPING

Bolivians do not cut their warps, but use a continuous yarn that is wound around and around two posts (or horizontal cross-bars) in a figure-8 pattern. Each figure-8 forms one complete circuit of yarn—called a *bout*—as it is wound around the posts (Figure 2). The bouts are always wound carefully one above the other. In following the directions in this book, always begin winding the bouts behind the left post.

The warp is counted in bouts. When a bout is wound with a single yarn—as in the borders—it is

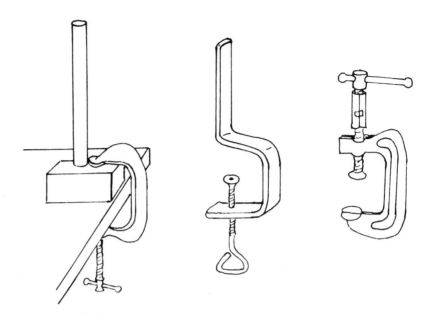

I. Here are three types of warping posts: (left to right) a dowel in a wood block, secured with a C-clamp, a Kircher warping clamp, and a C-clamp with its threads wrapped with heavy paper.

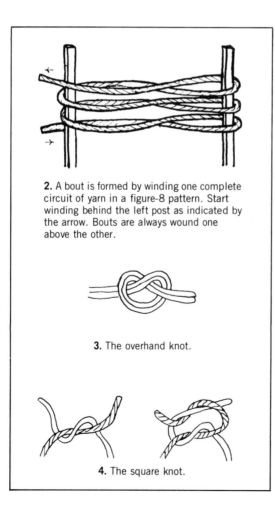

2. A bout is formed by winding one complete circuit of yarn in a figure-8 pattern. Start winding behind the left post as indicated by the arrow. Bouts are always wound one above the other.

3. The overhand knot.

4. The square knot.

called an *s-bout* and is composed of two warp ends. In the pattern areas, there are usually two contrasting yarns wound together in the bouts, sometimes more. The following terms are used throughout this book to specify the type of bout needed for a project:

S-bout: a single-yarn bout (2 warp ends)

D-bout: a double-yarn bout (4 warp ends)

T-bout: a triple-yarn bout (6 warp ends)

Q-bout: a quadruple-yarn bout (8 warp ends)

Warping directions are shown in the following order: border / pattern / border. A beginner should start with a warp that is no longer than about a yard. For each group of bouts, the ends are tied together with a square knot at the left post.

Either end of the warp may be chosen for the beginning of the weaving. Since the end at the left post has the knots, the choice usually depends on how the ends are to be finished. When the band is to have fringes it doesn't matter, but for the sample bands, plan to begin with the unknotted loops at the right post.

Tying Knots. Two familiar knots will be used frequently. The *overhand knot* (Figure 3) is a simple knot used to tie two parallel ends together. To tie a *square knot* (Figure 4) it helps to have a little chant, such as "left over right, then right over left."

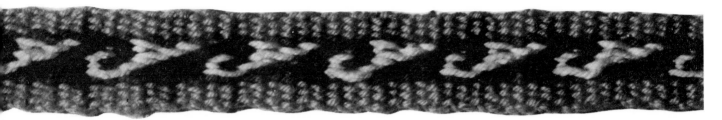

Complementary-Warp Uneven Twill Band (3 d-bouts) with a carpet warp.

Complementary-Warp, Uneven-Twill Band

The interlocking scroll motif introduced in this band is very popular around La Paz, the capital city. Coca bags and larger weavings are often patterned with many of these narrow bands in a variety of different colors. Sometimes two scrolls are placed "back-to-back," giving the appearance of a succession of small hearts.

Preparing the Warp. Wind the warps around two posts in figure-8 bouts, starting behind the left post: 4 s-bouts color M / 3 d-bouts colors L & D /4 s-bouts color M. (For the four s-bouts, you might like to have three of one shade and the fourth of a contrasting color.) When winding multiple-yarn bouts, keep the individual yarns in order by running them between your fingers (Figure 5). For each color group, tie the ends with a square knot at the left post.

Insert a generous length of cord through the warp loops at the left post. Tie it tightly around the loops with a knot, then knot the ends with an overhand knot to form an extra loop (you will use this later for attaching the warp to a stable object for weaving). Enclose the loops at the right post with a safety pin or loose cord loop. The bouts will now be kept in order if they should accidentally slip off the posts during the following steps. Do not remove the warp from the posts until so instructed.

The Warp Cross. Midway between the two warping posts, the warps criss-cross each other. This is called the *warp cross*. Find the warp cross (Figure 6) by putting your fingers within the end-loops, one hand by each post, and sliding them toward each other. Move this cross closer to the right post, where your weaving will begin. (Reduce tension by unscrewing a clamp slightly.) In this book, one side of the warp cross is called the *near* side (nearest the weaver) and the other is called the *far* side (furthest from the weaver).

The entire original warp cross (when viewed from either end of the warp) appears as shown in Draft A. Transfer the cross so it is between your two fingers of the left hand with the palm of the hand facing up. This way you can inspect it. When you wound the d-bouts for the pattern area, you took a dark and a light yarn together for the figure-8, making four warp ends. These four warp ends constitute two light-dark warp pairs (L–D pairs). In the lease, the two L–D pairs of a bout appear as shown below the draft.

To prepare the warps for heddle installation, the warp cross needs to be rearranged so all the light warps are on the near side of the lease cross and all the dark warps are on the far side. In this way each light warp will be to the left of its dark partner. The light warps will form the basis of heddle 1 (H 1) and the dark warps are for heddle 2 (H 2).

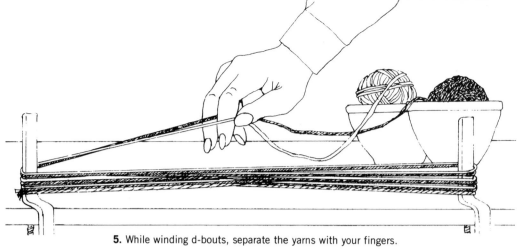

5. While winding d-bouts, separate the yarns with your fingers.

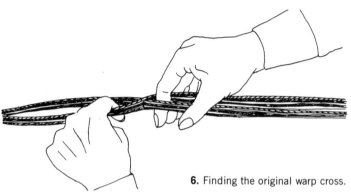

6. Finding the original warp cross.

Rearranging the Warp Cross. You should be positioned by the right post, with your left two fingers in the two sheds of the original warp cross and your palm facing up. Your right hand will also be used palm up, so your fingers can easily hold and manipulate the warps.

Transfer the right-hand border warps to two fingers of the right hand. Then, taking each L–D pair one pair at a time from the warp cross, first put the dark warp on the far finger, then put the light warp on the near finger, as shown in Figure 7. Do likewise with the next L–D pair. Continue in this manner until all the warps have been placed in the alternating warp order shown in Draft B. The two L–D pairs of each d-bout should appear as in the diagram below the draft. Hold this new lease cross by inserting lease sticks (or a large safety pin) in the two new sheds.

Preparing Heddle 1. It's a good practice to color-code the heddles. Although not important for this simple band, you will find color coding helpful in later projects for identifying the various heddles. Use light-colored Knit-Cro-Sheen for H 1. It is smooth, strong, and not as thick as carpet warp. Otherwise, carpet warp may be used. Heddle 1 is a *multiloop heddle*.

With the heddle yarn at the right, open the near shed (having light warps) and insert the end of the heddle string into the shed from right to left, positioning your hands as shown in Figure 8. When making the heddle loops, make sure that the warps are taken in order or you will not be able to operate the heddle. Using your right thumb, push the left border warp to the left so it is under the

first joints of the left two (or three) fingers. Lift the heddle string and wind it once around the left fingers, enclosing the single warp (Figure 9). Working from left to right across the warp, continue to push over each consecutive warp, enclosing each in turn in a heddle loop, as the string is wound around the fingers. When you have finished making all the loops, you may need to adjust the size of some of the loops so they are all uniform.

Cut the heddle string, leaving several inches of extra yarn. Tie the ends in a square knot on top of the left fingers (Figure 10). Pinching the knot area with the right fingers, remove the left fingers from the loops. Bind the loops firmly together by bringing each of the ends through the center of the loops in opposite directions and tying very firmly with the first half of a square knot. Then complete the square knot and trim off the surplus ends.

Preparing Heddle 2. Use either a dark cord or a doubled piece of dark carpet warp to make this heddle (H 2). Tie a simple loop around the warps, making it large enough to encircle two or three fingers (Figure 11). This type of heddle is called a *shed loop*.

You can now remove the warp from the posts and attach it to a stable object. If the hanger-loop at the far end is not large enough, add another cord loop.

Checking the Heddles. Grasp the near end of the warp and pull taut. Lift H 1 and put your left index finger in the shed near you. Then lift H 2

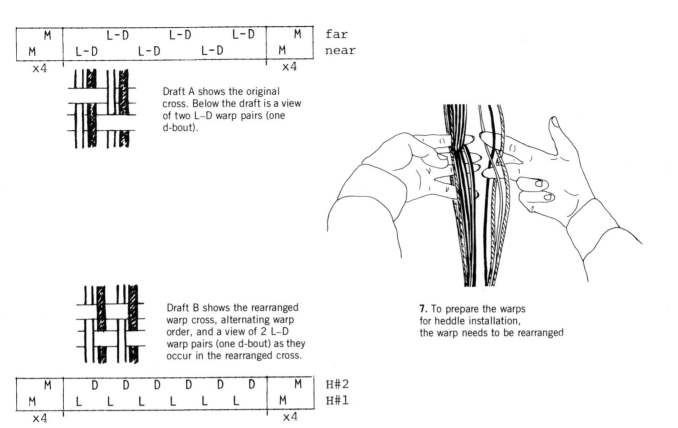

M		L-D		L-D		L-D		M	far
M	L-D		L-D		L-D			M	near
×4								×4	

Draft A shows the original cross. Below the draft is a view of two L–D warp pairs (one d-bout).

Draft B shows the rearranged warp cross, alternating warp order, and a view of 2 L–D warp pairs (one d-bout) as they occur in the rearranged cross.

7. To prepare the warps for heddle installation, the warp needs to be rearranged

M		D	D	D	D	D	D	M	H#2
M	L	L	L	L	L	L		M	H#1
×4								×4	

and widen the shed with your right hand to see if the shed can be cleared past H 1 down to the left finger as shown in Figure 12. If the shed cannot be cleared, H 1 needs to be remade because the warps were not taken in consecutive order. Return the warp to the posts and repeat the previous steps as needed.

Weaving Preliminaries. Bolivians treat the ends of their bands in a variety of ways, as described further in Chapter 4. Braided fringes are suggested for this first narrow band. Inserting rag filler (or a rolled strip of paper toweling or napkin) for a few inches (as shown in Figure 13) will leave space to braid later, and also provide practice in using the heddles. Insert the filler in the sheds made by alternately lifting H 1 and H 2. Beat the weft down after opening each new shed by pressing it with the side of your hand or a strong finger. After a few inches, end with the filler in the shed made by H 2.

You will need about a yard of carpet warp (color M) for the weft. Let it hang unwound so it is easier to pull out if you need to. Begin by inserting the weft into a shed made by lifting H 1, with the short tail of the weft at the left. Then lift H 2 and pass the weft to the left, tucking in the short tail. Pull the weft snug; it should not show between the warps. Continue with alternate heddles for several more rows, beating the weft down firmly after each new shed is formed. You are producing a warp-faced plain weave with horizontal stripes due to the alternating warp order. Since plain weave tends to spread more than the float-pattern weave, the weft should be pulled more

snugly for this section than for the pattern. End with a dark row, with the weft at the left. You are now ready to begin learning the pick-up for the pattern. In order to do this, you will first need to learn about the pattern diagram and the picking technique.

Understanding the Pattern Diagram. Since Bolivians learn to weave when they are very young, they are familiar with the motifs used in their neighborhoods and with the manipulations needed to weave them. They do not have to work with pattern diagrams, but for us it is far easier to have a guide to follow.

Because the band is warp-faced, with no weft showing, a rectangular grid or graph provides better proportion than a squared one. There is a horizontal row represented for each weft row (see the pattern diagram, part c) and a vertical row or lane for each L–D warp pair (and consequently two lanes for each d-bout). In order to have the pattern double-faced, the L and D warps in each L–D pair are treated as opposite partners, or as *complementary-warp pairs*. This means that when one of the pair is shown above the weft, the other must be below it. This can be seen in the lanes of the grid. When the rectangle in the grid is empty, the L warp is picked up to be above the weft. A dark line or a dot in the rectangle indicates that a D warp is picked. Dots are the same as lines, but are sometimes used for the places where the light floats around dark warps tend to conceal them. (A *float* is a warp that goes over two or more wefts.) The arrows show the direction of the weft. The encircled number shows the number of pattern

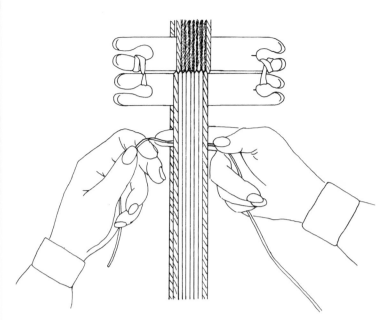

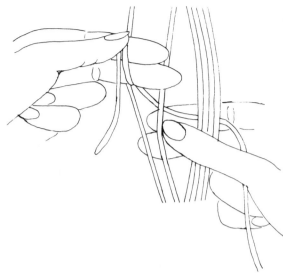

8. To begin heddle 1, insert the end of the heddle string into the shed from right to left.

9. Wind the heddle string around the left fingers, enclosing a single warp in every loop. Continue from left to right, enclosing each warp in a heddle loop.

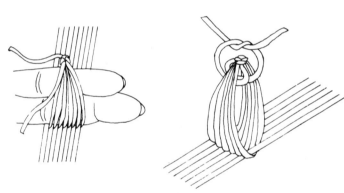

10. When you have finished making the heddle loops, tie the ends in a square knot, then bind the loops firmly together, as shown on the right.

11. Heddle 2 (H 2) is prepared as a shed loop.

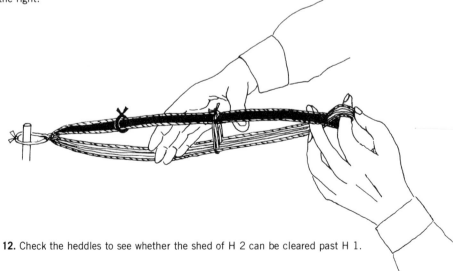

12. Check the heddles to see whether the shed of H 2 can be cleared past H 1.

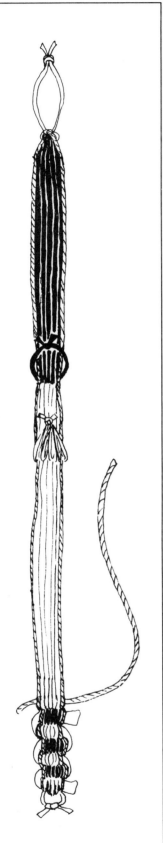

13. When your warp is ready for weaving, it should look like this.

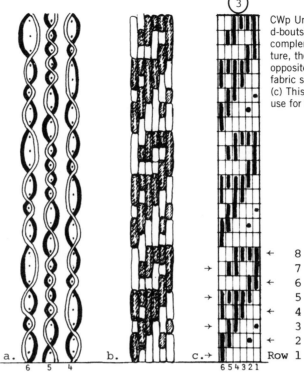

③

CWp Uneven-Twill Band (3 d-bouts). (a) In a complementary-warp structure, the L–D warp pairs act as opposite partners. (b) This is a fabric sketch of the pattern. (c) This is the pattern draft to use for weaving the band.

	Row	
←	8	2L,4D*
→	7	1L,2D*,2L,1D*
←	6	4L,2D*
→	5	5D*,1L
←	4	1D*,1L,2D*,2L
→	3	1L,2D*,2L,1D*
←	2	2D*,2L,1D*,1L
←	1	1D*,5L

a.   b.   c.→

bouts. Only the pattern area is included in a pattern diagram; the border warps are not indicated. This type of pattern diagram is called a float grid or float diagram, because most of the pattern is caused by floats. The instructions at the right of the pattern are for you to check your understanding of the code, but try to do the pickup from the diagram itself.

Picking Technique. Bolivian weavers select the warps for the motifs from a *picking cross*. This cross is formed on two fingers of the left hand, with the palm facing down. For the first row lift H 1, locking in the weft at the borders, and insert your left index finger in the shed. This is the *near* finger of the picking cross. Then, pulling the band taut with your finger in the shed, lift H 2. Open the shed with your right hand, and insert your left middle finger in that shed as the *far* finger of the cross (Figure 14). Check to be sure you have a good cross with no "floaters" between the fingers. The fingers can be slid back and forth on the warp to help put the yarns in order.

First pick up (and pull to the right) the border warps from the near finger. Notice that their partners on the far finger also move to the right and drop. Because you pick from the right, you must read the pattern from right to left. Look at the pattern for Row 1: you are to pick 5L, 1D*. Pick the 5L, and notice that their partners drop. Next pick up the ID* (from the far finger), and notice that its L partner (which is to its left on the near finger) does not drop and you need to push it off. The asterisk (*) after the D is to remind you

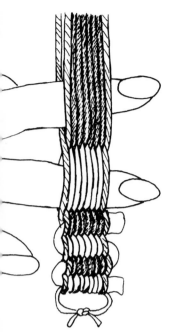

14. A picking cross is formed by the warps between the near and far fingers of the left hand.

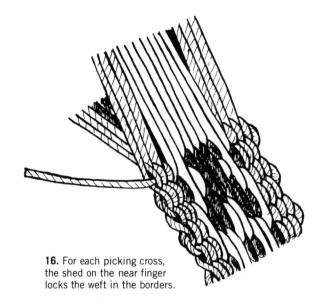

16. For each picking cross, the shed on the near finger locks the weft in the borders.

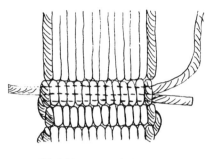

17. Add a new weft in the same shed as the old one.

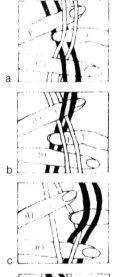

15. It is important to pick the warps as complementary pairs. When you pick the L warps, the D partners drop (as shown in a and b). When you pick the D warps, you must drop the last L partner (as shown in c and d).

of this. As you do the picking, think "one D, drop." End the row with the border warps from your near finger. Open this new shed, beat down the previous weft and pull it taut, then pass the weft to the right.

In the alternating-warp setups in this book, each light warp is to the left of its dark partner. When the left one of the L–D pair (L) is picked up and pulled to the right, its partner (D) will drop. However, when the right one (D*) is picked, its partner (L) needs help in dropping and must be pushed off (Figure 15).

To form the picking cross for Row 2, lift H 2, locking the weft in the borders. Insert your near left finger in the shed, then lift H 1 and enter your far finger. Pick the border warps from your near finger, pulling them to the right. This time the last partner does not drop, so push it off. (Color gives a clue, so it helps to have at least one bout next to the pattern area in a color that contrasts with the pattern colors.) Then pick 1L, 1D* (drop), 2L, 2D* (drop) and end with the left border warps. Beat, pull previous weft taut, and pass weft to the left.

To help you keep your place in the pattern diagram, it helps to know which way the picking cross is formed in relation to the direction the weft is to be passed. For each picking cross, the shed on the near finger locks the weft in the borders (Figure 16). This is H 1 when the weft is to

pass to the right and H 2 when the weft is to pass to the left. Continue upward, following the pattern row by row. To help you keep your place you can also use a marker such as a ruler or a card. Check that your weft is going in the direction of the arrows.

Adding a New Weft. When you run out of weft, overlap the old end with a new one in the same shed, leaving a short tail on each side of the band (Figure 17). Later, pull the tails taut on each side and trim off the excess yarn.

Finishing the Ends. You started this band with a filler, which will now be removed for a fringed end. When you have woven as far as you can, remove the heddles and pull out the filler. The end fringes are often braided. Four-strand round braids make a neat finish for narrow bands such as this one (see Chapter 4).

Suggestions. You have now learned many of the basic techniques, but you need practice. Perhaps you'd like to try another similar band with other colors, other yarns, and perhaps more s-bouts in the borders. Remember to have the s-bout next to the pattern in a contrasting color. Turn to the end of this chapter to read some suggestions that may help you improve your technique. Then go on to the 4-bout pebble band.

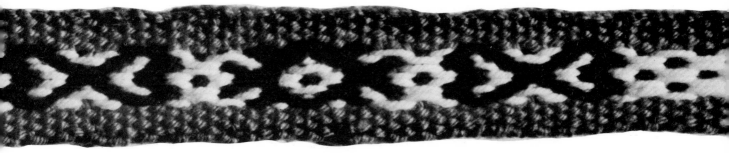

Pebble Weave Band (4 d-bouts) in carpet warp.

Pebble Weave Band

Aymara weavers have a great wealth of small motifs from which to choose when they produce pebble weave bands. Bird and duck motifs are popular around Lake Titicaca. Near the high mountain peaks weavers often use small animals as motifs, especially the viscacha, a gray-furred, long-tailed rodent that looks like a rabbit with a squirrel's tail. The viscacha supposedly is seen only ''in the moonlight.'' Delicate geometric patterns may be used in combination with the animal motifs or as motifs by themselves.

Pebble weave is produced with a simple two-heddle setup in either of two ways: with an alternating warp order or with an irregular one. Each method has its advantages and disadvantages. You will use the alternating warp order for this project. This band gives you an opportunity to practice the basic techniques introduced with the previous band. You will also learn some of the special features of pebble weave and get acquainted with some of the smaller geometric motifs.

Preparing the Warp. Wind the warp around two posts in figure-8 bouts, starting behind the left post: 3 s-bouts color M / 4 d-bouts colors L & D / 3 s-bouts color M. Attach the hanger loop to the warps at the left post, and enclose the warps at the right post in a safety pin. Make sure the pin is positioned with the pointed side within the loops so it may be easily removed later (Figure

18). Find the warp cross, move it toward the right post, and rearrange the cross as shown in Draft C. Use lease sticks (or a substitute) to hold the new cross. Prepare H 1 as a multiloop heddle and H 2 as a shed loop. Take the warp from the posts, attach the hanger loop to a stable object, and check the heddles. (It's even better if you check them while the warp is still on the posts.)

Weaving Preliminaries. This band will demonstrate how to make a neat tab end with the help of a safety pin. Enter the weft in the end-loops beside the pointed side of the pin, with the short tail at the left. Lift H 2, clear the shed to the pin, making sure that the yarns are even and snug. Pass the weft to the left, tucking in the tail. Lift H 1, beat firmly, and pass the weft to the right. You may continue to use the alternate heddles for several rows, pulling the weft snug for the plain weave. End on a dark row, with the weft at the left. Before you begin on the pattern, read through the following section on pebble weave patterning.

Pebble Weave Patterning. Like the previous band, this one also has complementary-warp float patterning. In this band, however, there is regular repetition of *tie-downs* in alternate or odd-numbered rows. In the pebbled light area, these tie-downs appear as dark pebbles, and in the pebbled dark area as light pebbles. In view A of Fig-

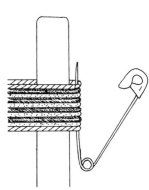

18. To have a neat tab end on your band, insert the pointed side of a safety pin into the end-loops at the right end of the warp.

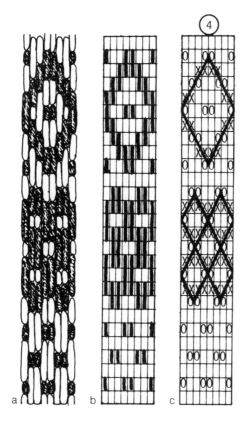

M		L–D		M	far
M		L–D		M	near
×3		×4		×3	

M		D	D	M	H#2
M		L	L	M	H#1
×3		×4		×3	

Draft C shows the pebble weave band with 4 d-bouts. The top draft represents the original warp cross. The bottom draft shows the rear-ranged warp cross, with an alternating warp order.

19. A special grid has been devised for pebble weave. The fabric sketch is shown on the left, the float grid in the middle, and the rectangular pebble grid on the right.

ure 19 the light and dark warps are drawn as they appear on the face of the fabric. View B shows the face of the fabric as it appears when diagrammed on a float grid.

There is a third way of diagramming pebble weave that is helpful, both for recording the traditional motifs and creating new ones (view C). In this grid, 00's (pebbles) are positioned where the dark warps regularly appear in the light ground, which is the pure unmodified fabric structure. Where dark warps are picked up to form a design (thus modifying the pure structure) XX's are placed in the rectangles. A diagonal line is added between the 00's of the previous and following rows to represent the visual effect of the dark floats.

Look at the pebble weave diagram to observe the following additional characteristics of the pebble weave diagram system:

1. Alternation of Rows. The diagram shows the pebble rows, where the weft goes from left to right (the arrow faces right), and the design rows where the weft goes from right to left (the arrow faces left).

2. Alternation of Pebble Rows. The diagram indicates that a row with a single light warp at the edge will be called an L-edge row, and a row with a single dark warp at the edge will be called a D-edge row.

3. Diagonal Lines between Dark Pebbles (00). These represent the visual effect of the dark floats. Each diagonal between pebbles is used to indicate two dark design row warps picked up (XX).

4. Empty Rectangles. Each space where there is no diagonal line between pebbles indicates two light warps picked up.

Your beginning motifs will be provided on this pebbled rectangular grid. Later, in Chapter 3, an even more simplified method will be presented.

Picking a Light-Edge Pebble Row. Your weft was brought to the left in the shed made by lifting H 2. Your warp is now ready for you to pick the first pebble row, shown as Row 1 near the bottom of the pattern diagram. Form a picking cross with the H 1 warps on the near finger and the H 2 warps on the far finger. Pick the right-hand border warps from your near finger. Then pick the L-edge pebble row: 1L, 2D*, 2L, 2D*, 1L. Finish by taking the left border warps from the near finger. Beat down in the picked shed, and pull the previous weft taut. Pass the weft through to the right.

Weaving Sequence. Follow the sequence shown on the pattern diagram, using the printed instructions merely as a check on your understanding of the diagram. Plan to pick each row taking the border warps from the near finger, thereby locking in the weft. There is a repeat of four rows in the sequence. Row 1, which you have already woven, is listed first.

1. Pebble Row, L-edge. Form a picking cross with the H 1 warps on the near finger and the H 2 warps on the far finger. Pick as shown for Row 1: 1L, 2D*, 2L, 2D*, 1L, taking the border warps from the near finger. Beat, and pass the weft to the right.

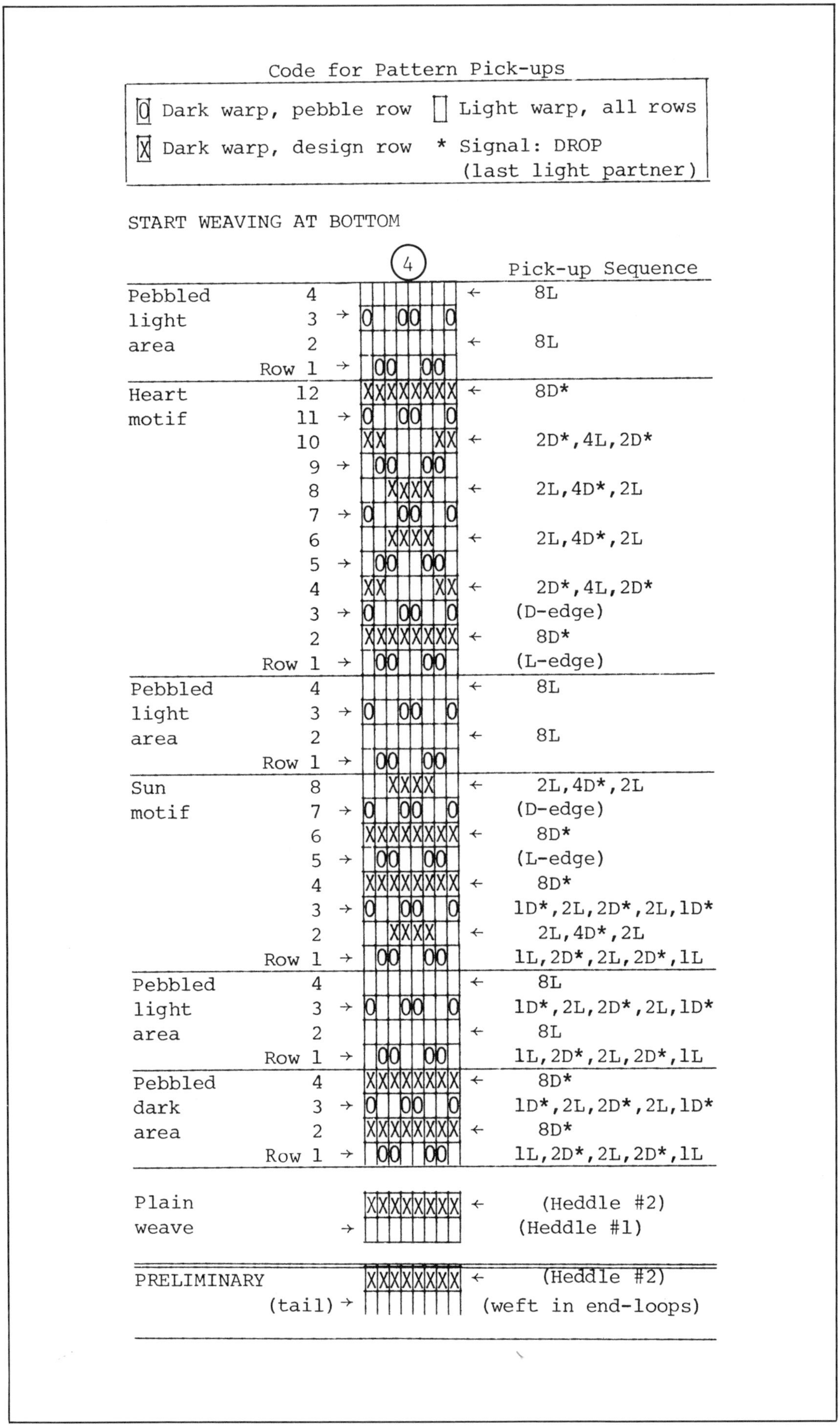

⟨0⟩ Dark warp, pebble row	⟨⟩ Light warp, all rows
⟨X⟩ Dark warp, design row	* Signal: DROP (last light partner)

START WEAVING AT BOTTOM

④ Pick-up Sequence

Area	Row	Dir		Pick-up Sequence
Pebbled	4	←		8L
light	3	→	0 00 0	
area	2	←		8L
	Row 1	→	00 00	
Heart	12	←	XXXXXXXX	8D*
motif	11	→	0 00 0	
	10	←	XX XX	2D*,4L,2D*
	9	→	00 00	
	8	←	XXXX	2L,4D*,2L
	7	→	0 00 0	
	6	←	XXXX	2L,4D*,2L
	5	→	00 00	
	4	←	XX XX	2D*,4L,2D*
	3	→	0 00 0	(D-edge)
	2	←	XXXXXXXX	8D*
	Row 1	→	00 00	(L-edge)
Pebbled	4	←		8L
light	3	→	0 00 0	
area	2	←		8L
	Row 1	→	00 00	
Sun	8	←	XXXX	2L,4D*,2L
motif	7	→	0 00 0	(D-edge)
	6	←	XXXXXXXX	8D*
	5	→	00 00	(L-edge)
	4	←	XXXXXXXX	8D*
	3	→	0 00 0	1D*,2L,2D*,2L,1D*
	2	←	XXXX	2L,4D*,2L
	Row 1	→	00 00	1L,2D*,2L,2D*,1L
Pebbled	4	←		8L
light	3	→	0 00 0	1D*,2L,2D*,2L,1D*
area	2	←		8L
	Row 1	→	00 00	1L,2D*,2L,2D*,1L
Pebbled	4	←	XXXXXXXX	8D*
dark	3	→	0 00 0	1D*,2L,2D*,2L,1D*
area	2	←	XXXXXXXX	8D*
	Row 1	→	00 00	1L,2D*,2L,2D*,1L
Plain		←	XXXXXXXX	(Heddle #2)
weave		→		(Heddle #1)
PRELIMINARY		←	XXXXXXXX	(Heddle #2)
(tail)		→		(weft in end-loops)

Pebble Weave
Pattern Diagram
(4 d-bouts).

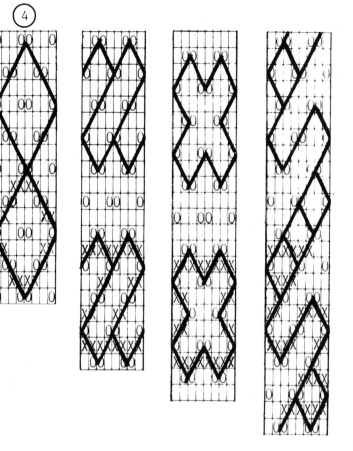

④

20. Here are more motifs
for pebble weave
with 4 d-bouts.

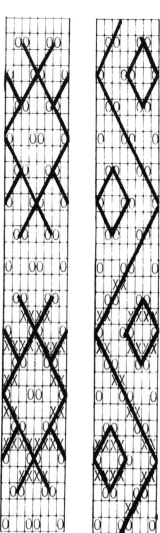

2. Design Row. Form a picking cross with the H 2 warps on the near finger and the H 1 warps on the far finger. Pick as shown for Row 2, taking the border warps from the near finger. Beat, and pass the weft to the left.

3. Pebble Row, D-edge. Repeat as for Row 1, but pick for the D-edge pebble row, as shown for Row 3: 1D*, 2L, 2D*, 2L, 1D*.

4. Design Row. Repeat as in Row 2, picking for Row 4. Continue according to the pattern diagram and its directions.

Getting More Practice. When you have become comfortable with the basic techniques and can weave the motifs on the pattern diagram, you may wish to review the suggestions for improving your techniques at the end of this chapter. Then you might repeat some of the same motifs or try some others, shown in Figure 20. *Always check the initial pebble row of the pattern to see whether it has a light edge or a dark edge.* You may need to weave another design row of all light, for more background, to have the proper pebble row for the motif you select. There are two repeats of each motif. Select a motif and start weaving at the bottom with the proper pebble row. The lower motifs have the XX's entered in the design rows, the upper repeats do not. If you need the XX's, you may either repeat from the lower unit or draw them in on the upper one.

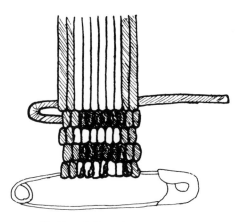

21. For a better edge, leave a loop of the weft at the edge, then pull it taut after the shed for the next row is formed.

SUGGESTIONS FOR IMPROVING YOUR TECHNIQUES

After you have made a beginning at this new way of weaving, you might consider some ways to improve your techniques, so it will be easier for you to handle warps that are wider or more sticky.

Lifting Heddles. Develop your own method of lifting the heddles so you avoid friction of warps and heddles. The most important thing is to try not to work the heddles back and forth on the warps. Strumming is a big help with a sticky warp. It can be done with a tool, or by fanning out the warps to the side between your fingers and thumb, then releasing them gradually.

For the two bands in this chapter, the way the picking cross is formed for the rows partially determines the lifting technique. When the weft is on the right, the picking cross is formed with the H 2 warps on the near finger. They usually lift quite easily. As you are reaching up to lift H 2, it helps to give H 1 a little tug on the way, to straighten the heddle loops so they won't be in the way of lifting the warps. For wider bands or sticky warps, it also helps to clear the dark warps past H 1 in sections, a few warps at a time, with your fingers and thumb in a "quacking" motion until all are cleared through. (Be sure to insert the near finger in the shed after lifting the H 2 warps!)

To complete the picking cross, H 1 will lift more easily if you hold the band with more tension on the dark warps than on the light ones. This is achieved by pressing the dark warps firmly between your left thumb and finger while rotating your hand toward you.

When the weft is on the left, the picking cross is formed with the H 1 warps on the near finger. These warps will lift best if you pull back on the dark warps while you are lifting H 1. This will also aid in lifting H 2 to complete the picking cross.

Beating and Weft Control. To have distinct pick-up patterns, the weft must be well beaten down with the side of the hand or a strong finger after each new shed is picked and before the next weft is shot. This presses in the weft of the previous row, which should then be grasped firmly and pulled fairly taut so no weft shows between the warps.

To maintain a uniform·width and even selvedges, leave a loop of weft at the selvedge when it is inserted (Figure 21). Then watch the edge to keep it even, when you pull it taut later. Since plain weave areas tend to spread more than the areas with pattern floats, they need to have the weft pulled more tightly.

Pick-Up Methods. Each weaver develops her own picking technique, and every weaver differs in the way her hands are held while picking. Suggestions are given here to get you started in developing your own picking style. Experiment with the methods below and then adjust them to suit your own preference. The important thing is that your hands feel comfortable, especially when weaving for an extended period of time. Try to keep your hands as relaxed as possible, yet still

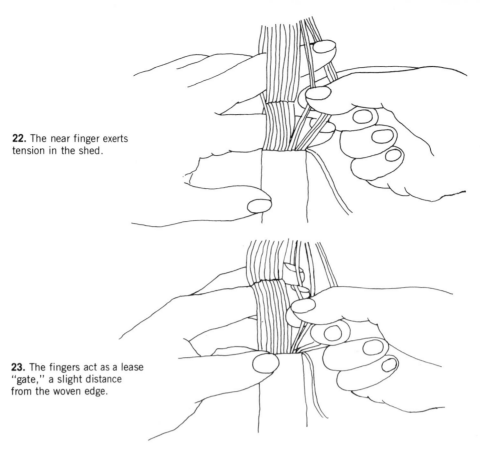

22. The near finger exerts tension in the shed.

23. The fingers act as a lease "gate," a slight distance from the woven edge.

maintain enough tension on the warp to perform the necessary manipulations. During the picking, the fingers may slide back and forth if needed to put the warps in proper order.

In one method (Figure 22), the near finger of the left hand maintains tension on the warps by pressing toward the body in the shed, against the fabric. The far finger is spread a comfortable distance (one to two inches) from the near finger. The warps are picked from the far side of each of the left fingers. These fingers are raised and lowered as necessary while picking to aid in positioning the yarns. During picking, the unpicked warps are dropped only from the far left finger. Unpicked warps on the near finger are allowed to remain there until the finger is removed, at which time they drop automatically.

In the other method, the picking cross is held (as above) between the two left fingers, but this time a short distance from the fabric, which is held lightly in place between the thumb and other fingers. According to the situation, these fingers may have their tips apart or together. When together, they act as a gate to keep the warps from

slipping off (Figure 23). Much of the picking may then be done "on the outside," on the near and far sides of the fingers. But some picking is also done between them when they are open. Unpicked warp partners are dropped from both fingers as the picking proceeds. It is easier to pull the warps off the fingers when the near finger is not so close to the woven edge. The picked warps are held by the right middle finger, leaving the forefinger and thumb free to do the picking.

If you use a backstrap or frame loom so that both hands are free, try making the picking cross with your left palm up, beyond H 1. Then only the picked warps need to be lifted through H 1.

Unweaving. If you wish to remove several rows of weft, there is a way to do it fairly easily. Lift the border warps of H 1 on the left side and those of H 2 on the right side. Pull these yarns back toward you, on top of the woven edge. This will expose the weft on each side in turn. A yarn needle can then be inserted under the weft so it can be grasped and pulled out of its shed. Peel back the border yarn layers as you continue.

A small Chuspa (detail) with two kinds of pattern bands: the center band is pebble weave and the side bands show a 5-bout version of the complementary-warp uneven twill motif.

Ancient Peruvian Belt. This shows both sides of the unfinished belt, which was worked with a five-color warp. Courtesy of the Museum of Natural History, New York.

Chapter Three

Band Projects

Very little can be found in weaving literature about the actual techniques used for the warp-faced, double-faced pattern weaves characteristic of most Bolivian fabrics. Some writers have devised floor-loom methods for a few weaves that use four to six harnesses, whereas the Indian may use only two for the same weave and has greater possibilities for flexibility in design. We learned most of the techniques presented in this book directly from the Bolivian Indians. When this was not possible we carefully analyzed the fabrics, then reproduced them on the basis of known Indian methods. Adaptations for contemporary American looms are described in Chapter 5.

When you are familiar with the basic techniques and have woven the narrow bands in Chapter 2, you are ready to try the "recipes" in this chapter. For each new way of patterning, directions will be given for weaving a small sample band. If you leave it only partly woven, with the heddles still in, it will be handy for later reference and review.

The techniques are grouped according to the methods used to produce them. The two-heddle weaves are the easiest. Those with four heddles are somewhat harder. Most difficult are the three-color weaves. While the techniques are arranged in a logical progression, it is not necessary to take them in the given order.

After you have mastered the techniques for a particular sample band, you may wish to try one or more projects in that pattern weave before going on to another sample band. For help in additional projects, see Chapters 5 and 6.

GENERAL DIRECTIONS

The basic techniques introduced in Chapter 2 will be used to produce the bands in this chapter. Follow the general procedures summarized below unless otherwise instructed. A warp length of about 2 feet/160.96 cm is useful for these samples. A tab end is planned for the beginning of each band like the pebble band in Chapter 2.

Part of the fun of weaving Bolivian patterns is in playing with color. Try out different combinations as much as possible. The yarns chosen must have a high degree of contrast to obtain distinct patterns. Usually one light and one dark color are chosen for the pattern area and a medium color or two are chosen for the border. For polychrome effects you would need two or more dark or light colors. In addition to the symbols L, M, and D for the light, medium, and dark yarns, B may be used to indicate a suitable color for the border. As in Chapter 2, the sample bands should be woven with cotton yarns. Later you can experiment with other yarns.

For some bands you will be warping the borders with d-bouts that require two yarns of the same color. Before beginning to wind the warp, you will need to divide your border-colored yarn into two balls. The second ball needs only enough yarn to make the border bouts.

When rearranging the warp cross, always carefully follow the draft. There may be several steps involved when there are more than two heddles. Special directions for the three-color warps appear in the introduction to that section at the end of this chapter.

All heddles should be the multiloop type in which there is a separate heddle loop for each individual strand of yarn unless otherwise indicated. In some cases two yarns instead of a single yarn are enclosed in a heddle loop. Sometimes a warp is operated by more than one heddle. Use a shed loop as a heddle only where indicated. Always check the heddles to assure proper installation before beginning to weave.

Always pick the warps so one warp of the complementary pair is above the weft and the other is below the weft. Remember to push down the partners which do not drop automatically.

TWO-HEDDLE WEAVES (ALTERNATING WARP)

Creative freedom of design is particularly evident in fabrics woven with only two heddles. Bolivian weavers in different areas have developed distinctive styles of color and design. The basic complementary-warp structures were described more fully in Chapter 1. Five patterning versions, woven with alternating warp order, are included in this section: pebble weave, CWp uneven twill, modified intermesh, stepped diagonals, and CWp floats on plain weave.

Band 1. Pebble weave (8 d-bouts) with alternating warp order.

Band 1: Pebble Weave

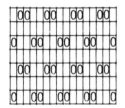

a. rectangular
   pebble grid

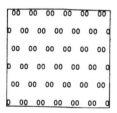

b. simplified
   pebble grid

1. A simplified version of the pebble grid makes it easier to record designs.

Interesting design variations in pebble motifs can be obtained by slightly altering the basic weaving rhythm. Techniques that make possible design flexibility are introduced in this section, as well as the simplified method of diagramming patterns. This band is similar to the one in Chapter 2, but has eight d-bouts instead of four.

A wealth of traditional designs occur in pebble weave, in bands of different widths. Many of these are provided for you in the Appendix. The simplified diagram system shown in this chapter will free you to create your own designs. Read through the instructions quickly first to get the general idea, then you will know where to find the information as you need it.

Simplified Diagram System. Wider motifs have so many warp ends that it is difficult or impractical to diagram them on the rectangular pebble weave grid, so we have developed a simplified grid on which it is much easier to sketch and "read" the design. The two versions of the pebble weave grid are shown in Figure 1. In the simplified version, the rectangles have been removed so only the 00's that indicate the pebbles remain. The design row XX's are removed also, leaving only the diagonal lines drawn between the pebbles of the previous and following pebble rows. The simplified grid is also reduced in size.

Sketching patterns on the grid in Figure 2 will prepare you for weaving designs directly from the

simplified grid. You may choose either to try sketching a traditional motif, or perhaps you'd like to design some of your own. (The darkened 00's in the motifs will be explained later.)

If you want to avoid marking directly on the grids in the book, there are several options. If a copy machine is available, make a copy of the practice grid. If not, type one of your own. Use squared paper to draw the pebble grid (2 squares = 1 rectangle), or use tracing paper.

As you may have noticed in Chapter 2, pebble weave motifs are built from two kinds of diagonal lines, those that slant to the left and those that slant to the right. These two are combined to form most patterns, with occasional modifications for horizontal lines. These diagonal lines are drawn from the 00's in any pebble row to the 00's in the next pebble row. Begin by drawing your motifs on the rectangular grid. First sketch in the diagonal lines. Then fill in the design row XX's, marking two XX's for each diagonal line. You may also wish to jot down the pickups beside the grid (for example: 2D*, 4L, 2D*). Finally, transfer the same motif to the simplified grid.

To learn to read a motif in the simplified system, you must learn to count how many warps to pick up. With the rectangular grid present it is easy to count the warps, but it is slightly more difficult when the rectangular grid is removed. Both the light and dark warps are counted *diagonally* between the 00's. Each diagonal line

CODE

◧ = dark warp,
    pebble row

⊠ = dark warp,
    design row

☐ = light warp,
    either row

Each diagonal line
between 00's = two
dark warps in the
design row (XX).

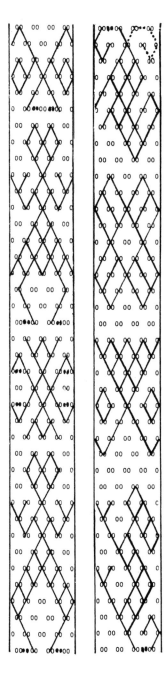

2. Use the practice grid to sketch designs.

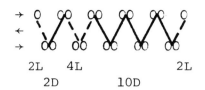

2L   4L   2L
2D   10D

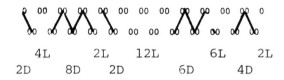

4L   2L   12L   6L   2L
2D   8D   2D   6D   4D

3. For the design row warps, count diagonally in a horizontal zigzag course (a line = 2D, a space = 2L).

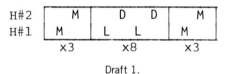

Draft 1.

---

indicates that two dark warps are to be picked up; each diagonal space (without a line) indicates that two light warps are to be picked up. In using the simplified pebble grid, the warps are counted by two's in the design-row spaces between the pebble rows. Always start with the single pebble (0) at the right edge and count the light or dark warps to be picked up, by two's, diagonally in a horizontal zigzag course. You will soon be able to do this visually as you go. For wider patterns it is sometimes helpful to enter some small numbers to help you keep count. Figure 3 shows how to count the light and dark warps by observing the diagonal lines and spaces.

Preparing the Warp. Wind the warp yarns in the following order: 3 s-bouts M / 8 d-bouts L and D / 3 s-bouts M. Rearrange the warp cross as shown in the draft for Band 1. Install H 1 as a multiloop heddle and H 2 as a shed loop.

Start the weft in the end loops beside the safety pin, with the short tail at the left. Instead of beginning with alternating heddles as before, form a picking cross with the H 2 warps on the near finger and the H 1 warps on the far finger. Pick the borders from the near finger and all the lights from the far finger. Pass the weft toward the left, tucking in the tail. Form another picking cross, this time with the H 1 warps on the near finger. You are now ready for Row 1 of the right-hand motif in Figure 4. Weave until you come to the leg of the bird in Row 5. This pebble row has been modified. Now follow directions for horizontal line modifications that follow.

Horizontal Lines. The lines of pebble weave designs are typically diagonal, since they relate to the twill part of this pattern weave. Some patterns or motifs may also have straight, horizontal lines that are produced by modifying the pebble rows.

There are two kinds of modifications. A dark warp can be replaced by a light warp or vice versa. In each case, the warp that would ordinarily be lifted for a pebble row is replaced by its partner warp. These two modifications are noted on the pattern grid as shown in Figure 5. Darkened 0's are added to the pebble row to indicate that a light warp is to be replaced by its dark partner. Crossed-out 0's indicate that a dark warp is to be replaced by its light partner. To make these modifications, simply pick the warps as indicated by the pattern diagram. The other motif in Figure 4 and some of the motifs in Figure 2 will provide further practice.

When there is an acute angle formed by a horizontal line with the diagonal line of the motif, longer floats result. When the horizontal line forms a triangle, the solid area of floats may be desirable, but it is often better visually to have a spot of contrast, or *seed*, within the triangle as shown in Figure 6 and in the lower geometric motif in the left column of Figure 2. The seed also ties down the floats within the triangle.

To form a seed, the replacement warps in the horizontal line must each be picked up on the ''wrong'' side of their complementary-warp partners during the picking of the modified pebble row. Figure 7 shows how this is done so the partner warps are crossed. It is easiest to pick a light

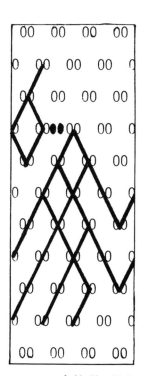

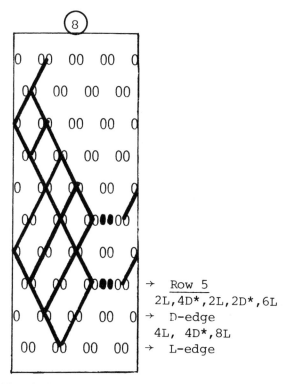

→ Row 5
   2L,4D*,2L,2D*,6L
→ D-edge
   4L, 4D*,8L
→ L-edge

4. Motifs with horizontal lines for Band 1.

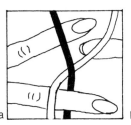

5. Two kinds of pebble row modifications are used to produce horizontal lines. The dark warp replaces the light in the top diagram; the light warp replaces the dark in the bottom diagram.

6. A "seed" motif for Band 1.

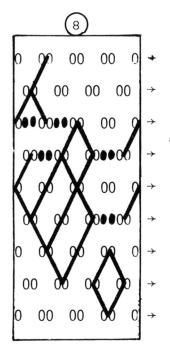

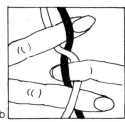

7. To produce a "seed," the complementary warps must be crossed. View a shows picking the light replacement warp. View b shows picking the dark replacement warp.

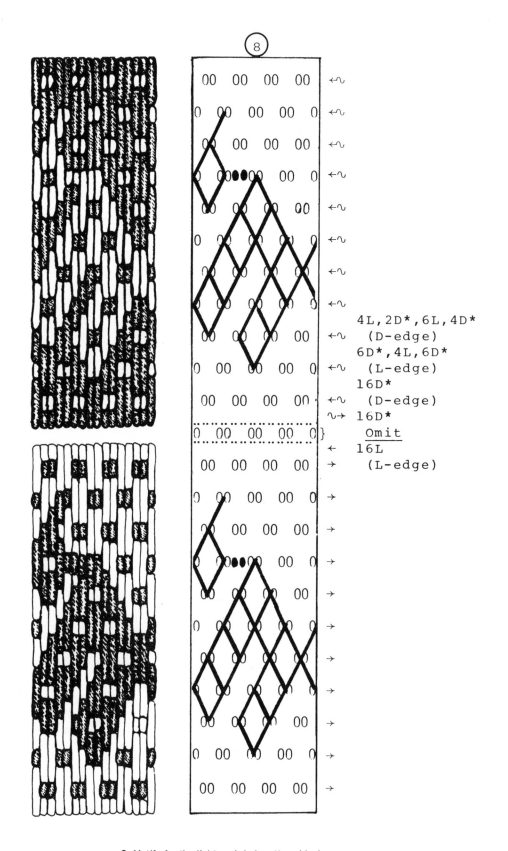

8. Motifs for the light and dark pattern blocks.

warp as a replacement, since merely reaching under the dark warp to pick the light partner causes them to cross (view a). To pick a dark warp as a replacement, first position the picking finger to the left of the light partner. Then reach down between the two left fingers and pick the dark warp from beneath the near left finger (view b). Don't worry if you can't master the seed technique immediately. You can come back to it later when you've had more experience.

Pattern Blocks. The Bolivians often weave motifs in blocks, alternating a dark motif on a light background with a light one on a dark background. You can do this with a mental reversal of the pattern, using any suitable motif.

Two changes in the basic techniques are necessary to produce a band with alternating pattern blocks. First, one pebble row must be omitted at the point of change from one background color to another. Second, the omission of the pebble row causes a reversal in the direction of the weft for the pebble and design rows from the weft direction used in the previous block. These two changes are shown in Figure 8.

More Adventures with Pebble Weave. You have been learning how to produce a two-color pebble weave pattern with an alternating warp order and two heddles. In the Appendix you will find sample sheets of pebble grid and a variety of traditional patterns.

Later in this chapter, there is information for doing pebble weave with an irregular warp order, in which the pebble rows are heddle-controlled: Band 8 is a two-heddle pebble weave for which only the design rows need to be picked, and Band 9 is a doubled pebble variation. Band 15 is a three-color pebble that is not reversible. Bands 16 and 17 give directions for weaving the reversible three-color pebble weave with the alternating warp order and more heddles. (Band 16 is a tripled variation.)

In Chapter 5 you will find information on how to do pebble weave with either two or four heddles on a variety of looms—backstrap, Bolivian-type frame, inkle, and floor loom. Chapter 6 has ideas for additional projects.

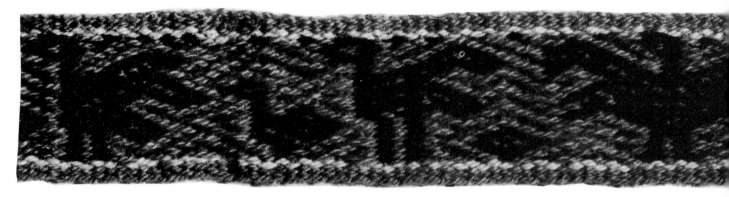

Band 2. A complementary-warp uneven twill pebble band.

```
H#2 | M M L | D   D | L   M M
H#1 | M M L | M   M | L   M M
            x12
```

Draft 2.

Band 2. Complementary-Warp Uneven Twill

In addition to its use for abstract designs, often with interlocking scrolls, this twill is used in Bolivia for wide pattern bands filled with fanciful creatures. In the community where this style has developed to an art, the color is traditionally red, along with a darker color that is usually dark green, purple, or maroon. The dark and light faces of the fabric used for the pattern and background areas (Figure 9) are due to the 2/1 and 1/2 interlacement of the complementary warps with the wefts.

To expand your experience with this weave in the beginning 3-bout band in Chapter 2, a wider band is provided here that has a variety of bird motifs. The detail at the end of the wings is typically used in many designs. We suggest that you use traditional colors, with red for the M color.

Preparing the Warp. Wind the warp yarns in the following order: 2 s-bouts M, 1 s-bout L / 12 d-bouts M and D / 1 s-bout L, 2 s-bouts M. Rearrange the warp cross as indicated in Draft 2. Install H 1 as a multiloop heddle and H 2 as a shed loop. Insert the weft with the tail to the left, lift H 2, pass the weft toward the left, and tuck in the tail.

Weaving Sequence. Lift the heddle that will lock in the borders and insert the left near finger in the shed. When the weft is at the left, lift H 1 for the near finger, and when the weft is on the right, lift H 2 first for the picking cross. Then lift the other heddle to complete the cross. Pick the borders from the near finger. Pick the pattern row by row as indicated by Figure 10, dropping the complementary partners. A dark warp to be picked is represented by either a dot or a vertical line in the rectangle.

9. The light and dark faces of the weave come from the 2–1 and 1–2 interlacement of the complementary warps with the weft.

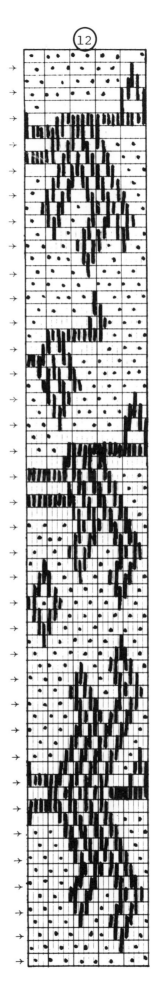

10. The pattern diagram for CWp uneven twill.

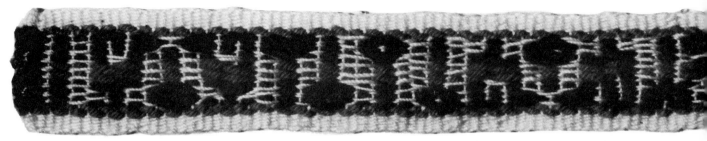

Band 3. Modified intermesh.

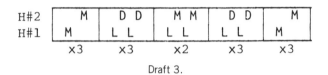

H#2		M	D D	M M	D D	M
H#1	M		L L	L L	L L	M
	x3		x3	x2	x3	x3

Draft 3.

Band 3. Modified Intermesh

Modified intermesh patterns are characterized by intricate abstract designs with zigzag lines and interlocking scrolls. A Spanish influence is noticeable in the traditional horse motif that is frequently used within the geometric framework. The weaver often uses commercially spun yarn to overtwist for her weaving, which reflects the fact that there are many outside contacts in the community where this weave is produced.

Preparing the Warp. Fabrics woven with this technique are traditionally warped with a thin white yarn (usually cotton) and a thicker dark-colored wool yarn, usually a warm rust, gold, or brown shades. The dark warps are customarily varied with a few ends of a brighter color in the center of the band. This not only provides richness in color, but also makes it easier to count the warps during the pattern pickup. Wind the warp yarns in the following order: 3 s-bouts M / 3 d-bouts L and D, 2 d-bouts L and M, 3 d-bouts L and D / 3 s-bouts M. Rearrange the warp cross as indicated in Draft 3. Install H 1 as a multiloop heddle and H 2 as a shed loop. Insert the pointed side of the safety pin into the end loops of the warp. Insert the weft alongside the pin with the short tail to the left. Lift H 2 and pass the weft to the left, tucking in the tail.

Pattern Diagram. Modified intermesh motifs are diagrammed on the rectangular grid. It is helpful to indicate the position of the color variations of the dark warp on the pattern diagram by drawing colored vertical lines between the bouts of different colors.

At first, modified intermesh designs seem amazingly complex. However, these motifs are not as complicated as they appear if they are broken down into their separate parts, or building blocks. Many geometric designs are built from components such as those shown in Figure 11. The animal motifs are not as regular.

Dark warps to be picked up are represented by either a dot or a vertical line in the rectangle. Look at the pattern diagram (Figure 12) and notice how the rows alternate. In the odd rows, when the weft is passed from left to right, there are areas of the background where only light warps are picked; in the pattern areas, L and D are picked alternately, to tie down the dark floats. In the even rows, when the weft goes from right to left, areas of all-dark warps are picked for the pattern, and L and D are picked alternately in the background area to tie down the light floats. This system permits neat horizontal lines, which is a characteristic of this weave in contrast to regular intermesh. Variations in design can be made in many ways.

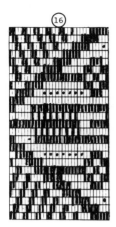

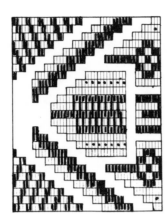

11. Intricate modified intermesh patterns seem less complex when broken into their component parts.

Weaving Sequence. Follow the sequence below to pick the warps for the pattern in the diagram (Figure 12). The method is the same as Band 2.

1. Odd rows (with some all-light areas). Form the picking cross with the H 1 warps on the near finger and the H 2 warps on the far one. Pick the border warps from the near finger. Pick the pattern as indicated by the diagram. Pass the weft to the right.

2. Even rows (with some all-dark areas). Form the picking cross with H 2 warps on the near finger, H 1 warps on the far finger. Pick the border warps from the near finger. Pick the pattern as indicated by the diagram. Pass the weft to the left.

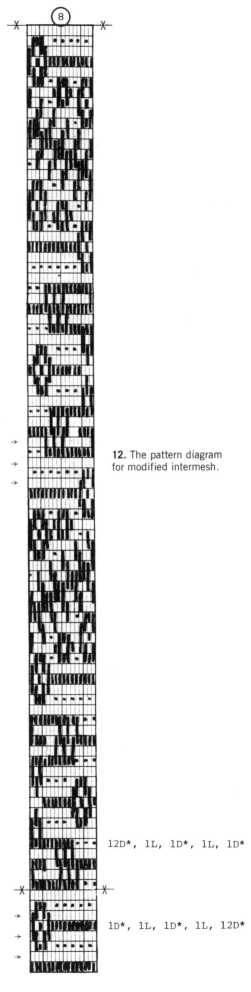

12. The pattern diagram for modified intermesh.

12D*, 1L, 1D*, 1L, 1D*

1D*, 1L, 1D*, 1L, 12D*

Band 4. Stepped diagonals.

H#2		M		D D		M		D D			M
H#1	M		L L			M		L L			M	
	x4		x5			x2		x5			x4	

Draft 4.

Band 4. Stepped Diagonals

Weavings with stepped diagonal bands are occasionally seen in highland Bolivia. These bands are usually filled with simple geometric repeat patterns. Although stepped diagonal patterning resembles pebble weave, there are differences. At the edges there are paired warps instead of a single light or dark warp. The tie-downs are not as regular as the pebble weave ones. All the warp floats span three wefts, except for an occasional five-span float. There are no two-span floats in the pattern.

Preparing the Warp. The project band is woven with two pattern stripes separated by a nar-row plain-weave area. You may wish to warp this band using different sets of colors in the two pattern areas. Wind the warp yarns in the following order: 4 s-bouts M / 5 d-bouts L and D / 2 s-bouts M / 5 d-bouts L and D / 4 s-bouts M. Rearrange the warp cross as shown in Draft 4. Install H 1 as a multiloop heddle and H 2 as a shed loop. Start the weft in the end loops beside the safety pin, with the short tail at the left. Lift H 2 and pass the weft to the left, tucking in the tail.

Weaving Sequence. The sequence used for Band 2 is also used for this weave. Follow the pattern diagram (Figure 13), row by row.

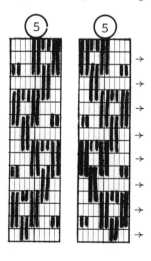

13. The motif for stepped diagonals.

Band 5. CWp floats on plain weave.

Band 5. CWp Floats on Plain Weave

This technique seems to be quite uncommon in Bolivia and we know of only a few examples of this weave. While this technique is found in other parts of the world, the Bolivian version, unlike most of its foreign relatives, is double-faced. We have not observed this weave in process.

Preparing the Warp. Because an odd number of warp ends is necessary to have a center thread, a half bout is used in warping this band. Wind the warp yarns in the following order: 2 s-bouts M / 8½ d-bouts L and D / 2 s-bouts M. Rearrange the warp cross as shown in Draft 5A. Install H 1 as a multiloop heddle and H 2 as a shed loop. Enter the weft in the end loops beside the safety pin, with the short tail at the left. Lift H 2 and pass the weft to the left, tucking in the tail.

Weaving Sequence. Picked rows are alternated with solid color rows to form the motifs. In Figure 14 the pattern on the right is formed by light floats in the upper motif and by dark floats in the lower motif, which symbolizes a fish. The pattern floats are picked as complementary-warp pairs, so the design is in reverse on the back. The background has horizontal stripes of plain weave. To weave *dark motifs,* alternate the two following rows.

1. Plain Dark Row. Lift H 2. Pass the weft to the left, leaving the left near finger in the shed with the weft.

2. Pattern Row. Lift H 1 to complete the picking cross. Pick the borders from the *far* finger. Pick the pattern warps as indicated by the diagram, dropping complementary partners. Pass the weft to the right.

Weave *light motifs* by alternating the two rows below:

1. Plain Light Row. Lift H 1. Pass the weft to the right, leaving the left near finger in the shed with the weft.

2. Pattern Row. Lift H 2 to complete the picking cross. Pick the borders from the *far* finger. Pick the pattern warps as indicated by the diagram. Pass weft to the left.

Changing the Warp Setup for Another Version. The band shown on the left in Figure 14 has an even number of warp bouts. Each diamond is split in half vertically, with the floats on one half light, on the other half dark. The diamonds may be woven further apart by using more rows of plain weave, or may be woven with no plain weave at all between them.

You may try this pattern on the same project band by omitting the 17th L–D pair, either by cutting it off or just letting it hang unwoven. If you were starting a new band like this, you might prefer to have your warps in another arrangement, so each heddle lifts half the light and half the dark

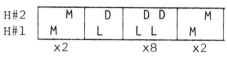

H#2		M	D	D D		M
H#1	M		L	L L		M
	x2			x8		x2

Draft 5A.

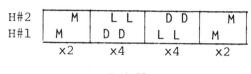

H#2		M	L L	D D		M
H#1	M		D D	L L		M
	x2		x4	x4		x2

Draft 5B.

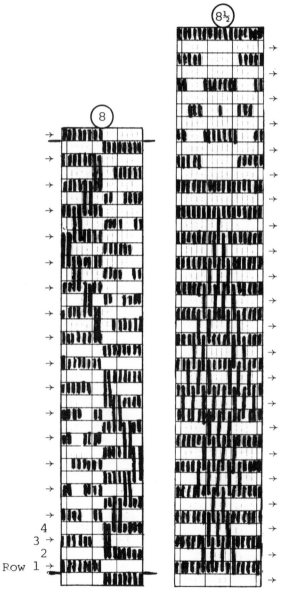

4
3 →
2
Row 1 →

14. Motifs for CWp floats on plain weave .

warps, as shown in Draft 5B. You might wish to rearrange the warps in your sample band, and install new heddles, not including the extra warp pair.

In order for successive warps to be on alternate heddles, there needs to be a reversal from the usual order of the L and D warps in the complementary warp pairs. In the left half of the pattern, the D warps are each to the *left* of their L partners, as shown in the draft. This should be remembered during the pick-up, because you will then need to drop the last D partner when you pick the light warps. For example, in Row 3, pick from the right: 6L, 2D*, 2L*, 6D. You can easily adapt this simple diamond design to a band that is narrower or wider.

FOUR-HEDDLE WEAVES (ALTERNATING WARP)

Two different weave structures—intermesh with complementary warps, and "one-weft" double cloth—are produced with alternating warps in four-heddle setups. Intermesh is favored by Aymara weavers. One-weft double cloth is most often produced by the Quechuas. A wide range of color and design variations are noticeable from one region to another in both of these techniques.

This is a Bolivian example of an intermesh band.

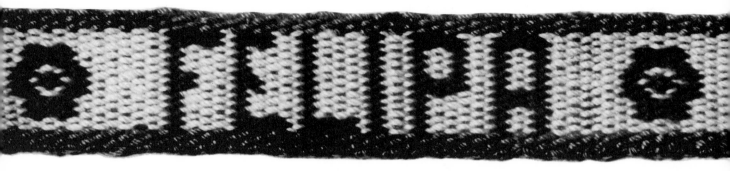

Band 6. Intermesh.

Band 6. Intermesh

Beautiful alphabet letters and numerals have been created by the Aymara weavers for incorporating names and dates into various items. We saw lettering that was particularly attractive on a city bus, when an Aymara lady sat in front of us. She leaned forward because of the baby in her awayo, which made it easy to see the fabric well enough to study the details of the letters. They were well proportioned and had serifs. The serif alphabet in the Appendix grew from that observation. You may omit the serifs if you prefer.

Although intermesh is considered to be double-faced, it is not as truly reversible as the other two-color complementary-warp structures. There is a tendency for ''feathering'' along diagonal lines of the design, on one side of the fabric or the other. In a capacho that was loaned to us for study, the weaver had managed to have all the feathering on the back side of the fabric.

Preparing the Warp. Knit-Cro-Sheen is recommended for this band. Before beginning to warp, divide your medium-color yarn into two balls. Wind the warp yarns in the following order: 2 d-bouts M / 12 d-bouts L and D / 2 d-bouts M.

Heddles 2 and 3 are installed first, one on each side of the original warp cross, without any rearranging of the cross. Insert lease sticks to hold the original cross. Make multiloop heddles for the paired warps on each side of the cross, having an L–D warp pair in each heddle loop, as shown in Draft 6A. Remove the lease sticks.

Next the warps are rearranged for the installation of H 1 and H 4. Bring the original warp cross in front of H 2 and H 3, placing it between the two left fingers. Rearrange the warps as indicated in part B of the draft. Insert lease sticks to hold the warps in position. Install H 1 on the light warps. Then lift the H 4 warps back through H 2 and H 3, and enclose them in a shed loop. This will result in the complete heddle arrangement shown in Draft 6 C.

Insert the weft alongside the pin in the end loops with the tail to the right, lift H 3, and pass the weft to the right, tucking in the tail. Lift H 4 and pass the weft to the left.

Pattern Diagram. A special version of the rectangular grid is used to diagram intermesh patterns (Figure 15). Plain rows indicate the design rows. Staggered dots in alternate rows serve to show the effect of the tie-down rows, which are woven by alternately lifting H 2 and H 3. Since the order of warping placed the L–D pairs of H 2 to the left of the L–D pairs of H 3, the right-hand dot of the row corresponding to H 2 is always to the left of the right-hand dot of the H 3 row. Each design-row warp will float to the nearest dot in the adjoining rows, giving the characteristic intermeshed effect. Three-span floats appear in the

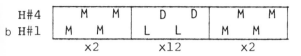

H#3		M–M		L–D		M–M	
a H#2	M–M		L–D		M–M		
	×2		×12		×2		

H#4	M	M	D	D	M	M	
b H#1	M	M	L	L	M	M	
		×2		×12		×2	

H#4	M		M	D	D	M	M
H#3		M–M			L–D		M–M
H#2	M–M			L–D		M–M	
c H#1	M		M	L	L	M	M
		×2		×12		×2	

Draft 6.

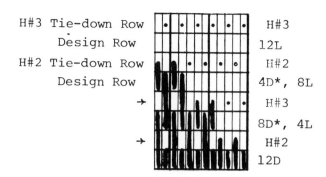

H#3 Tie-down Row		H#3
Design Row		12L
H#2 Tie-down Row		H#2
Design Row		4D*, 8L
→		H#3
		8D*, 4L
→		H#2
		12D

15. A special version of the rectangular grid is used for intermesh.

diagram whenever the same color is to be picked above and below the dot.

Although the intermesh grid may appear the same as that used for modified intermesh, it is actually different in what it represents because of the way that the tie-down heddles are customarily installed without rearranging the warp cross. Each dot shows where an L and a D warp are lifted together as a pair, so both are above the weft in that lane; no warp is above the weft between the dots (Figure 16). This represents a basic difference between this grid when used for intermesh as compared with the significance of the dotted areas found in the modified intermesh grid. There the dot shows where only the D partner is above the weft in that lane. One of the warps of the next L–D pair is above the weft in the next lane.

Weaving Sequence. Picked design rows are alternated with heddle-controlled tie-down rows to produce intermesh designs. Heddles 2 and 3 are used alternately on the tie-down rows. It is essential to alternate the tie-down rows. It is also imperative for all but the simplest block patterns to precede your first design row with the proper tie-down row, to establish the proper left-right relationship with the warps in the following design row.

You are now ready to weave the motifs in Figure 17, following the sequence below. Begin in the lower right corner of the pattern, first weaving the rows of plain dark and plain light ground. Since some of the heddle strings tend to become enmeshed in the warps, it is a good idea to watch which heddles may need to be pulled for

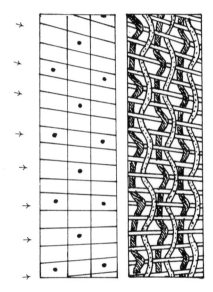

16. Although the intermesh grid (top) may appear the same as that used for modified intermesh (bottom), it is actually different in what it represents.

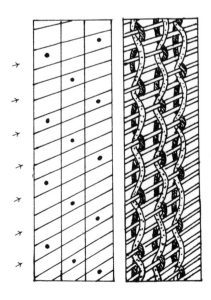

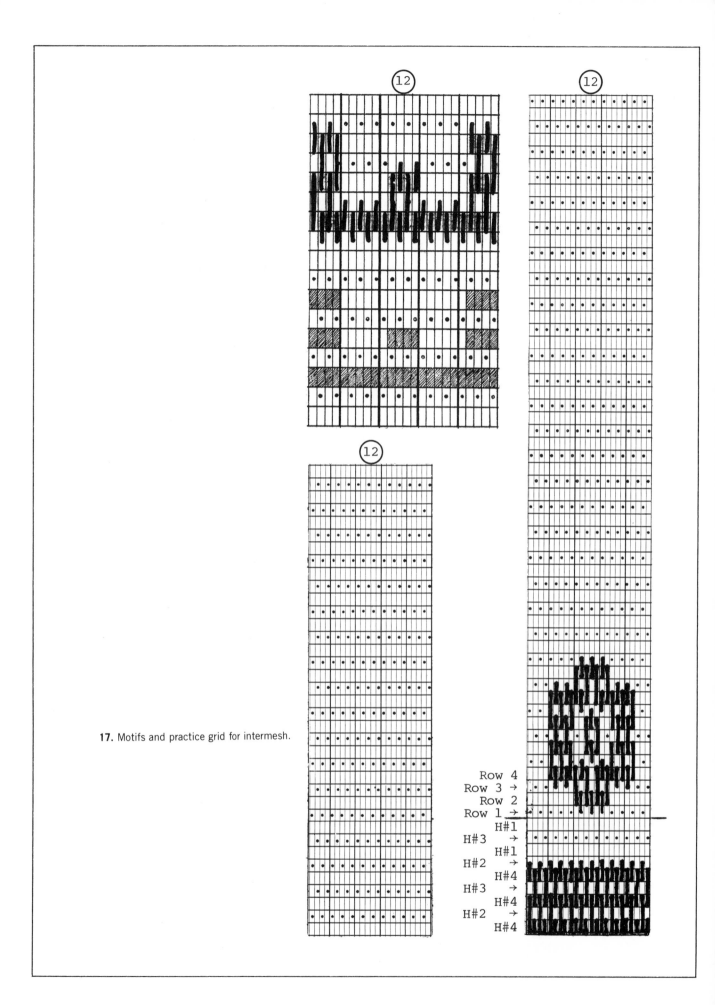

17. Motifs and practice grid for intermesh.

Row 4
Row 3 →
Row 2
Row 1 →
H#1
          →
H#3
    H#1
          →
H#2
    H#4
          →
H#3
    H#4
          →
H#2
    H#4

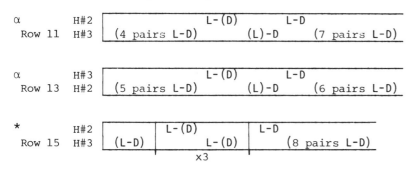

Pick yarns in parentheses:

```
α          H#2   ┌─────────── L-(D) ──────── L-D ──────────────┐
Row 11     H#3   │ (4 pairs L-D)        (L)-D         (7 pairs L-D) │
                 └─────────────────────────────────────────────────┘

α          H#3   ┌─────────── L-(D) ──────── L-D ──────────────┐
Row 13     H#2   │ (5 pairs L-D)        (L)-D         (6 pairs L-D) │
                 └─────────────────────────────────────────────────┘

*          H#2   ┌──────┬── L-(D) ──┬── L-D ──────────────┐
Row 15     H#3   │ (L-D) │   L-(D)   │ (8 pairs L-D)        │
                 └──────┴───────────┴──────────────────────┘
                          x3
```

18. Motif with altered tie-down rows.

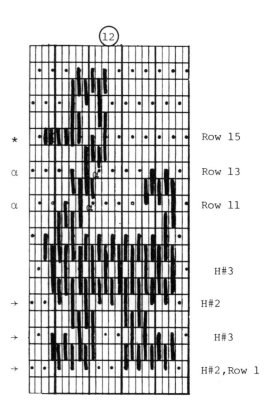

Row 15
Row 13
Row 11
H#3
H#2
H#3
H#2, Row 1

straightening before lifting the heddle you need. The following sequence is used for weaving a pattern:

Row 1: Heddle 2 Tie-Down. Lift H 2. If the shed is difficult to obtain, it will help to pull H 2 and H 3 in opposite directions while lifting H 2. Pass the weft to the right.

Row 2: Design Row. Form a picking cross with the H 4 warps on the near finger and the H 1 warps on the far finger. When you lift H 4, open the shed up to H 3, insert your thumb first and then your fingers into the shed in front of H 3, repeating likewise for H 2 and H 1. With the sample warp you may be able to merely "snap" through the heddles, but with wider or stickier warps you will need to lift the warps through each heddle separately, and often by sections of the width. Pick the borders beside the background color. Pick the pattern warps as indicated by the diagram. Pass the weft to the left.

Row 3: Heddle 3 Tie-Down. Lift H 3. Pass the weft to the right.

Row 4: Design Row. Repeat as for Row 2. Pass the weft to the left.

After you have woven the motif, you might like to try some lettering. Space is provided in Figure 17 for you to draft your name or initials. You may want to refer to the intermesh alphabet in the Appendix for help in drafting. To draft a letter, first fill in the dark warps in design (undotted) rows with shading. Then ink in the intermeshed effect by drawing a line through each darkened rectangle, extending it to the nearest dot in the adjoining row. If there is a darkened rectangle on

each side of a dotted one, this represents a three-span float and the line should show it (see the upper left-hand corner of Figure 17).

Altering the Tie-Down Rows. Ordinarily the tie-down rows are controlled by H 2 and H 3. For special design possibilities, alterations may be made to produce smooth horizontal lines in the tie-down rows or to prevent "feathering" in a diagonal line.

The right side of the duck's neck in Figure 18 will feather unless the tie-down rows are altered. This is indicated on the pattern diagram by the Greek letter alpha. In the rows where this alteration is to be made, make a picking cross with the proper tie-downs on your near finger and the other set on the far finger. Then pick as indicated below the duck.

It is possible to predict where the feathering will occur. A dark diamond shape on a light background will feather on the right-hand side of the diamond on the front of the fabric, with the opposite on the back. When the diamond is light on dark, the feathering is on the left-hand side of the diamond. Alterations will be required wherever a "gap" occurs in the diagonal line. To correct the feathering, make a picking cross as you did for the duck's neck. Where a gap is, take one warp of the motif color from the far finger as a substitute for the warp of the same color in the L–D pair at the edge of the motif on the near finger (Figure 19).

The beak of the duck in Figure 18 is also formed by altering a tie-down row. Vertical lines are drawn in the dotted rectangles and in the

75

LEFT SIDE OF LIGHT MOTIF

L-D	(L)-D	L-D	H#3
(L-D)	L-(D)	(L-D)	H#2
dark background	*gap*	*light motif*	
L-D L-D	(L)-D	L-D	H#2
(L-D)	L-(D)	(L-D) (L-D)	H#3

RIGHT SIDE OF DARK MOTIF

L-D	L-(D)	L-D L-D	
(L-D) (L-D)	(L)-D	(L-D)	
dark motif	*gap*	*light background*	
L-D	L-(D)	L-D	
(L-D)	(L)-D	(L-D)	

upper: H#2 tie-down row
lower: H#3 tie-down row

19. Alterations may be made in the tie-down rows to control "feathering."

empty ones between them to show the appearance of the alteration. In altering a tie-down row, the opposite color warp from the alternate tie-down heddle is substituted for the warp that ordinarily occurs in that row. The substitution is made by forming the picking cross as you would to correct feathering. In the case of the beak, the H 3 warps are on the near finger and the H 2 warps are on the far finger. Then pick the warps for this row as indicated below the motif.

Other Borders. It is not hard to produce a band with plain-weave borders on either side of inter-mesh weave. This causes a relief effect in the in-termesh section and makes it possible to weave a wider band without quite so many pattern warps to handle. Borders with several narrow stripes of various colors also look attractive beside inter-mesh pattern areas.

To warp a plain-weave border, wind the border yarns as s-bouts. Each of the border warps will be included in two heddles. Include the warps on the far side of the cross with H 2 and H 3. The warps on the near side of the cross are included in H 1 and H 4. A good project for experimenting with this technique would be a band with a series of bookmarks, each with the recipient's name woven into it. Short fringes make a nice finish for such pieces. To allow room for the fringes weave a few shots of filler (rag strip) before and after each bookmark.

The idea of having alternate blocks with light and dark grounds was explained in the directions for Band 1. This can also be done with intermesh. If one plans to do alternating blocks it is fun to have two colors for the borders so the block effect can be carried across the entire warp, including the borders. To warp the borders, wind the border bouts with two different medium colors instead of a single color. The borders are picked, as usual, from beside the background color of the block. For intermesh, the usual tie-down row may be used between the rows of solid ground color at the point of reversal from one background color to the other, so it is not necessary to reverse the direction of the weft for the weaving sequence as it was in Band 1. The same designs can be woven in each block by mentally reversing the lights and darks.

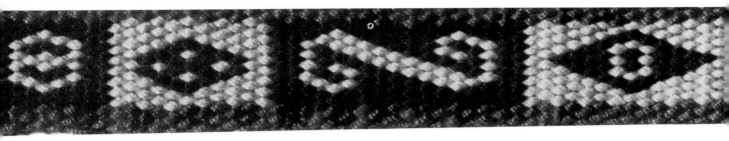

Band 7. One-weft double cloth.

Band 7. One-Weft Double Cloth

This weave is different from most of the Bolivian pattern weaves in that the pattern is not formed by floats. Patterns therefore do not have some of the design limitations found in other weaves. One means of identifying the weave is to find the ''pockets'' between the cloth layers in the larger plain areas of the design.

Preparing the Warp. Divide your medium color yarn into two balls before beginning to warp. Wind the warp in the following sequence: 2 d-bouts M / 8 d-bouts L and D / 2 d-bouts M.

The warp cross is rearranged for the four heddles in two steps as shown in Draft 7. First, the far side of the original cross is rearranged for H 3 and H 4. Second, the near side of the cross is rearranged for H 1 and H 2. Because the heddles tend to bunch together during weaving, it is a good idea to color-code them.

Insert lease sticks into the two sheds of the warp cross. Working only with the warp above the far stick of the lease, rearrange each L–D pair and the border warps as shown in the draft. Hold this new lease by inserting a second set of lease sticks. Install H 3 as a multiloop heddle and H 4 as a shed loop. Attach the two heddles to each other as shown in Figure 20 with the tops of the heddles at least an inch apart. Remove the far set of sticks.

Working only with the warps above the near stick of the lease, rearrange each L–D pair and the border warps as for the far side of the cross. Insert lease sticks to hold the new lease. Install multiloop heddles for H 1 and H 2. Remove both sets of lease sticks. This will result in the total heddle arrangement as shown in Draft 7.

When weaving a tube there is a pairing of warps where the layers join on one side. In the sample band this pairing occurs on the left side. To avoid this, one warp end may be added or subtracted. Since the border on the sample band is so narrow, it is best to add a warp. This extra warp end is added at the left side of the band after the heddles have been installed. Tie a second shed loop as H 5 to include this warp and H 3 and H 4 (Draft 7C).

Begin the weft beside the pin in the end loops, with the short tail to the right. Lift H 5 and pass the weft to the right, tucking in the tail.

Understanding the Pattern Diagram. Become acquainted with the diamond grid system as shown in Figure 21. There is a small diamond for each warp above the weft in every row of the upper layer of the fabric. Small ovals in the diamonds indicate the pattern-color warps; the rest is background. The slant of the weave *must* be coordinated with the slant of the pattern diagram, as shown by the direction of the zigzag edges. To achieve this matching when beginning

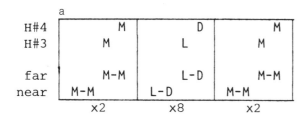

a

	×2	×8	×2
H#4	M	D	M
H#3	M	L	M
far	M-M	L-D	M-M
near	M-M	L-D	M-M

b

	×2	×8	×2
H#4	M	D	M
H#3	M	L	M
H#2	M	D	M
H#1	M	L	M

c

	×2	×8	×2
H#5 M	*M M*	*L D*	*M M*
H#4	M	D	M
H#3	M	L	M
H#2	M	D	M
H#1	M	L	M

Draft 7.

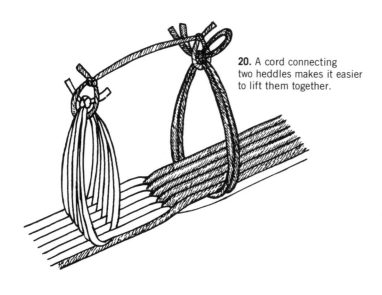

20. A cord connecting two heddles makes it easier to lift them together.

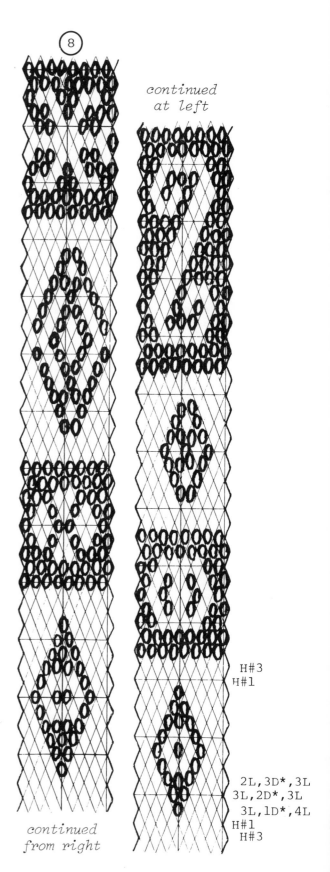

⑧

continued at left

H#3
H#1

2L,3D*,3L
3L,2D*,3L
3L,1D*,4L
H#1
H#3

continued from right

21. Motifs for "one-weft" double cloth.

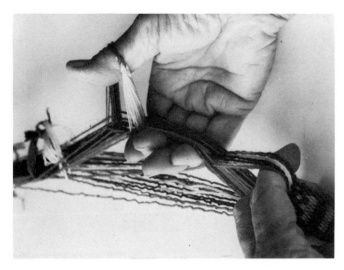

22A. Special manipulations are needed to obtain the shed for the lower weft shot. This photo shows lifting H 5 (or H 3 and 4) for the left-slant row.

22B. This shows lifting H 1 and H 2 for the right-slant row.

to weave a motif, you may either select a suitable motif or weave another row of plain ground. In some cases it will work to turn the motif upside-down.

Weaving Sequence. In the pickup, the warps are treated as complementary pairs, but in two separate sets. One set is on H 1 and H 2, the other on H 3 and H 4. First the pickup for the upper weft shot is made and the weft is passed. Then the warp layers are manipulated for the lower shot, with no further picking needed for the design on the lower surface. Note that the heddles lifted last are the ones used for the next row's pickup. Begin at the lower right corner of the pattern diagram in Figure 21. Use the following sequence to weave the left-slant row:

1. Upper Face Shot. Form a picking cross with the H 1 warps on the near finger and the H 2 warps on the far finger. Pick the border warps from the near finger. Pick as indicated by the pattern diagram. Pass the weft to the left, leaving your left index and middle fingers in the shed.

2. Lower Face Shot. With the left fingers in the shed with the weft, lift H 5. Put three or four fingers of the right hand in the shed, and bring the warps forward to form a cross. Slide your fingers back and forth on each side of the cross if needed to put the warps in order. Snap both hands to a vertical position to open the lower shed (Figure 22). Enlarge the lower shed and beat. Pass the weft to the right. (If you do not add the extra warp, lift H 3 and H 4, instead of H 5).

The following steps are used to produce the right-slant row:

1. Upper Face Shot. Weave as for a left-slant upper face shot, except make the picking cross with the H 3 warps on the near finger and the H 4 warps on the far finger.

2. Lower Face Shot. Repeat as for the left-slant lower face shot, except form the lower shed by lifting H 1 and H 2 instead of H 5.

Border Warps. If you are doing blocks with the background alternately light and dark and you have a border of one color, there will be an extra little float on the right if you always pick the borders from beside the background color each time you change from a dark block to a light one. This may not bother you. However, if you want to avoid this in a one-color border, there are two options. Either you may have H 1 or H 3 on your near finger every time, even for the dark blocks, and take the borders always from the near finger; or you may put the dark warps on your near finger for the dark blocks, but take the borders from beside the light warps. If you are weaving a band in which the border colors alternate along with the background colors, there is no way to avoid the extra little float.

When there is no shift in the color of the background, pick it in the following manner. When the background is all light, put the heddle with the light warps on your near finger for the picking cross, and take the border warps from your near finger. If you are doing a band with an

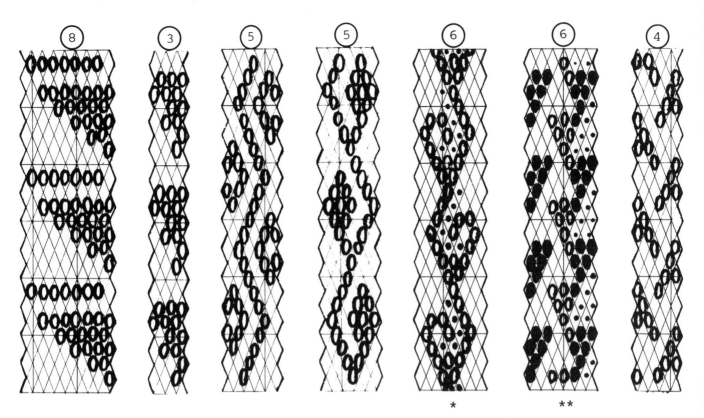

23. Motifs for border designs. * Warp Order: 2 d-bouts L and D, 2 d-bouts M and D, 2 d-bouts L and D. ** Warp Order: 2 d-bouts L and D, 2 d-bouts L and M¹, 2 d-bouts M² and D.

all-dark background, it is better to have the dark warps be the ones you put on your near finger.

A Special Nontubular Edge. Two narrow bands were found with an unusual bicolor edge. Instead of being woven as a flattened tube, the band was woven as two layers of cloth, each with its own selvedge color. It required two wefts in colors to match the selvedges. The same background color was used throughout the pattern area, with the layers held together where the warps interchanged for the design. At intervals on each edge of the band, there was an exchange of the two selvedge colors, involving an adjustment of the selvedge warps and the matching wefts.

The Beaded Edge. The beads that embellish the edges of a wincha are usually attached during the weaving of the band. The beads are strung on a single, double, or triple strand. A string of beads is attached to each edge as follows. After the desired number of beads are separated from the others, the strand is anchored firmly at the edge by the weft loop as it is snugged into place. Sometimes loops of very tiny beads are spaced so closely together that they form a hollow beaded tube along the edge.

Wider Bands. When you have mastered the basic technique you may like to try doing a somewhat wider band. Many of the Bolivian bands are done with 28 or 30 bouts in the pattern area. There is often a tubular border, which may be separated from the pattern area by a narrow border design that acts as a seal for the "pock-

ets." A variety of these border designs are shown in Figure 23. A band with 30 d-bouts and one of the narrower border designs might have about 150 warp ends. Knit-Cro-Sheen is easier to use at first, but later you might like to try Cottolin or a fine hard-twist wool.

In doing wider, more elaborate double cloth patterns, tension control becomes important. While a wider band can be woven with finger-tension, Bolivian weavers prefer to use a backstrap, which frees the hands for the necessary manipulations. There is also another solution to the problem of tension control in a wider band. With the addition of supplementary heddles, it is easy to do Bolivian double cloth on the inkle loom. See Chapter 5 for backstrap and inkle instructions, and for additional suggestions for weaving wider double-cloth bands.

Use of a Secondary Weft. Only one weft is needed for this flattened tubular structure if you are weaving a belt. However, when warp-faced pattern bands of double cloth are used in wider pieces, in combination with sections of plain weave, a secondary weft is used. The weft that goes across the whole piece is used for one surface of the double-cloth band, and a second, finer weft is used for the other surface of the pattern band. This finer weft is usually extended into the plain weave a thread or two on each side of the band.

Double-Faced Reinforced Double Cloth. In one awayo, the pattern bands appeared to be

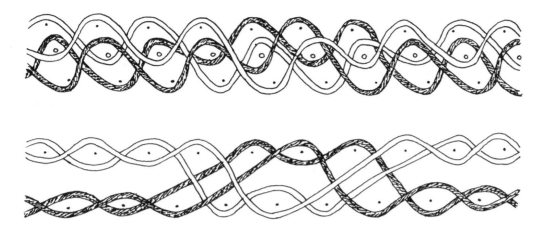

24. A reinforced version of warp-faced double cloth may be woven with the use of an inner weft. There are then no "pockets" between the layers of cloth.

warp-faced double cloth, but the layers of plain weave could not be separated in the pocket areas. The two sets of warp were not only woven into the usual two complete surfaces of plain weave, but the layers were also locked together by an inner weft that went over two, under two in the center of the fabric, between the two outer layers (Figure 24). There was no change in the effect on the surface. The inner weft, which went across the width of the fabric, was thicker than the fine weft used only for the two surfaces of the double-cloth band. From analysis of the fabric, it appeared that the weaver had made her lower shed for the lower weft shot in the usual manner, but also used the upper shed for the inner weft before picking for the next upper pattern shot. In that way, the inner weft separates the warps on H 1 and H 2 from those on H 3 and H 4, in every row of the weaving. Another unusual feature of the same awayo was a pattern band that was woven as double cloth on one end and as pebble weave on the other end. It illustrates the flexibility available to the weaver.

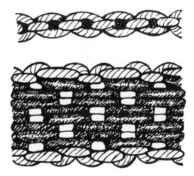

25. A beautiful chain-like border can be produced with a one-bout selvedge.

TWO-HEDDLE WEAVES (IRREGULAR WARP)

All the previous pattern bands had warps in alternating order, with the light warps to the left of their dark partners. However, in this section, the warps are arranged in a different order, so there are some different picking rules.

Two pebble bands are included in this section, the standard pebble weave, using the same pattern diagrams as Band 1, and doubled pebble.

This is a Bolivian example of a pebble-weave band woven with heddle-controlled tie-downs. Courtesy of the Museum of the American Indian.

Band 8. Pebble weave band with an irregular warp order.

Band 8. Pebble Weave

In the irregular warp method, the pebble rows are heddle-controlled, so that only the design rows need to be picked. Some weavers prefer this method, finding it faster and more rhythmic.

This band introduces the one-bout selvedge, which is also picked in a different manner. Using this method for the borders produces a neat chain-like edge as shown in Figure 25. It is more apparent when done with coarse yarns.

Preparing the Warp. Wind the warp yarns in the following order: 1 s-bout M / 6 d-bouts L and D / 1 s-bout M. Rearrange the warp cross as shown in Draft 8. Notice that the warp order in each heddle corresponds to the order of warps in the pebble rows, with the light-edge row for H 1 and the dark-edge row for H 2.

In transferring the warps from the left to the right hand, it is helpful to concentrate on only the dark-edge row that is being formed on the far right finger. After transferring the border warps, take one L–D warp pair at a time, placing the proper one on the far finger first, then its partner on the near finger. Continue across the warp, so the far finger has the proper order: D LL DD LL DD LL D. You should end at the left edge with a single dark on the far finger and a single light on the near one. Transfer the remaining border warps and check your order.

Install H 1 as a multiloop heddle and H 2 as a shed loop. Insert the weft in the end loops, with the tail at the left. Lift H 2 and pass the weft to the left, tucking in the tail.

Weaving Sequence. Start with a few rows of plain weave by lifting the heddles alternately. Observe that the effect is different from the horizontal stripes you had with your warps in alternating order, and that it is almost a checkerboard design (Figure 26). This difference often makes it possible to identify the method the weaver used when examining fabrics and photos of pebble weave. End with your weft at the left.

When you start to weave the plain light pebbled area, you will need to learn some new methods for the picking technique. Only the design rows need to be picked, because the pebble rows, or return shots, are heddle-controlled. For the chain-link selvedge, the selvedge yarns cross when the weft enters the shed, and do not cross when the weft leaves the shed (Figure 27).

1. Pebble Row (L-edge). Lift H 1. Pass the weft to the right.

2. Design Row. With your near finger in the shed of H 1 with the weft, form a picking cross by lifting the other heddle for the far finger. Pick the right selvedge yarn from the *far* finger, then pick all the light warps in order, going to the near finger and the far finger as needed. Finish by tak-

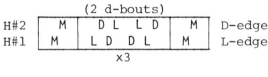

	(2 d-bouts)		
H#2	M	D L L D	M	D-edge
H#1	M	L D D L	M	L-edge

×3

Draft 8.

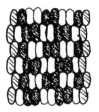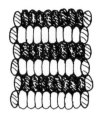

26. By observing the plain-weave areas in a pebble band, it is possible to know which warp order the weaver used (irregular is on the left; alternating on the right).

ing the left selvedge warp from the *near* finger. Pass the weft to the left.

3. Pebble Row (D-edge). Lift H 2. Pass the weft to the right.

4. Design Row. With your near finger in the shed of H 2 with the weft, repeat as for Row 2, picking the selvedge from the far finger on the right and from the near finger on the left. Pass the weft to the left.

For a plain dark pebbled area, repeat the same four-step sequence, but pick all the dark warps instead of the light ones. Observe the same rules for the selvedge. Continue to use the heddles alternately for the pebble row shots. If you have trouble remembering which heddle should come next, it can easily be checked by merely lifting the left-hand heddle loop enough to see whether the left selvedge would cross if you would lift H 1 (Figure 27). If the selvedge yarns do not cross, then you know that you should lift H 2 instead for the return shot. It avoids friction on your warps to check with just the left loop rather than by using the whole heddle.

Weave another space of the light pebbled area. Before you start on your first motif, you must have your weft in the proper pebble row. In Figure 28, the first row is an L-edge row in which your weft needs to be passed to the right in the shed of H 1. It may be necessary to weave another light design row first, if you are not in the right place.

When you were picking the warps in the plain pebbled areas, you perhaps noticed that although you were picking the design row warps by twos, you always began and ended with a single one on either finger. In picking for a pattern, you will need to do this for each of the groups of colored warps, that is, each color starts and ends with a single one on either finger, but there may be pairs to pick off a finger in-between. Often the partners of the warps you pick will drop off, but sometimes when you are changing from one color to the next, you will need to push off a partner of the warp that you have just picked. The clue for this is that each time you start a new color, there should be just a single yarn of a color at the right on each left finger. If there is an extra one, it is the partner of the warp you just picked and must be pushed off.

Start at the bottom of the motif and weave, row by row. Remember that for the picking cross, your near finger is in the shed with the weft. Also remember the rules for the selvedge warps. Weave a space of plain light pebbled area between the motifs.

The same motif may be used to experiment with weaving short horizontal lines by forming triangles at the four corners. Mark the horizontal modifications in the proper pebble rows with darkened 0's. Although experienced weavers can simply reach down to the lower warp layer and bring up the proper exchange warp, it is easier to make sure you are getting the proper partner by making a picking cross. For each of these two pebble rows, *before* passing the weft, form a picking cross with the H 2 warps on the near finger and the H 1 warps on the far finger. Pick both selvedge warps this time from the near fin-

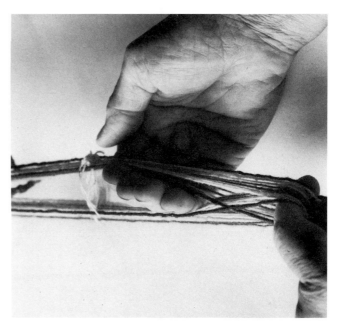

27A. For the one-bout selvedge, the edge warps should be crossed where the weft enters the shed, not where it leaves the shed. Avoid friction by lifting only the left loop of H 1 to check whether it will cross the edge warps.

27B. In this case, H 2 is the one that will cross the left edge warps.

ger; pick 5D, 2L, 5D, and pass the weft to the right. In this way you have exchanged two dark warps at each side for the light ones that would have been in this row, forming triangles with floats in them. If you wish to try a seed as shown for Band 1, cross the dark exchange warps with the ones they're replacing, by bringing them up on the wrong side of their opposite partners. To have the proper shed on the near finger for the picking cross of the following design row, lift H 2 again and insert the near finger.

Other motifs are provided for you to try in Figure 29. Two are of the continuing type, and one of these has a horizontal line as part of the design. This method lends itself particularly well to traditional narrow multicolor bands (Figure 30). Each side has a different visual effect.

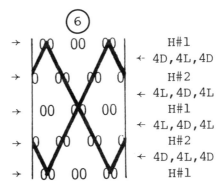

```
 6
→  00    00   00      H#1
                   ←  4D,4L,4D
→  0    00   00   0   H#2
                   ←  4L,4D,4L
→  00    00    00     H#1
                   ←  4L,4D,4L
→  0    00   00   0   H#2
                   ←  4D,4L,4D
→  00    00    00     H#1
```

28. A motif for pebble weave with instructions for an irregular warp order. Alternate rows are heddle-controlled.

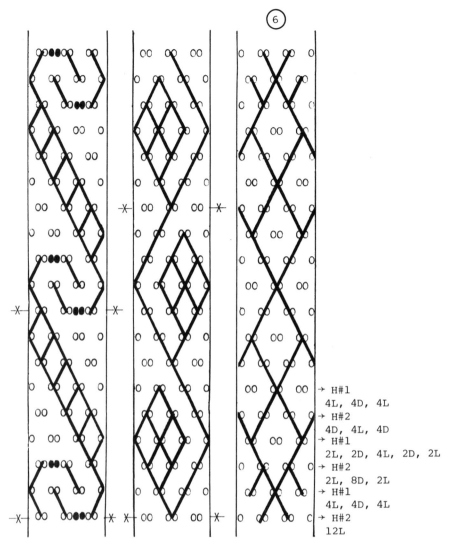

⑥

→ H#1
4L, 4D, 4L
→ H#2
4D, 4L, 4D
→ H#1
2L, 2D, 4L, 2D, 2L
→ H#2
2L, 8D, 2L
→ H#1
4L, 4D, 4L
→ H#2
12L

29. Motifs for pebble weave bands.

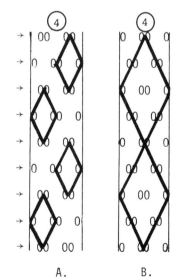

④ ④

A. Warp Order:

   1 s-bout green / 2 d-bouts blue-green & white,
   2 d-bouts red-violet & yellow / 1 s-bout green

B. Warp Order:

   1 s-bout red / 1 d-bout navy & white, 2 d-bouts
   yellow & red, 1 d-bout navy & white / 1 s-bout red

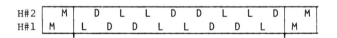

H#2		M		D	L	L	D	D	L	L	D		M
H#1	M		L	D	D	L	L	D	D	L		M

A.   B.

30. Motifs for multicolor pebble weave bands.

Band 9. A doubled pebble weave band.

Band 9. Doubled Pebble Weave

A wide multicolor belt with a staggered flower or diamond design is a common doubled pebble item woven by the Aymaras. The designs appear spread out because there are twice as many warps per unit as there are in pebble weave. A doubled version of the pebble weave pattern grid is used for the pattern diagrams. Pebble weave patterns may be used by doubling them, but geometric rather than animal motifs should be chosen.

Two variations of the chain-link selvedge are included with this band. Both coordinate well with the sequence for irregular warp pebble. The first is merely a multiple of the one-bout selvedge, with several warps taken from a finger in place of one. The second variation gives a double chain-link effect and requires four s-bouts. It is attractive and worth trying.

Preparing the Warp. For a traditional effect in this band, choose red (M), yellow (L) and dark green (D)—the colors of the Bolivian flag. Wind the warp yarns in the following order: 2 s-bouts M, 2 s-bouts D / 4 d-bouts L and M, 4 d-bouts M and D / 2 s-bouts L, 2 s-bouts M. Rearrange the warp cross as shown in Draft 9. Install H 1 as a multiloop heddle and H 2 as a shed loop. Insert the weft alongside the pin, with the short tail to the left. Lift H 2 and pass the weft to the left, tucking in the tail.

Weaving Sequence. The weaving sequence is the same as for irregular warp pebble weave, with the pebble rows being heddle-controlled. The traditional motif (Figure 31) introduced for this band is commonly woven with a color combination that simulates a three-color effect. Use the M color for the background and colors L and D for the pattern as indicated. As you weave, take a look at the back side of the band. Some consider that the "right" side.

1. Pebble Row (L-edge). Lift H 1, pass the weft to the right.

2. Design Row. With the near finger in the shed of H 1 with the weft, form a picking cross by lifting the other heddle. Pick all the right border warps from the far finger. Pick the pattern warps as indicated by the diagram, pushing down the partners that do not drop automatically. Pick all the left borders from the near finger. Pass the weft to the left.

3. Pebble Row (D-edge). Lift H 2 and pass the weft to the right.

4. Design Row. Repeat as for Row 2, except that the near finger of the picking cross is with the weft in the shed of H 2. Pass the weft to the left.

Double Chain-Link Border. The same sequence is followed, except that the border warps are picked differently. For each *color group* of

H#2	M	D	L L M M M M L L	D D M M M M D D	L	M	L&D-edge
H#1	M	D	M M L L L L M M	M M D D D D M M	L	M	M-edge
	x2	x2				x2	x2	

Draft 9.

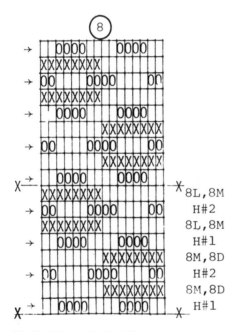

31. Motif for doubled pebble weave.

four warps, a warp is first picked from the far finger, and then one is taken from the near finger, as indicated below. Pick the warps shown in parentheses.

Row 2. Design row with near finger in shed of H1:

M (M)	D (D)	L (L)	M (M)
(M) M	(D) D	(L) L	(M) M
left border			right border

Row 4. Design row with near finger in shed of H2:

M (M)	D (D)	L (L)	M (M)
(M) M	(D) D	(L) L	(M) M
left border			right border

88

WEAVES WITH SUPPLEMENTARY ELEMENTS

Weaves with supplementary-warp patterning are more common in Europe and some other countries in Latin America than they are in Bolivia. In the one area where the fabrics with supplementary warps are prevalent, two colors of supplementary warps are used on the paired-warp plain-weave ground. Instead of being double-faced like most Bolivian fabrics, this one has a mixture of long floats on the back.

Although we have only seen three examples of the one-color supplementary-warp weave, this weave is presented first in this section as Band 10. It is basically woven in the usual manner for supplementary warp, but two specimens had the unusual feature of having parts of the design woven as for complementary warps, which makes both sides of the fabric attractive.

The method for supplementary weft is presented in Band 12 also. The back side is plain white. It is not found often, but is used for narrow hat bands and straps, and was found in two chuspas as well.

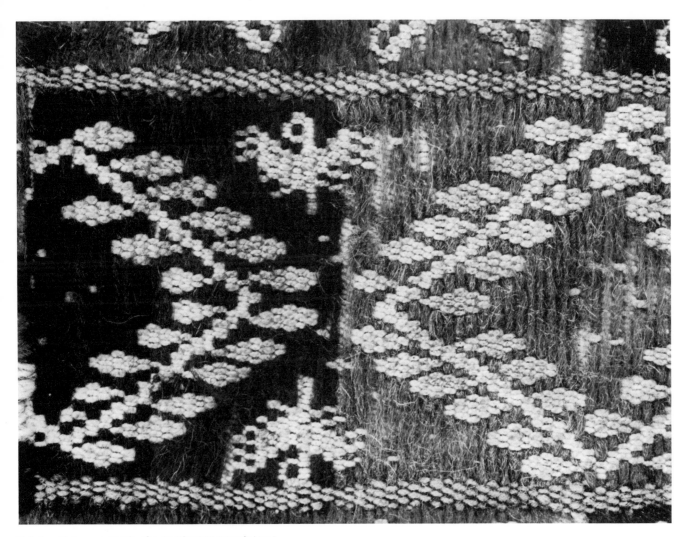

This is a Bolivian example of a supplementary-weft band.

Band 10. One-color supplementary-warp band.

Band 10. One-Color Supplementary Warp

The plain-weave ground has paired warps and the supplementary warps are placed so that each one is between the two warps of a pair, but on the opposite heddle. This gives a staggered effect to the warp order. The ground warps are of finer yarn, and are of various colors in different bands.

Preparing the Warp. Choose a fine yarn for the ground warp (G or ·), and a somewhat heavier yarn for the pattern warps (P). Before beginning to warp, divide your ground-color yarn into two balls. The second ball should have enough yarn for 4½ bouts. Wind the warp yarns in the following order: 3 s-bouts B / 4 t-bouts G, G and P, plus one end each of G and P / 3 s-bouts B. (As another option, the yarns can be wound without the extra ball by winding the two colors separately as s-bouts, and half s-bouts. This works better if you have someone to help you at one post.) Rearrange the warp cross as shown in Draft 10. Install H 1 as a multiloop heddle and H 2 as a shed loop. Insert the weft alongside the safety pin, with the short tail to the left. Lift H 2 and pass the weft to the left, tucking in the tail.

Pattern Diagram. Supplementary-warp patterns are drawn on the rectangular grid. Vertical lines within the rectangles indicate the pattern color warps. Empty rectangles indicate which of the supplementary warps are *not* above the weft in each row. In the odd rows, the weft goes from left to right, and the picking cross is made with the shed of H 1 on the near finger. For the even rows, it is the opposite. The ground-weave warps, which are not shown on the pattern diagram, are taken each time from the near finger of the picking cross. An exception, in the case of the version with some complementary-warp treatment, will be described later.

Weaving Sequence. The pattern in Figure 32 is drawn to be woven in the standard one-color supplementary-warp manner:

1. Odd-Numbered Rows. Form the picking cross with the aarps of H 1 on the near finger. Pick the border warps from the near finger. Pick the ground-weave warps from the near finger and the pattern warps from either finger, according to the pattern diagram. Pass the weft to the right.

2. Even-Numbered Rows. Lift H 2 for the near side of the picking cross. Again pick the border and ground-weave warps from the near finger, and pick the pattern warps from either finger according to the pattern diagram. Pass the weft to the left.

Some of the diagonal lines of the pattern bands

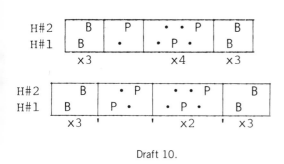

Draft 10.

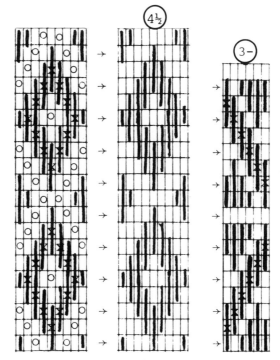

32. Motif and substitution chart for one-color supplementary-warp weave.

may be treated as for complementary warps (Figure 32). Two kinds of substitutions are indicated by symbols on the pattern diagram. An x means to pick up the pattern warp from the far finger, but dropping off the ground warp that is at its immediate right on the near finger. An o means to drop the pattern warp from the near finger, but picking the ground warp that is at its immediate right on the far finger. When the o occurs at the right edge, there will be no ground warp to pick,

but the pattern warp is still dropped from the near finger.

A slightly different warp order is used in the narrower pattern shown in Figure 33, as indicated beside the diagram. This will make a good project for further practice. The weaving sequence is the same as for the diamond pattern and it may be woven with or without the complementary-warp treatment in the diagonal lines.

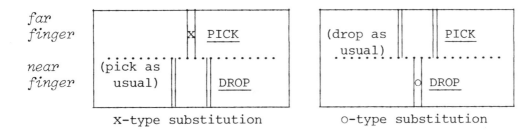

33. A narrower motif for a one-color supplementary-warp.

Band 11. A two-color supplementary-warp band.

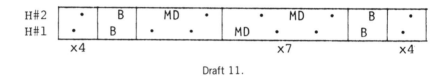

H#2	•	B	MD	•		•	MD	•	B	•
H#1	•	B	•	•	MD	•	•		B	•

x4　　　　　　　x7　　　　　　x4

Draft 11.

Band 11. Two-Color Supplementary Warp

Like the one-color version in Band 10, the ground weave for this band is also a plain weave with paired warps, but in this case the ground weave is a natural white. The pattern yarns are larger in scale, and are s-twist, z-doubled for one or both of the colors. The two colors used for the pattern warps may be varied across the width of the band, as in a belt. There are longer floats on the back, causing the fabric to have a right and a wrong side. In the community where this weave is in common use, it may be found in a great variety of items such as ponchos, incuñas, capachos, chuspas, and belts.

Preparing the Warp. The warp may be wound with q-bouts, using an extra ball of the ground color, or it may be wound as s-bouts and half s-bouts, without the extra ball. With a helper, the latter method is better, especially for a larger weaving on a frame as is done in Bolivia.

Wind the warp yarns in the following order: 4 s-bouts L (the ground warp), 1 s-bout B / 7½ q-bouts L, L, M, D plus one end L / 1 s-bout B, 4 s-bouts L. Rearrange the warps according to Draft 11. A dot symbol is used in the draft to represent the L-ground warps. Install H 1 as a multiloop heddle and H 2 as a shed loop. Start the weft in the end loops alongside the safety pin,

with the tail to the left, lift H 2 and pass the weft to the left, tucking in the tail. Lift H 1 and pass the weft to the right so it will be ready for the extra row below the motif.

Pattern Diagram. As for Band 10, these supplementary-warp patterns are drawn on the rectangular grid, and the empty rectangles indicate where the pattern warps are *not* above the weft in each row. Since there are two colors of pattern warps, the dark warps are shown as vertical lines in the rectangles, and the medium-colored warps are shown by dots. Only one *or* the other is picked from each pair, except in the tie-down spots, which are usually in the last shot of the float. Their purpose is to prevent the floats from being too long on the back side. These spots have been entered on the beginning motifs as short horizontal lines, to indicate that both warps in the M–D pair are to be picked. You may not need these marks after a while; if you do you can draw them in.

Weaving Sequence. Before beginning with the regular sequence, do the extra row below the motif (Figure 34). It is an all-light row with no pattern warps. Lift H 2, insert your near finger, and form a picking cross with the other heddle.

92

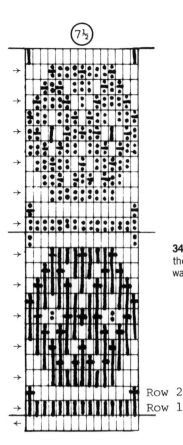

Row 2
Row 1

34. The beginning motif for the two-color supplementary-warp weave.

(You do not need the cross for this kind of row, but it will be easier to lift H 1 for the next row if you lift it now.) Pick the border warps and all the ground warps from your *near* finger, dropping the pattern warps. Pass the weft to the left.

1. Odd-Numbered Rows. Form the picking cross with the H 1 warps on the near finger. Pick the border and ground warps from the near finger, and the pattern warps as shown in the pattern diagram. Pass the weft to the right.

2. Even-Numbered Rows. Form the picking cross with the H 2 warps on the near finger. Pick the border and ground warps from the near finger, and the pattern warps as shown in the pattern diagram. Pass the weft to the left.

For the narrow horizontal lines, there is a tendency for the pattern warps to be pulled down by the tension used in weaving. It may be helpful to insert a small cord under the picked pattern warps temporarily before opening the next shed. It is also helpful to do this at the horizontal beginning line of a motif. The cords can be easily removed later. Additional motifs are provided in Figure 35.

If you would like to draw some designs of your own, plan so your design fits the order of the pattern warps on the heddles. One way of checking for this relates to the location of the tie-down pairs in the last shot of the float. The M–D tie-downs consistently are picked from the near finger of the picking cross. In this warp draft, the edge M–D warp pairs are on H 2, which is on the near side of the picking cross in the even rows, when the weft goes toward the left, and the center M–D pair is on H 1, which is near when the weft goes to the right. Ideas such as these may help you check your plan.

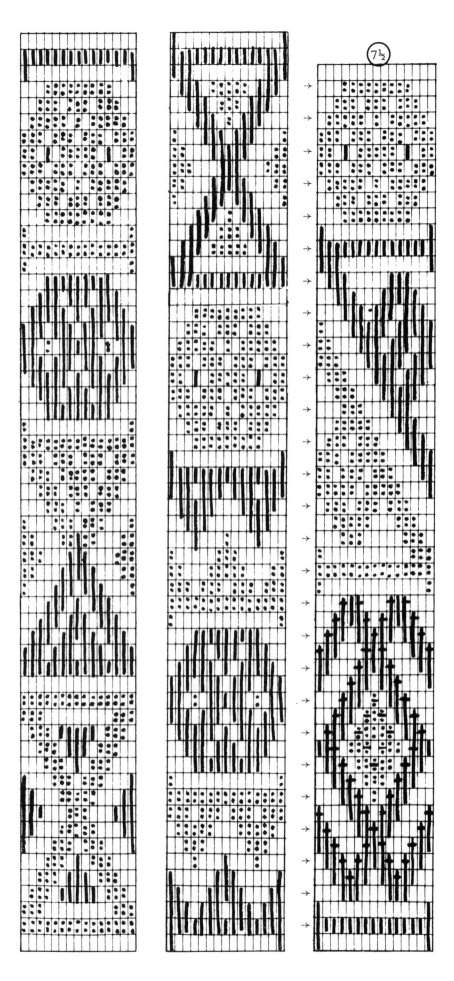

35. Additional motifs for two-color supplementary-warp.

Band 12. A supplementary-weft band.

```
H#2    │ D │ M │ L │ M │ D │
H#1    │ D │ M │ L │ M │ D │
              x12
```

Draft 12.

Band 12. Supplementary Weft

In this patterning version, light warp-faced plain weave forms the pattern, and colorful supplementary-weft floats fill in the negative spaces of the design. The supplementary weft is concealed inside the shed when not in use, so the reverse of the fabric is all white. The narrow bands produced by this technique for hat bands and bag straps are commonly warped with sewing thread. For a chuspa, the warp may be not quite so fine.

Preparing the Warp. Knit-Cro-Sheen and Cottolin are recommended for this band, with Knit-Cro-Sheen for the warp and cottolin for the weft. If desired, the border warps may be wound with Cottolin so they will harmonize with the supplementary-weft colors. Wind the warp yarns in the following order: 1 s-bout D, 1 s-bout M / 12 s-bouts L / 1 s-bout M, 1 s-bout D. The warp cross does not need to be rearranged for this technique (Draft 12). Install H 1 on the near side of the cross. Install H 2 as a shed loop on the far side of the cross.

Two wefts are used in this weave, a structure weft (a) and a supplementary weft (b). The structure weft is the same yarn as the border warps. A doubled strand is used for the supplementary weft, with several color changes incorporated into the fabric as it is woven. Insert the structure weft (a) in the end loops beside the safety pin, with the short tail to the left. Lift H 2 and pass the weft to the left, tucking in the tail. Weave a few rows of plain weave, ending with H 1. Lift H 2, insert the supplementary weft (b) to the right, then also the structure weft (a) to the left, in the same shed but going in the opposite direction.

Pattern Diagram. Supplementary-weft motifs are diagrammed on the diamond grid. There is a diamond for each warp above the weft in every row of the weave. Ovals in the diamonds indicate the light-color pattern warps; the rest is background and will be hidden by the supplementary-weft floats. The slant of the weave must be coordinated with the slant of the pattern diagram, as may be observed by the zigzag edges. The pickup for the rows that slant to the left is made from H 1. If the slant is to the right, the pickup is made from H 2.

In the narrow bands we examined, the weft color was changed each time a main diagonal line in the pattern was begun. These places are marked on the pattern in Figure 36 with a dotted line through the rows. Directions for changing the color of the supplementary weft are given at the end of this section.

Weaving Sequence. Left-slant rows are alternated with right-slant rows. To begin, lift H 1, pick the border warps and insert supplementary weft (b) under the borders and over all the light warps to the left, then lift H 1 again and pass

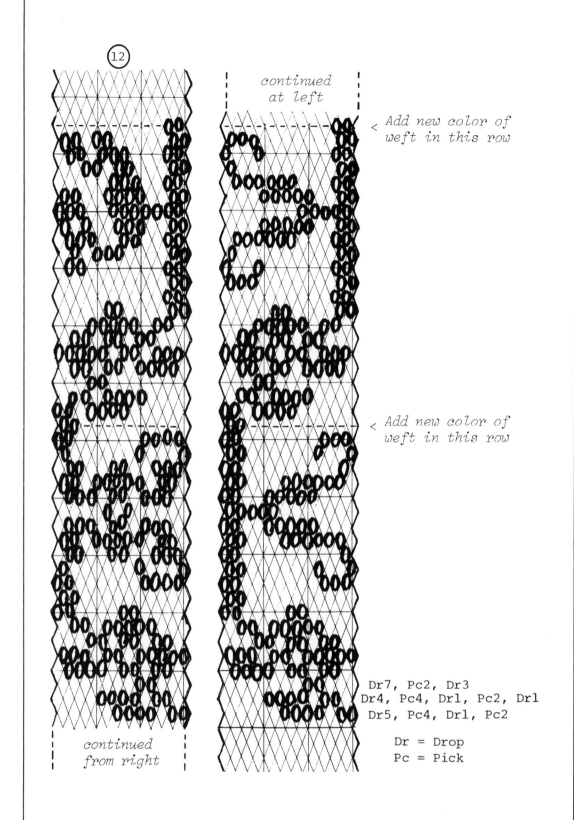

⑫

continued
at left

< Add new color of
  weft in this row

< Add new color of
  weft in this row

continued
from right

Dr7, Pc2, Dr3
Dr4, Pc4, Dr1, Pc2, Dr1
Dr5, Pc4, Dr1, Pc2

Dr = Drop
Pc = Pick

36. Motifs for supplementary weft weave.

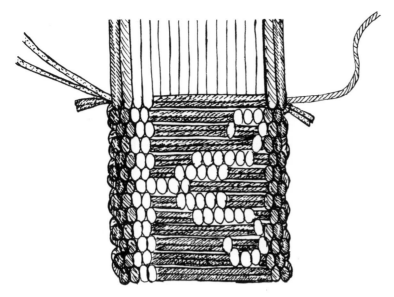

37. To change the color of the supplementary weft, begin the new one along with the structure weft in the last row of a color section.

structure weft (a) to the right. Next try the first row of the pattern. Lift H 2, pick and drop the warps according to the pattern diagram, pass weft (b) to the right. Lift H 2 again and pass weft (a) to the left.

Careful attention must be given to "snugging" in the wefts to keep the pattern in proper proportion and maintain an even width. After changing sheds, snug in first the structure weft and then the supplementary weft. Pull only hard enough to make the fabric warp-faced. If you pull too hard the pattern will become elongated.

Another way to avoid elongating the motifs is to beat the fabric firmly. This can be done with the edge of a ruler or small sword. The fabric should be beaten just after snugging in the wefts from the previous row, before picking the pattern. Your edges will be neater if you pass the structure weft (a) under the supplementary weft (b) at the selvedges, as you continue. The weft ends can be trimmed off later.

The next row of the pattern is a left-slant row. Continue weaving in the following sequence until you come to the dotted line indicating a color change:

1. Left-Slant Row. Lift H 1. Pick borders and pattern warps as indicated. Pass supplementary weft (b) to the left. Lift H 1 again and pass structure weft (a) to the right.

2. Right-Slant Row. Lift H 2. Pick border and pattern warps as indicated. Pass supplementary weft (b) to the right. Lift H 2 again and pass the structure weft (a) to the left.

To change the color of the supplementary weft, pick the row and pass the weft for the "old" color as usual. Then lift the same heddle again, but before passing the structure weft, enter the weft of the "new" color (c) in the shed so it will go in the direction opposite to that of the structure weft, which should now be entered in the same shed (Figure 37). Proceed as usual with the new color in place of the previous one. The ends may be trimmed later.

THREE-COLOR WEAVES

Some of the most exciting adventures for us the authors have been gaining insights into the intricacies of the three-color pattern weaves. Margie's first experience was at the side of one of her Aymara students, when she learned how to weave Band 13, with its little "H"'s and jewel-like squares of two bright colors. Fabric analysis led to more understanding and wonder, but the major breakthrough involved a bumpy two-hour ride in a very crowded, small *collectivo* to the breathtaking height of 15,500 feet. We had been invited to spend the night in the home of an Indian teenager. To her dismay Adele could not endure the altitude, but fortunately Margie was able to stay and learn the basics for the techniques of the three-color pebble weave. Much time has since been spent in fabric analysis and experimental weaving.

The three-color version of one-weft double cloth will be explained at the end of this section, as Band 22, but all the bands preceding it are varieties of float patterning. The first two, Bands 13 and 14, have layers of floats first on one face, then on the other; the other seven have complementary-warp patterning.

In these three-color float patterns, one of the three colors serves as a *common color*, which shows both on the face and the back of the fabric. The other two colors are held in layers, with one color in the upper layer showing on the face, the other color in the lower layer and showing only on the back, until the point of color shift when these layers exchange positions. The color is often shifted in a horizontal line, resulting in alternate blocks, but sometimes the shift is in a diagonal line, or an even more complicated shape.

In Bands 13 and 14, when two of the colors are forming the pattern on one face of the fabric, the third color merely floats as a layer on the other face. For the bands with complementary-warp patterning, the interlacement to separate the color layers is a little more complex. When the patterns are composed of 3-span floats, as in Bands 19 and 20, the third-color warp is hidden under the floats by interlacing there over one, under one with the weft. In pebble weave, where 2-span floats are combined with 3-span floats, a thinner secondary weft is used to aid in separating the color layers. In a study of numerous examples, it was found that the secondary weft is usually in alternate rows, either the pebble rows or the design rows. Sometimes it is used to separate the layers in every row if the design has mostly diagonal lines with 2-span floats, or for special smaller areas of color shifts such as the eye of a bird. For the 3-color complementary-warp uneven twill, the thinner secondary weft is used in every row.

Special manipulations are needed to achieve some of these results, and additional heddles are often used. Although Bands 20 and 21 are customarily woven with only two heddles, the other float-pattern bands have the three colors in separate heddles. The rearrangement of the warp trios, L, M, and D, may be done either with a one-step three-finger method as described for Band 13, or with a two-step two-finger method as described for Band 14. The latter method is recommended for Bands 16, 17, 18, and 19, while the former method is good for Band 15.

Since the common color is usually light, the L's are usually placed at the left of the other two colors of the trio and are operated by H 1. To be consistent, the M's are next toward the right in H 2, and the D's are at the right in H 3. In Band 18, red is the common color and is at the left in H 1, followed by L and D. The arrangement of the colors in the warp trios must be kept in mind during the picking of the pattern, so the proper warps are dropped. The directions for these bands are written on the basis that the weaver has mastered some related two-color-pattern weaving techniques.

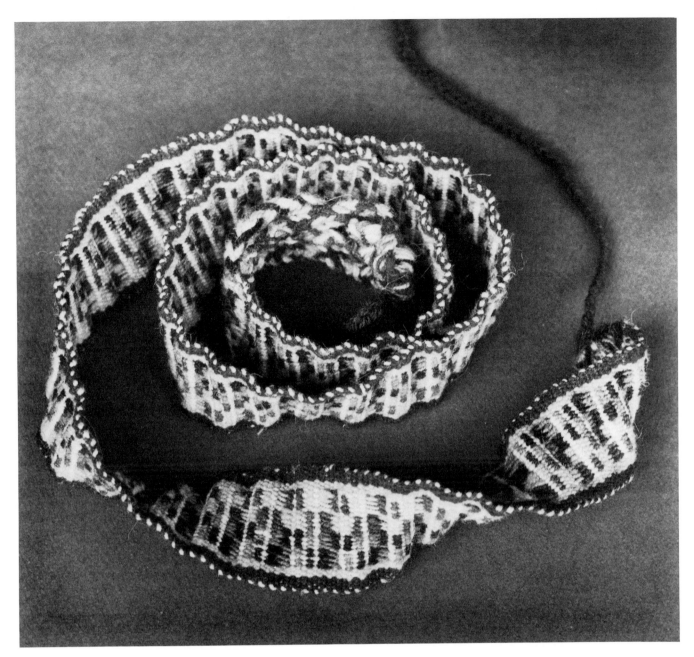

Here is a Bolivian example of a crinkle-weave belt.

Band 13. A layered-weave band in three colors.

Band 13. Layered Weave in Three Colors

This weave is ordinarily used as a pattern stripe in wider pieces such as incuñas and awayos. The Indians use three heddles to produce this weave, one for each of the colors. Even a beginner can enjoy weaving this band!

Preparing the Warp. It is traditional to warp this pattern with white for the common color, and bright contrasting colors such as red and green for the other two colors. Wind the warp yarns in the following order: 2 s-bouts B / 3 t-bouts L, M, and D / 2 s-bouts B. Rearrange the warps in the following three-finger method:

Have three lease sticks ready. In transferring warps from the original cross, use three fingers of the right hand, palm up. The index finger is the far finger, the ring finger is the near finger, and the middle finger is in between. (See Draft 13.)

Transfer the border warps to the right hand with their cross between the middle and ring fingers. Then take each trio in turn, putting the D warp on the far finger, the M warp on the middle finger, and the L warp on the near finger, ending by transferring the borders in the same manner as before. When finished, replace each of the three fingers with a lease stick. Install H 1 as a multiloop heddle for the L warps and the near bor-

ders. Install H 2 as a multiloop heddle for the M warps and the far borders. Then tie a shed loop around all the D warps and the far borders (again) for H 3. Attach H 2 and H 3 to each other, about an inch apart.

Weaving Sequence. A pattern of white "H"'s is woven on one side of the fabric with one of the colors while the third color floats on the back side. The pattern and float sections alternate on each side of the fabric for several repeats and then there is a shift of the color layers, so the third color becomes the color used on the face. Sometimes the outer lane on each side of the band is omitted for a band with only two t-bouts. This band may also be patterned in squares instead of "H"'s.

Begin the weft alongside the safety pin with the short tail to the left. Lift H 2 and H 3 together and pass the weft to the left, tucking in the tail. Then follow the sequence in the pattern (Figure 38). Notice that a picking cross is needed only for Rows 2 and 5, and that in each case it is made with the near finger in the shed with the weft. Consequently, the borders are then taken from the *far* side of the cross.

H#3	B		D		D		B
H#2	B		M		M		B
H#1	B	L		L			B

| x2 | x3 | x2 |

Draft 13.

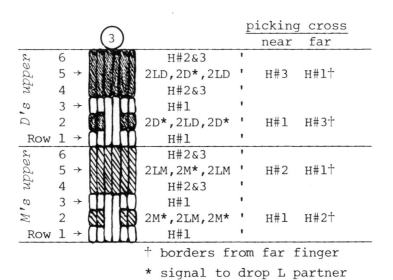

38. Motif for a layered weave in three colors.

Band 14. A crinkle belt.

Band 14. Crinkle Belt

If you are a spinner, this band is for you! The unique "crinkle" effect of this belt used in central Bolivia is largely due to the overtwist of the yarns, in combination with the length of the float sections that appear alternately on the two sides of the fabric. If you use yarn of ordinary twist, your result will still be attractive, but it will lack the crinkle unless you use special manipulations to shorten the floats. The weave is related to Band 13, but no picking is required since the checkerboard pattern is heddle-controlled for both the design and the switching of the colors. The instructions that follow are based on an analysis of the fabric, and on the setup taught to Margie by the Indian mother. The two-step, two-finger method of rearranging the warp will be described here, and will also be used in weaving Bands 16, 17, 18, and 19.

Preparing the Warp. Wind the warp yarns in the following order: 2 s-bouts B / 10 t-bouts L, M and D / 2 s-bouts B. Mark the center of the pattern section before rearranging the warp cross. Rearrange the cross in the following manner: Transfer the border warps to two fingers of the right hand, and then take the trios (L, M, and D) in turn. When the common color is L, the M and D yarns are first placed on the far finger as a pair, then the L warp is placed on the near finger (Draft 14A). Install lease sticks to hold the new cross in position. Insert the heddle string under all

the warps on the near lease stick, and install H 1 as a multiloop heddle. Then tie a shed loop around all the warps on the far lease stick for H 4. (This is all that is necessary for Bands 20 and 21.)

Use H 4 to lift the far warps onto the left fingers, then slide the heddle back, out of the way. Drop the border warps for now and transfer the M–D pairs in turn to two right fingers according to the draft, with H 3 warp being placed first on the far finger, and then the H 2 warp on the near finger. (Often the D warps are on the far finger and the M warps are on the near finger, but watch for exceptions as in this band and in Bands 16 and 18.) Put a lease stick under the warps for H 2 and tie a small shed loop around the warps for H 3. Install the H 2 warps in a multiloop heddle and attach the tops of H 2 and H 3 to each other about an inch apart.

For the crinkle band, an extra heddle is recommended for the far border warps. Pick them up from H 4 and insert a heavier heddle string only under these border warps. In the usual manner for multiloop heddles, make a two-loop heddle with one loop for each set of border warps. After binding the top of the loops, separate them and bind them in the cross-wise direction (Figure 39). Then knot and trim the ends. This border heddle is called Hb in the text.

Weaving Sequence. A firm but not too strong

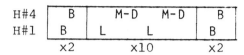

H#4	B	M-D	M-D	B
H#1	B	L	L	B
	x2	x10		x2

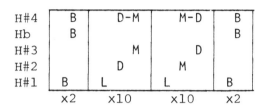

H#4	B	D-M	M-D	B
Hb	B			B
H#3		M	D	
H#2		D	M	
H#1	B	L	L	B
	x2	x10	x10	x2

Draft 14.

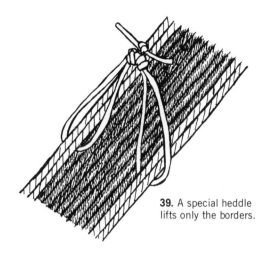

39. A special heddle lifts only the borders.

motion is used in beating. If the fabric is beaten too firmly, the light-colored rows tend to disappear. A double-weave sword, an inkle shuttle, or a ruler with a sharp edge may be used for beating.

Insert the weft alongside the safety pin, with the short tail to the left. Lift H 4 and pass the weft to the left, tucking in the tail. Then weave according to the sequence shown in Figure 40, lifting the heddles as indicated.

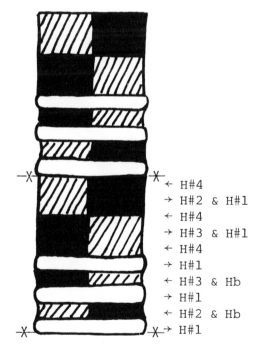

```
← H#4
→ H#2 & H#1
← H#4
→ H#3 & H#1
← H#4
→ H#1
← H#3 & Hb
→ H#1
← H#2 & Hb
→ H#1
```

40. Motif for a crinkle belt.

Band 15. A three-color non-reversible pebble weave band.

H#3	B		D		D	B
H#2	B		M		M	B
H#1	B	L		L		B

×6

Draft 15.

Band 15. Three-Color Nonreversible Pebble Weave

Customarily, when Bolivians weave a 3-color complementary-warp structure, it is double-faced, or reversible. There is evidence that a non-reversible version of 3-color pebble weave has been woven in Peru. Although we do not actually know whether this practice is ever carried out in Bolivia, we have woven suitable patterns in this way, using either an irregular warp order or an alternating order. With the former method, the colors tend to separate unless certain yarns are used. The latter method is included here as an introduction to the 3-color double-faced pebble bands because it is easier and quicker to weave. It is a useful technique for fabrics in which the floats on the back will not be seen. Only one weft is needed.

Preparing the Warp. Wind the warp yarns in the following order: 1 s-bout B / 6 t-bouts L, M, and D / 1 s-bout B. Rearrange the warp cross into three colors as shown in Draft 15, using either the 3-finger method of Band 13 or the two-step method of Band 14. Install multiloop heddles for H 1 and H 2, connecting them about an inch apart with a cord so they can be lifted together easily when needed. H 3 is a shed loop. Begin the weft in the end loops with the short tail to the left. Lift H 3 and pass the weft to the left, tucking in the tail.

An Adjusted One-Bout Selvedge. If you prefer, you may have a two- or three-bout selvedge as in Band 1. Although the chain-like one-bout selvedge is more easily produced with an irregular warp order as in Bands 8 and 9, it is suggested here so you may learn how to have it with an alternating warp order too. Special manipulation is needed so the warp ends on each side follow the rule that the edge two warps should cross when the weft enters the shed, but should not cross when it leaves the shed. To help you at first, the letters n and f have been entered beside the pattern diagram to indicate whether the selvedge warp should be picked from the near or far finger of the picking cross.

Weaving Sequence. Special kinds of motifs must be chosen for this type of band. Each motif must have a definite center area that can be completely outlined by the dark color (Figure 41). The medium color may be used for the center area of the motif and the light color for the background, as suggested for this band (Figure 42) or it may be vice versa.

The method of weaving is similar to that of Band 1 with a few differences. In the pebble rows, the L and M warps are picked together as one in place of the L warps. In the design rows, the colors are picked singly. In the background

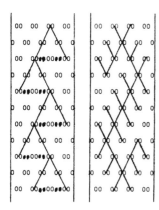

41. Motifs for this band should have a center area that can be completely outlined with a contrasting color. The motif on the left is suitable; the one on the right is not.

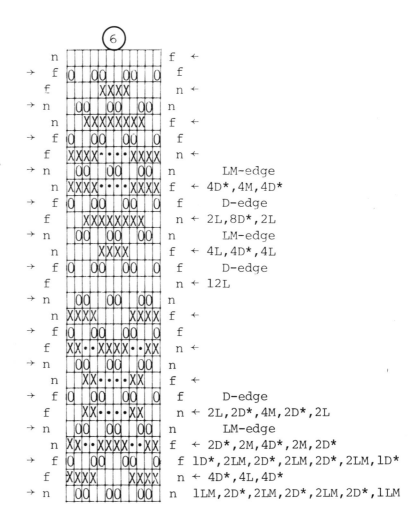

42. Motif for three-color non-reversible pebble weave.

areas, the L warps are picked as usual, but within the motif a single M warp is to be picked in place of each of the usual L warps. For rows having all three colors, it may help to have a 3-finger picking cross. The third color does not need to be lifted in rows having only two colors. Use the following sequence, adjusting the selvedge warps:

1. Pebble Row (L M-edge). Lift both H 1 and 2 together for the near finger, and H 3 for the far finger. Pick L M, D*, D*, L M, L M, D*, D*, L M, etc. Pass the weft to the right.

2. Design row. Lift H 3 for the near finger, and H 1 and/or H 2 for the far finger(s). Substituting M warps for L warps within the outline of the motif, pick the warps in the usual way as indicated in the pattern diagram. Pass the weft to the left.

3. Pebble row (D-edge). Form the picking cross as for Row 1, and pick D*, L M, L M, D*, D*, L M, L M, D*, etc. Pass the weft to the right.

4. Design row. Repeat as for Row 2. Pass the weft to the left.

Band 16. A three-color tripled pebble weave band.

Band 16. Three-Color Tripled Pebble Weave

The simple diamond design that often appears in the doubled pebble band is used here in an even broader version, with each warp unit tripled instead of doubled. Instead of the usual two sets of complementary warps (L and D), there are three sets (L, M, and D). A traditional combination is planned for this band, with the X's on the front side in a dark color, and the diamonds or "roses" in bright colors like red and yellow.

For three-color pebble, a secondary weft is used to separate the warp layers either in the design or pebble rows, or both. For this band it will be used for the design rows only, and both wefts will be passed in opposite directions in the pebble rows. In order to easily distinguish the primary weft (a) from the secondary weft (b), use the usual weft yarn for (a), and split it in half for (b). To split the yarn merely untwist the ends enough to divide the plies, put one half on each side of a post and pull the two parts, straightening the unsplit end with your left hand as you pull. If you prefer, a contrasting color may be used for an unusual edge appearance. Use weft (b) for the whole width of this band.

Since this is such a simple design, certain shortcuts may be made. A more complete introduction to the techniques for the three-color reversible pebble weave will be given for Band 17.

Preparing the Warp. Wind the warp yarns in the following order: 2 s-bouts B / 6 t-bouts D, L, and M / 2 s-bouts B. With the exception of H 1, which is to be prepared in a special way, rearrange the warp cross and install the heddles in the manner given for Band 14, according to Draft 16, with D warps on H 1, followed by L and M warps on H 2 and H 3.

Heddle 1 is installed on the dark warps, but it is made in three sections. First prepare the heddle for the dark pattern warps only; then make two small multiloop heddles for the near border warps, one on each side. Join the tops of these together with a cord, spacing them about an inch apart (Figure 43). Prepare the other heddles as described for Band 14, including Hb, for the far border warps.

Enter both wefts into the end loops, with the tail of weft (a) at the left, and the tail of weft (b) at the right. Lift H 4 and pass weft (a) to the left, then lift Hb and H 3 (M) and pass weft (b). Two more rows will make a handsome beginning for your band and give you some practice with the heddles. Lift H 1 and H 2, pass (a) to the right, then lift H 2 (L) and the same border warps above the D warps to pass (b) to the left. Lastly, lift the D warps only, plus Hb, and pass (a) to the left, then the same warps plus H 3, pass (b) to the

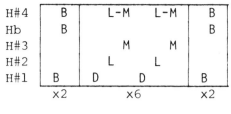

H#4	B		L-M	L-M	B
Hb	B				B
H#3			M	M	
H#2		L		L	
H#1	B	D	D		B
	×2	×6			×2

Draft 16.

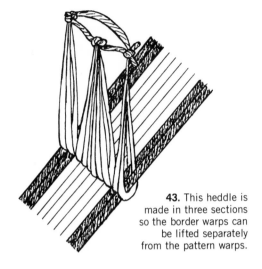

43. This heddle is made in three sections so the border warps can be lifted separately from the pattern warps.

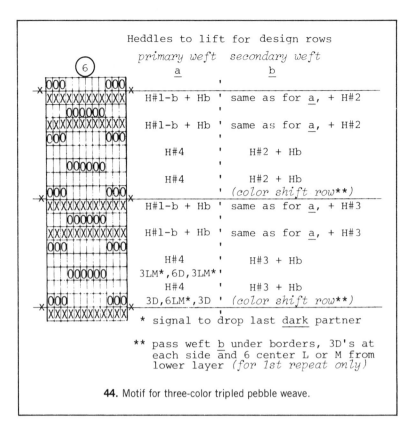

44. Motif for three-color tripled pebble weave.

right. The M warps of H 3 are now in the upper layer with the D warps and you are ready to begin the bottom row of the pattern diagram (Figure 44).

Understanding the Pattern Diagram. A tripled version of the pebble weave pattern grid is used for motifs of this band, with design rows alternating with pebble rows. Notice that the design rows are solid-colored, being all dark, medium or light. The D-edge pebble row is composed of 3 D, 6 L M*, 3 D, and the L M-edge row, of 3 L M*, 6 D, 3 L M*. When the dark warps only are to be picked, this is indicated in the instruction sequence by H 1−b. (−b = minus borders).

Weaving Sequence. The dark color is the common color in this pattern. The lower half of the pattern diagram (Figure 44) is repeated for two motifs with the medium warps in the upper layer, then the upper half is done twice with the light warps in the upper layer. The directions show which heddles to lift for the primary weft first, then for the secondary weft.

For the pebble rows, form the picking cross with the H 1 warps on the near finger and the H 4 warps on the far finger. Pick the borders from the near finger. Pick the darks as singles and the lights and mediums as pairs. Pass both wefts in the same shed except for the color shift rows. For the first row you weave, you do not need to make the color shift indicated on the diagram, but this is necessary thereafter whenever you are making the shift in the layers of the light and medium warps (see directions below).

Since each design row is a solid color, it is not necessary to form a picking cross for them. Continue upwards on the pattern diagram, keeping the different colors of warps in layers as indicated. After you have woven two repeats of the lower half and are ready to weave the first row in the upper half, follow the directions in the next paragraph for the color shift.

To make the color shift, pick the row and pass weft (a) as usual, leaving a finger in the shed. Keep the border warps and the 3 D warps at each side, dropping the L and M warps. Add to these the six center warps of the color that is to be on the upper surface in the following design row (M for row 1 of the lower half, L for row 1 of the upper half), by lifting the appropriate heddle and picking the six center warps. Clean the shed down to the woven edge. A yarn needle may be used to make the color change neater. Pass weft (b). The following design row will complete the shift of the layers.

Continue upward on the pattern diagram, keeping the L and M layers in order as indicated. In this way you can avoid unnecessary friction of your warps, and even a fairly sticky warp can be manipulated with rhythmic ease.

Band 17. A three-color reversible pebble weave band.

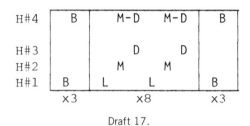

Draft 17.

Band 17. Three-Color Reversible Pebble Weave

Alternating blocks with motifs such as suns, animals, and birds are woven in reversible 3-color pebble weave in central Bolivia. Their colorful patterns bring richness and interest to awayos and chuspas. The light color is traditionally white and usually it is the common color. A favorite motif, the sun, has been chosen for this band. A popular color combination for it is: a white sun (L), in blocks of bright red (M) and dark green (D), with a border of gold (B). Some weavers like to bring the third color up for the center of the sun to add sparkle. A mental reversal of the pattern is needed for the white sun.

While this weave can be done in a narrow band using only the fingers for tension, it is easier if a backstrap or inkle loom is used because of the extra manipulations, especially when the warps are sticky or the band is somewhat wider. Refer back to Band 14 for instructions for rearranging the warp and preparing the heddles, and to Band 16 for suggestions for preparing the secondary weft.

The secondary weft that separates the color layers may be used in alternate rows, either the design rows or the pebble rows, or it may be used in every row, as it is in this band. After you have learned the method, you might like to try having it in alternate rows only, with a very thin weft so it doesn't show. For this band, pass it the entire

width. New manipulations and new types of sheds are involved.

Preparing the Warp. Wind the warp yarns in the following order: 3 s-bouts B / 8 t-bouts L, M, and D / 3 s-bouts B. Rearrange the warp cross and install the heddles for Draft 17, according to the directions given for Band 14. The border heddle Hb is not needed.

Begin both wefts in the end loops alongside the pin, with the tail of weft (a) to the left, and the tail of the thinner weft (b) to the right. Lift H 4 to pass weft (a) to the left and (b) in the opposite direction, tucking in the tails.

New Types of Sheds. Bolivian pickup weaving often involves some interesting manipulations of sets of warps in various types of sheds. Two special sheds are used in almost every row for this band, one for the separation of warps, the other for the addition of warps. Better sheds are made by inserting extra fingers and using a "tension snap" motion. With backstrap or inkle tension, shed sticks may be used in place of the fingers, and the "tension snap" is achieved when the flat sticks are suddenly rotated to vertical positions. Figure 45 illustrates finger versions of the separation shed (view a) and the addition shed (view b). The right thumb can be entered where the asterisk

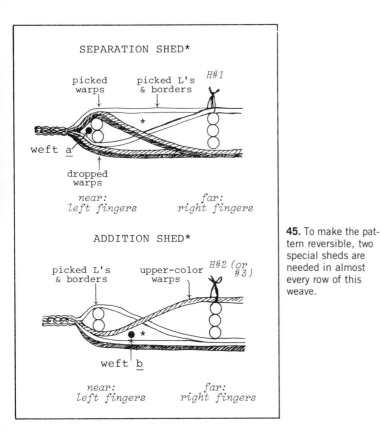

SEPARATION SHED*

picked warps   picked L's & borders   *H#1*

weft <u>a</u>

dropped warps

near: left fingers   *far: right fingers*

ADDITION SHED*

picked L's & borders   upper-color warps   *H#2 (or #3)*

weft <u>b</u>

near: left fingers   *far: right fingers*

45. To make the pattern reversible, two special sheds are needed in almost every row of this weave.

46. Motif for three-color reversible pebble weave.

is, then the rest of the hand can enlarge the shed.

Weaving Sequence. The thicker primary weft (a) follows the usual sequence for pebble weave. When it is at the left, it is a cue that you are to do a pebble row (odd-numbered) and that you should lift H 1 for the near finger of the picking cross. When it is at the right, you are to do a design row (even-numbered), and would lift H 4 for the near finger of the cross. For weft (a), M D warp pairs are picked in place of the D warps for the pebble weave pattern. For weft (b), the borders and L warps picked for the row are separated and kept, and then all the warps of the upper-layer color, either M or D, are added.

In this band, the backgrounds of the blocks are alternately D (first), then M, and L is used for the sun motifs and the bars between the blocks (Figure 46). Since the color shifts are made for each horizontal bar (a modified pebble row), directions for two rows will be given before beginning with the motif.

Preliminary Row A. Lift H 1, pass weft (a) to the right; add warps from H 3 (D), and pass weft (b).

Preliminary Row B. Lift H 4, pass weft (a) to the left; keep borders only, and add H 3 for (b).

The next time you will do these rows will be after the sun motif is completed, and at that time there should be a color shift. This is simply done by lifting the heddle for the next upper-layer color, H 2 for M instead of H 3 for D. Check the back of the fabric for neatness of the color line. You are now ready to start on Row 1 of the motif. Remember that the pattern is white against a dark background this time, and that the asterisk (*) in-

dicates you should drop a light partner.

1. Pebble Row (M D-edge). Form a picking cross with H 1 near, H 4 far, and pick: 1M D*, 2L, 2M D*, 2L, 2M D*, 2L, 2M D*, 2L, 1M D*, taking borders from the near finger. Pass weft (a) to the right. Lift H 1 to separate the picked L and border warps, and add to them all of the upper-color warps (D) by lifting H 3. Pass weft (b).

2. Design Row. Form a picking cross with H 4 near, H 1 far, and pick: 6M D*, 4L, 6M D*, taking borders from near finger. Pass weft (a) to the left. Lift H 1. This time it will separate the L's you picked, but will not lift the borders, so you must pick them up. Then add all of the upper-color warps (D) by lifting H 3. Pass weft (b).

3. Pebble Row (L-edge). Repeat as for Row 1, except pick: 1L, 2M D*, 2L, 2M D*, etc.

4. Design Row. Repeat as for Row 2, except pick: 4M D*, 8L, 4M D*.

Continue according to the pattern diagram. In the next motif, substitute the M warps for the D's by lifting H 2 instead of H 3.

Special Area Color Shift. When you have mastered this technique, you might like to use the third color for the center of the sun. This is easily done by merely replacing some of the center warps of the upper-color layer, when it is lifted for weft (b), by warps brought up from the lower layer. For the five middle rows of the motif, replace respectively 2, 4, 6, 4, and 2 of the center warps with warps of the lower-layer color.

Band 18. A three-color uneven twill band.

```
H#4 │   B   │ L-D     L-D │   B   │
    │       │             │       │
H#3 │       │   D      D  │       │
H#2 │       │  L      L   │       │
H#1 │   B   │ M      M    │   B   │
      x3        x13         x3
```

Draft 18.

Band 18. Three-Color Uneven Twill with Complementary Warps

Bolivian examples of this pattern weave sometimes have bird or animal forms, but more frequently they are abstract creations, often with diagonal lines and many times including interlocking scrolls. Two representative projects are planned for this band, the first with alternating blocks having a bird motif, and the second one abstract with special color shifts for diagonals and hexagons.

The methods used for this band are essentially the same as those used for Band 17, differing only because its twill structure does not require that the alternate rows be tie-down rows. Instead, every row is picked individually in such a way that the warp floats usually do not span more than two wefts.

The colors suggested for this band follow the tradition for the second project: red for the common color (instead of white), with white and black for the two color layers. This means that red should be rearranged at the left in the trios, and should be operated by H 1. Make your warp a yard long so you will have room to try the special color shifts after the bird motif.

Preparing the Warp. Wind the warp yarns in the following order: 2 s-bouts M (red), 1 s-bout B (gold) / 13 t-bouts M, L (white), and D (black) / 1 s-bout B, 2 s-bouts M. Rearrange the warp

cross and install the heddles for Draft 18 according to the directions given for Band 14, except attach H 3 and H 4 together, instead of H 2 and H 3. The border heddle (Hb) is not needed. Prepare a secondary weft as described for Band 16.

Insert both wefts in the end loops beside the pin, with the tail of weft (a) to the left and the tail of the thinner weft (b) to the right. Lift H 4 to pass weft (a) to the left and weft (b) in the opposite direction, tucking in the tails.

Weaving Sequence. Refer to Band 17 for background information on the use of the two wefts in the weaving sequence, and for information on the special types of sheds used for weft (b).

In this band, the backgrounds of the blocks are alternately D (first), then L, for the first project. Red (M) is used for the motifs and for the bars between the blocks. Since a color shift is made for each horizontal bar, directions for two rows will be given before beginning with the motif (Figure 47).

Preliminary Row A. Lift H 1, pass weft (a) to the right, add warps of H 3 and pass weft (b).

Preliminary Row B. Lift H 4, pass weft (a) to the left, keep borders and add H 3, pass (b).

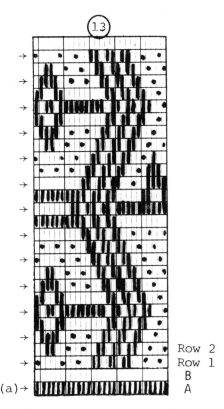

47. Motif with horizontal color shifts.

The next time you do these rows will be after the motif is completed, and at that time there should be a color shift. This will be explained after the motif. You are now ready to start on Row 1 of the motif. Remember that the red warps are the complements to the white or black ones that you pick, and must be dropped when the L or D warps are picked. There is also a mental reversal of the pattern, since the background in the first block is darker than the motif.

Row 1. Form a picking cross with H 1 near, H 4 far, pick near borders, and pick according to the pattern diagram, starting at the right. Each rectangle with a line or dot represents one red warp picked up (its complements will drop). Each empty rectangle means that you should pick up one L–D pair, and then you must be sure to drop the last red partner. For example, you would start picking: 1L D*, 1M, 2L D*, 1M, 2L D*, 2M, 1L D*, 2M, 1L D*, 2M, 2L D*, 1M, 2L D*, 1M, 4L D*, 1M. Pass weft (a) to the right. Lift H 1 to separate the picked M and border warps, and add to them the upper-color warps (D) by lifting H 3. Pass weft (b).

Row 2. Form a picking cross with H 4 near, H 1 far. Pick the near borders and pick the row according to the diagram, taking the M warps and the L D pairs as for Row 1. Pass weft (a) to the left. Lift H 1. This time it will separate the M's you picked, but will not lift the borders, so you must pick them up. Then add the upper-color warps (D) by lifting H 3. Pass weft (b).

Continue upward according to the pattern diagram, treating the odd-numbered rows like Row 1, and the even-numbered rows like Row 2. The

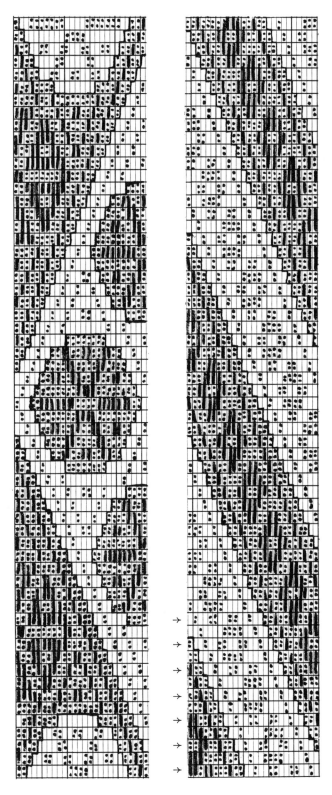

48. Motifs with diagonal color shifts on the right and with hexagons on the left.

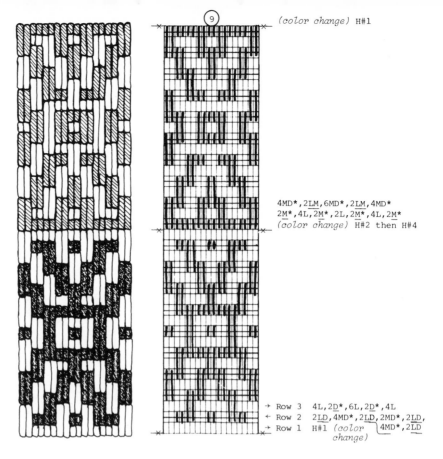

49. Motif for stepped diagonals.

(color change) H#1

4MD*,2LM,6MD*,2LM,4MD*
2M*,4L,2M*,2L,2M*,4L,2M*
(color change) H#2 then H#4

→ Row 3 4L,2D*,6L,2D*,4L
← Row 2 2LD,4MD*,2LD,2MD*,2LD,
→ Row 1 H#1 (color ⌐4MD*,2LD
　　　　　　　　change)

last row of the motif is a solid-colored row. After this, you are to repeat the two preliminary rows with a shift of the upper-layer colors. This is simply done by lifting the heddle for the next upper color, which at this time would be H 2 for the L warps instead of H 3 for the D warps. Check the back of the fabric for neatness of the color line. You are then ready to start on the next motif, Row 1, substituting H 2 for H 3 in the directions. After you have woven as many repeats as desired, end with the preliminary two rows to be ready to weave the pattern with diagonal color shifts.

Diagonal Color Shift. When you have mastered the basic technique, you are ready to try motifs that have a diagonal color shift, such as those in Figure 48. Look at the right-hand design on the pattern diagram. Notice the dotted rectangles, to indicate, the common color. Also observe that the line of color shift, which comes at the junction of the red and white diagonals, is indicated by a darkened line at the edges of the rectangles.

The weaving sequence is basically the same, except that warps from both H 2 and H 3 must be lifted before passing weft (b).

Row 1: Form a picking cross with the H 1 warps on the near finger and the H 2 warps on the far finger. Each rectangle with two dots in it represents one red warp picked up. Each empty rectangle *and* each rectangle with a vertical line in it

indicates you should pick up one L D pair. This means that for Row 1, starting at the right, you pick 1L D*, 1M, 2L D*, 2M, 2L D*, 2M, 2L D*, 1M, 2L D*; and 2M, 1L D*, 3M, 2L D*, 1M, 2L D*. Pass weft (a) to the right. Then lift H 1 to separate the picked M and border warps. Keeping a left finger with some tension under the separated warps, lift H 2 just enough to separate the white warps, and insert a right finger or two under them, back between H 1 and H 2. Check the pattern diagram to see which white warps will be in the upper layer. For Row 1, keep the 15 right-hand whites and drop the 11 on the left. Lift the 15 L warps and add them to the warps above the left finger. Next lift H 3 enough to separate the black warps. Drop the 15 right-hand D warps, and keep the 11 on the left. Lift these 11 D warps and add them to the warps above the left finger. Pass weft (b).

Row 2. Form a picking cross with H 4 near, H 1 far. Pick the near borders and the pattern as indicated, taking the M warps and the L D pairs as for Row 1. Pass weft (a) to the left. Lift H 1 to separate the reds, and pick the borders separately. Then add the black and white warps as indicated: 16 right whites, 10 left blacks. Pass weft (b).

When you are comfortable with the diagonal shift, you can go on to the hexagonal motif (Figure 48). Weave this in the same manner as the diagonal design, paying careful attention to the areas of color shift.

112

A Bolivian example of Bands 17 and 18. Collection of Phil Druker.

Band 19. A stepped diagonal band in three colors.

Band 19. Stepped Diagonals in Three Colors

The truly reversible effect of this three-color complementary-warp pattern weave is achieved in a way somewhat different from that of the three previous bands—16, 17, and 18. Only one weft is used and the third-color warp is hidden under the 3-span warp floats by interlacing with the weft over one, under one.

The pattern chosen for your sample band is from a Bolivian awayo in the collection of the American Museum of Natural History. We have found only a very few other examples of this weave in Bolivian fabrics. Experimentation with known Bolivian methods produced a suitable product, but final improvements came through drawing a series of vertical cross-sections to insure proper interlacement of the hidden third-color warp.

Understanding the Pattern Diagram. The diagram is related to the special manner of the pickup: warp singles are picked up in the odd-numbered rows, and warp pairs are picked up in the even-numbered rows. On the float grid (Figure 49), an extra horizontal line is drawn through the center of the even-numbered rows as a reminder that pairs are to be picked up there, a warp pair for *each* rectangle in the row.

Preparing the Warp. Wind the warp yarns in the following order: 3 s-bouts B / 9 t-bouts L, M, and D / 3 s-bouts B. Rearrange the warp cross and install the heddles for Draft 19 using the two-step, two-finger method as given for Band 14, but without the border heddle Hb. In this draft, L is the common color.

Begin the weft in the end loops beside the pin with the short tail to the left. Lift H 4, pass the weft to the left. You are now ready to start Row 1 of the first block. As another option, a contrasting stripe may be woven before the first block is begun. This requires more manipulation in exchanging the color layers. When the weft is first inserted into the end loops beside the pin, the tail should be long enough to use as a secondary weft for two rows, to aid in holding the M and D warps in separate layers. Then lift H 4, and pass the weft to the left. Pick up the border warps from H 4, and add to them the warps of H 2 (M); pass the tail to the right as a secondary weft. Lift H 1, and pass the weft to the right, then lift H 3 just enough to exchange the M and D layers, so that the D warps are now above the M warps, but the L warps are still on the top with their border warps. Pass the tail to the left between the M and D layers for its last shot. Lift H 4 one more time,

114

H#4	B	M-D	M-D		B
H#3		D	D		
H#2		M	M		
H#1	B	L	L		B
	×3		×9		×3

Draft 19.

pass the weft to the left, and you are ready for Row 1 of the first block.

Weaving Sequence. The border warps are taken from the near finger. When the weft is on the left, the picking cross is formed with H 1 warps on the near finger, and D warps of H 3 (first block) or M warps of H 2 (second block) on the far finger. Single warps are then picked for each rectangle, in the usual manner, keeping in mind the order of L M D in the trios, to drop the L partner when a D (or M) is picked.

When the weft is on the right, H 4 is lifted for the near finger, H 1 for the far one. An M D warp pair is picked for each rectangle with a vertical pattern line. If the rectangle is empty except for the horizontal line, the D warp only is picked from the M D pair, the M is dropped, and an L warp is picked in its place, to have an L D pair. (In the second block, drop the D, and pick the L M pair.) The asterisk (*) in the notation is a reminder to drop the L warp of the L M D trio.

When you have finished the plain light row at the end of the first block, you are ready for a color change. To exchange the M and D layers, lift H 2 first, (or H 3, second block), then lift H 4 to pass the weft. Check the back side for the neatness of the line. You may want to use a very fine secondary weft in the two boundary rows to aid in holding the M and D layers in respective positions.

This pattern is especially well suited to being woven on the inkle loom, with the help of supplementary heddles as described in Chapter 5.

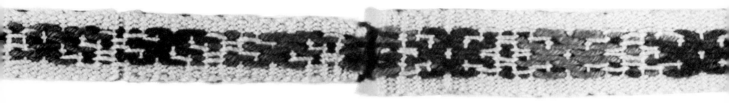

Band 20. Reversible three-color companion weave band, two variations.

Band 20. Reversible Three-Color Bands with Two Heddles

The three-color pattern weaves of Bands 20 and 21 are produced with only two heddles, and might be called companion weaves, since they have been found almost exclusively beside the wider two-color pattern bands of modified intermesh in chuspas and aksus.

This band, like the previous one, has 3-span floats under which the third-color warp may be hidden as it interlaces with the single weft. Because not all of its floats are in pairs, the motifs of Band 20 are more graceful than those of Band 19. Since this band is woven beside wider bands of modified intermesh, the warps are customarily wound on the oblique frame loom. The thinner white yarn is in the string heddle and the two colors of wool warp are on the shed rod. The method of weaving is related to the sequence for modified intermesh.

Two traditional motifs are provided for this band, the first one using four t-bouts, and the second one with only three. It is suggested that the 4-bout warp for Band 20 be made long enough to be used for Band 21 also, and that you prepare a separate band for the 3-bout pattern.

Preparing the Warp. Wind the warp yarns in the following order: 4 s-bouts L (thin white) / 4 t-bouts L, M, and D / 4 s-bouts L (thin white).

Rearrange the warp cross as shown in Draft 20, and install the heddles with the M D warp pairs in H 2. Insert the weft in the end loops beside the pin, with the tail to the left. Lift H 2 and pass the weft to the left. Lift H 1, and pass the weft to the right.

Pattern Diagram. In 3-color weaves done with two heddles, the color layers are not actually separated except by the picking choices. It helps to think of the basic weave as if it were merely heddle-controlled, with the single light warps on H 1 for the odd-numbered rows, and the paired M D warps on H 2 for the even-numbered rows. The 3-span warp pattern floats are made by substitutions in this basic order, which is reflected in the pattern diagram. In the light rows, color floats are caused by substitutions of upper-color (M or D) warps in place of the L warps; in the M D rows, L floats are caused by substituting a light warp in place of one of the M D warps (the L warp is kept with the upper-color warp).

The color shift for both these motifs is not on a straight horizontal line (Figure 50) as it was for the pattern blocks of Band 19. For the flower motif it is a "U" shaped line, and for the feather one it is a stepped diagonal line. The color shift is indicated on the pattern diagram by a heavy line,

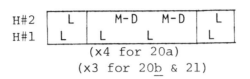

H#2	L	M-D	M-D	L
H#1	L	L	L	L

(x4 for 20a)

(x3 for 20b & 21)

Draft 20.

and also by speckles in the empty rectangles. A speckled rectangle with no horizontal line indicates a light warp is to be picked, just as an empty white rectangle does. The type of diagram presented for Band 19 is also used for these motifs. The pattern will not be truly reversible unless carefully picked as shown. Border warps are picked from the near finger of the picking cross, since the heddle for the near finger locks in the borders.

Weaving Sequence. It is planned that you do one picked row before the sequence begins for the flower motif (Figure 50). Make a picking cross with the H 2 warps on the near finger and the H 1 warps on the far finger. Pick 1L M, 2M D*, 2L M, 2M D*, 1L M. Pass the weft to the left. Rows A and B are given separately because they contain an overlap in the picking of the color layers, in preparation for the color shift.

Preliminary Row A. Lift H 1 for the near finger, H 2 for the far one. Pick 2L, 1D*, 2L, 1D*, 2L. Note that you have pairs on the far finger, but you pick only a single warp (D) in place of each L warp dropped. Pass the weft to the right.

Preliminary Row B. Lift H 2 for the near finger, H 1 for the far one. Pick 1M D*, 1L M, 4M D*, 1L M, 1M D*. Note that in two rectangles

you are keeping the M warp of the M D pair, but picking an L warp in place of the D warp. This is the last time for a while that you will be having the M choices for the upper layer. Since you do not have as good control of the order of the warps as if they were on a shed rod of a frame loom, you will need to watch that they do not get out of order and cross, affecting your color pattern.

Row 1. Continue with same sequence of heddles, picking single warps as indicated on the pattern for all odd-numbered rows (pick D warps to replace L warps).

Row 2. Continue, picking warp pairs as indicated on the pattern for all even-numbered rows (pick L D pairs to replace the M D pairs).

When you get to the next overlap section with rows A and B, follow the directions as indicated, then continue but have the M warps be your choices instead of D warps.

For the feather motif, woven with 3 t-bouts instead of four, the same two alternate rows (singles and pairs) are used. Take care to watch where the stepped diagonal line of the color change takes place: pick an L D pair for each speckled rectangle with a horizontal line and an L M pair for each plain white rectangle with a horizontal line in the even rows.

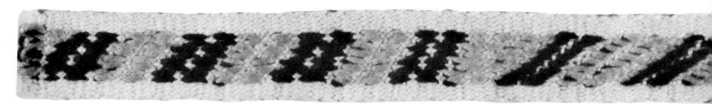

Band 21. Three-color twill companion weave band, two variations.

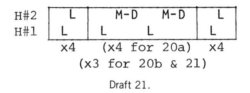

Draft 21.

Band 21. Three-Color Twill bands for Two Heddles

This band is also a companion weave with the same warp setup. It differs in structure from Band 20, being a type of twill with 2-span floats, and is therefore not truly reversible when woven with one weft. Two pattern versions are also provided for this band, but the method and pattern diagram are different because of the length of the floats.

The heddles are used alternately for the picking cross in the same way they were used for Band 20, with H 1 lifted first for the odd-numbered rows, and H 2 first for the even-numbered rows. Borders are picked from the near finger. For the first weft shot of each 2-span warp float, the M D warp pair is picked. On the second weft shot for the float, only the upper-color warp is picked. The warps are picked from both fingers as needed

for the design. In the pattern diagram (Figure 51), vertical lines in the rectangles indicate the D warps; dots indicate the M warps. A short horizontal line indicates the places where the pair is picked instead of a single warp. All others are picked as singles. Watch as you weave to be sure the proper colors are showing, and are not affected by crossing of the warps.

The first pattern has floats by pairs in a diagonal line, and resembles a doubled three-color CWp 2/1 twill. It is often used beside another similar band, with the diagonals at the opposite slant, giving a chevron effect. In the second pattern the warp floats are also aligned diagonally, but not as pairs. Both bands are easy to do.

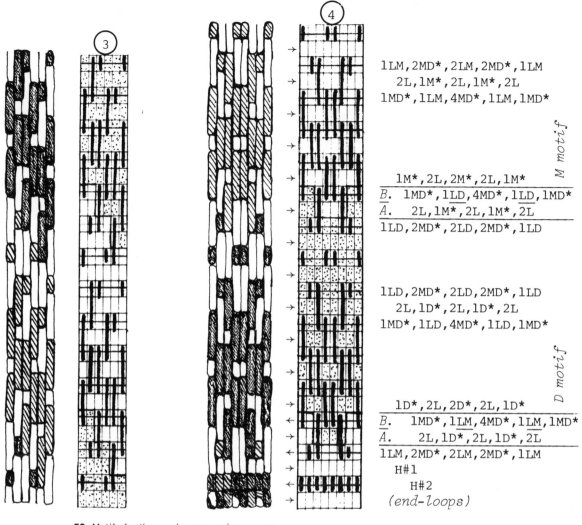

1LM,2MD*,2LM,2MD*,1LM
  2L,1M*,2L,1M*,2L
1MD*,1LM,4MD*,1LM,1MD*

M motif

    1M*,2L,2M*,2L,1M*
<u>B.</u> 1MD*,1<u>LD</u>,4MD*,1<u>LD</u>,1MD*
<u>A.</u>   2L,1M*,2L,1M*,<u>2L</u>
1LD,2MD*,2LD,2MD*,1LD

1LD,2MD*,2LD,2MD*,1LD
  2L,1D*,2L,1D*,2L
1MD*,1LD,4MD*,1LD,1MD*

D motif

    1D*,2L,2D*,2L,1D*
<u>B.</u> 1MD*,1<u>LM</u>,4MD*,1<u>LM</u>,1MD*
<u>A.</u>   2L,1D*,2L,1D*,<u>2L</u>
1LM,2MD*,2LM,2MD*,1LM
   H#1
    H#2
(end-loops)

50. Motifs for three-color companion weaves.

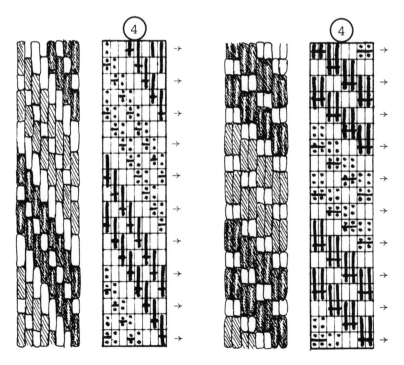

51. Motifs for three-color twill companion weaves.

Band 22. Three-color warp-faced double cloth band.

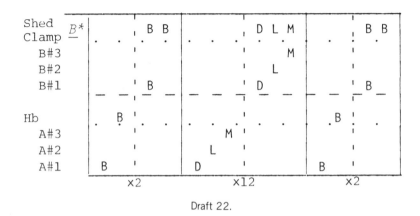

Draft 22.

Band 22. Three-Color Warp-Faced Double Cloth

This band should not be attempted until the two-color version, Band 7, has been mastered. Some instructions given there are not repeated here. It is one of the more difficult weaves because of its special manipulations and the tension problems that may be involved. It is advisable to make use of a backstrap.

The common color in this band is dark (D), providing a continuous background on the face and motifs on the back. The motifs on the face are alternately L and M; on the back, the L and M warps form alternate background blocks for the D motifs. In the first block, D and L warps are woven into two layers of cloth with the M warps hidden in between. In the next block, D and M warps form the double cloth, with the L warps hidden in between.

When the hidden warps are floating inside, there is no take-up on them and they tend to become slack. Measures to counteract this are suggested. Because so many warps are sandwiched between the layers of the fabric, belts and bands in this weave often have a padded appearance, giving an interesting sculptured effect to animal motifs. Ways to avoid friction on the warps and heddles are important. Knit-Cro-Sheen is recommended for use in your sample band.

Preparing the Warp. Be prepared with five lease sticks or suitable substitutes. Before beginning to warp, divide your border-colored yarn into two balls. Wind the warp yarn in the following order: 2 d-bouts B / 8 t-bouts L, M, and D / 2 d-bouts B. In tying the ends of the t-bouts, tie three knots, one for each color. This will make it easier to adjust for the slack of the warp sets, if necessary. Also, have one extra warp end for the outside edge of the left border because of the tubular construction. Allow it to remain to the side for now. (Later, weave it in.)

Six heddles plus a shed loop or clamp are used for this band, as shown in Draft 22. The heddles are numbered in two series. The set near the weaver is the A series, with the heddles numbered A1, A2, and A3. The set away from the weaver is the B series, with the heddles numbered B1, B2, and B3. It is a good idea to color-code the heddles. With some yarns it is better to form the heddles around three fingers instead of two to allow more room for making the sheds.

Insert lease sticks into the two sheds of the original cross. Lift the warps above the far stick of the lease with the left hand, and rearrange the warps onto the right fingers as follows. Taking the right-hand pair of border warps, place one on

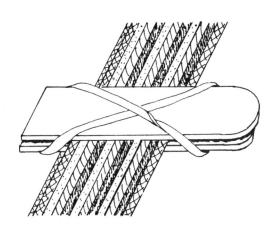

52. A shed clamp may be substituted as a heddle in place of the shed loop.

53. Motifs for three-color warp-faced double cloth.

the index (far) finger, then place the other on the middle (near) finger. Repeat with the other pair of border warps. Then taking each trio (L, M, D) in turn, place the L and M warps on the far finger, and the D warp on the near finger. Continue, and finish by placing the two left border pairs in the same way as the right ones. Insert lease sticks in place of the right fingers to hold the warps in position.

Install H B1 as a multiloop heddle for the D warps and the border warps by them. From the far lease stick, lift the L and M warps, without the borders, and rearrange them to the right hand, placing the M warp first on the far finger, then the L warp on the near finger, for each L M pair. Install H B2 and H B3 as multiloop heddles, for the L and M warps respectively.

Install a shed clamp (or shed loop) around all the series B warps, including all the border warps above the far stick of the original warp cross plus the extra warp end at the left edge. A shed clamp helps avoid friction on the warps and heddles. The warps are better spaced and they can be lifted easily by merely rotating the clamp a partial turn. It can be made from two short lease sticks or a tongue depressor. For this narrow band, cut the depressor in half. Place one piece under all the B series warps (plus the extra warp end) and the other piece on top of them. Bind the two sticks together with rubber bands as shown in Figure 52.

Now lift the warps above the near stick of the original warp cross and rearrange them in the same way as for the far side of the cross, instal-

ling multiloop heddles. H A1 is for the D warps and the near border warps. H A2 and H A3 are for the L and M warps respectively, without border warps. For the far A border warps, install Hb with each warp in its own loop (two loops at each side). It is easier to lift the heddles by groups if the heddles in each series have connecting cords. Be sure not to tie them too close together, or it will be difficult to lift them separately. Check the heddles.

To weave this band on the backstrap, there are various options for the beginning end. Perhaps the easiest for this sample is to use a thin stick or heavy wire in the end loops, tying it firmly to your waist beam. Insert the weft in the end loops, with the short tail to the right. Also insert the extra border warp in the same shed. Lift the whole B series, and clear the shed carefully to the end. Pass the weft to the right, tucking in the tail and the end of the border warp.

Weaving Sequence. With so many heddles, care must be taken to give them straightening tugs whenever necessary. If proper techniques are used, you should not have to move the heddles back and forth on the warps to lift them. At first, it is a good idea to count the warps in the lower layer before you make the lower weft shot.

You are now ready to begin weaving. No picking cross is needed for the plain background. Begin with the four rows of dark background, as follows:

Left-Slant Row. For the upper shot, lift H A1, and pass the weft to the left. With the left two

54. In three-color warp-faced double cloth, the unused warps float between the layers (top). When the lower cloth layer is not likely to be visible, the weaver sometimes does not separate the colors for the lower layer, which results in a mottled effect on the back of the fabric (bottom).

fingers in the shed with the weft, lift warps of H A3 (the hidden warps) and add them to the warps on your left fingers. Then lift all the B series warps by rotating the shed clamp, insert your right hand, snap fingers to a vertical position and find the lower shed. Pass the weft to the right in the lower shed.

Right-Slant Row. For the upper shot, lift H B1, and pass the weft to the left. With two left fingers in the shed with the weft, lift the warps of H B3 (the hidden warps) and add them to the warps on your left fingers. Then lift all the A series warps (with Hb), insert your right hand and find the lower shed. Pass the weft to the right in the lower shed.

Since Row 1 of the motif (Figure 53) is a left-slant row, repeat these two rows and you will be ready for the picking sequence. The pattern rows are done as follows:

Left-Slant Rows of Pattern. For the upper shot, form a picking cross with the H A1 (D) warps on the near finger and the H A2 (L) warps on the far finger. Pick the border warps from the near finger, and pick the pattern warps as indicated in the diagram. Pass the weft to the left, leaving two left fingers in the shed with the weft.

For the lower shot, lift H A2 (M, the hidden warps) and add them to those that are above the left fingers. Then lift all the B series warps and find the lower shed. Pass the weft to the right through the lower shed.

Right-Slant Rows of Pattern. For the upper shot, form a picking cross with the H B1 (D) warps on

the near finger and the H B2 (L) warps on the far finger. Pick the border warps from the near finger, and pick the pattern warps as indicated in the diagram. Pass the weft to the left, leaving two fingers in the shed with the weft.

For the lower shot, lift H B3 (M, the hidden warps) and add the warps to those that are on the left fingers. Then lift all the A series warps (with Hb) and find the lower shed. Pass the weft to the right through the lower shed.

In the next block of the pattern, picking crosses are formed with the D and M warps, and the L warps are the hidden warps. The sequence is then repeated.

Adjustment of Warp Tension. If trouble develops because of the slackness of either the L or M warp layers, an extra loop can be added for taking up the slack.

To adjust the L warps, lift all the heddles except H A2, in such a way that the L warps will drop. Separate them out below and clean the shed to the far end. Attach a loose loop around them which may be connected to the post with a cord. For the M warps, do the same thing, lifting all the heddles except H A3 so the M warps will drop.

Variation with a Mottled Effect on the Back. Usually the third-color warps float between the layers as shown in Figure 54. Occasionally, however, when the back side of the fabric will not be visible (like inside a coca bag) the weaver does not lift the third-color warps before passing the lower shot of weft and there is a mottled effect on the back side of the pattern band.

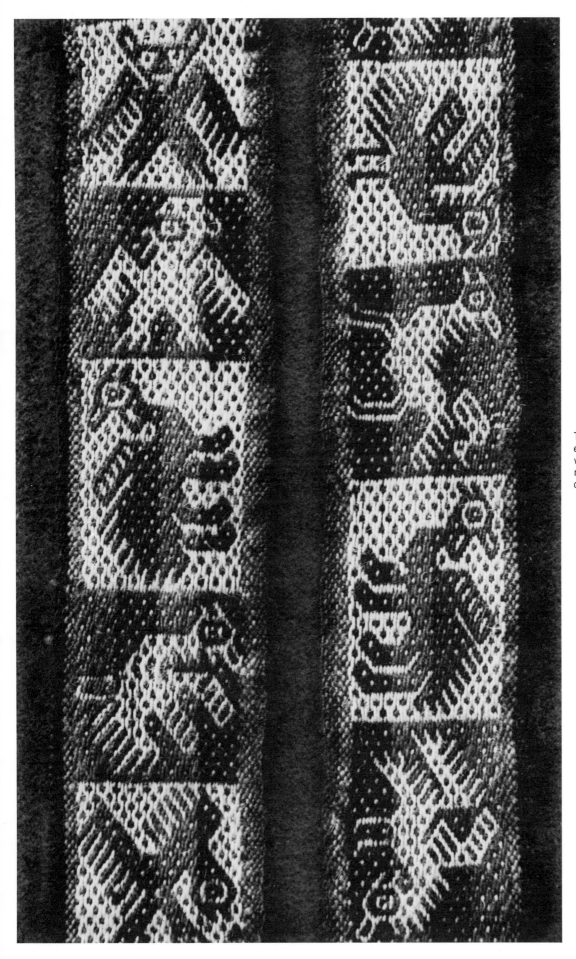

This band is a Bolivian example of pebble weave with an alternating warp order. Collection of Lynn Meisch.

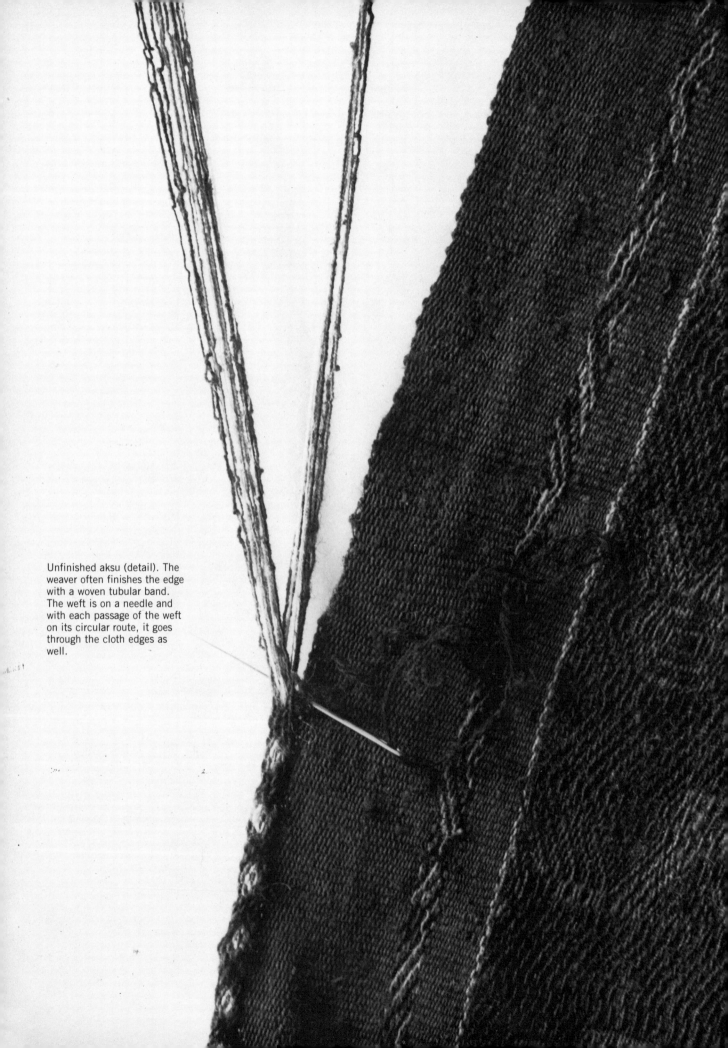

Unfinished aksu (detail). The weaver often finishes the edge with a woven tubular band. The weft is on a needle and with each passage of the weft on its circular route, it goes through the cloth edges as well.

Chapter Four

Embellishments

The Bolivian weaver-artist completes her composition with any of a rich variety of embellishments. From her yarn palette she chooses colors to use in ways that are often ingenious, for edge trimmings, tassels, wrappings, braids, or other finishes.

RIBETES

The weaver often finishes the edges of her coca bag, aksu, or lliklla with a woven tubular band, or *ribete*. This not only keeps the edges from fraying, but is also a decoration. The weft is on a needle, and with each passage of weft in its circular route, it goes through the edges of the bag or cloth and is firmly attached as it is woven. Each time a new shed is prepared, the previous weft must be beaten down with the fingers and the weft pulled tight to make the weave warp-faced before the weft is passed through.

The bands may be woven flat for purposes of

study, or as a round tubular cord, but it would be more fun to try doing one of them as a tubular edge on a small bag made of felt or other suitable material. Fold the bag and baste the side seams. There are several ways of applying the binding, as shown in Figure 1. In view a, two separate warps are prepared, one for each side seam. For this arrangement the top edge needs to be folded or suitably finished. Tassels can finish the bottom corners. In view b, two warps are also used; each starts at a top corner, goes along one side of the top, then down a side seam. For view c, one tube finishes the whole top and one side seam, and another tube is used for only one side seam. Only one warp is needed for view d, which starts at a lower corner, is split in half and woven separately for each side of the top, then rejoined for the other seam. In planning the length of your warp, allow generously for take-up and the space for your heddles.

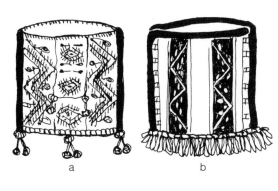

a   b

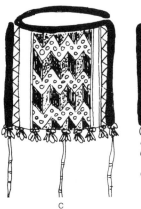

c

d

1. There are four ways to apply a ribete to a chuspa, as shown by the dark lines around each bag.

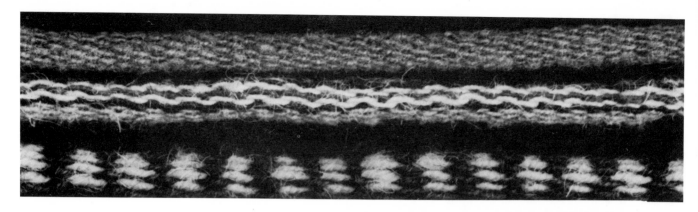

Tube 1. Plain weave tubes.

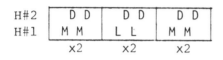

Draft 1.

Draft 1.

2. Motif for Tube 1c.

Tube 1. Plain Weave

To become familiar with the process, it is suggested that you start with a plain weave tube that has horizontal stripes due to an alternating warp order. Wind the warp yarns in the following order: 2 d-bouts M and D / 2 d-bouts L and D / 2 d-bouts M and D. Rearrange the warps and install the heddles as shown in Draft 1.

With your weft threaded on a needle, run it through the end loops and stitch them securely to your bag at the starting point. With your left forefinger in the end loops for tension, and your left thumb anchoring the weft, hold the bag in your left hand with the edge to be bound held up. Stick the point of the needle into the cloth from the right, near the edge of the bag. Raise H 2 with your right hand, opening the shed with the right fingers, and shift your left forefinger into the shed to hold it. Then reach into the shed with your right hand, pull the needle through the cloth toward the left, and bring the weft through the open shed from left to right. Stick the needle into the cloth again near the last stitch. Repeat with alternate heddles until the tube is finished (Figure 2). If you choose to do the bottom tube (d) in the diagram, you will find that you can use the same heddles, but need only half the warps as needed for each side of the top.

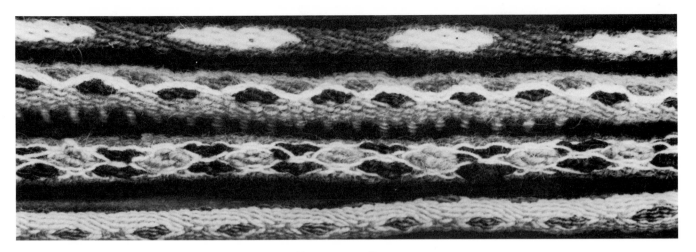

Tube 2. Plain weave with unwoven sections.

```
H#2 │  B  │  D  │  L  │  M  │  B  │
H#1 │  B  │  D  │  L  │  M  │  B  │
      x5    x2    x2    x2    x5
```

Draft 2.

Tube 2. Plain Weave with Unwoven Sections

A colorful meander effect is obtained by simple means in this tube. The warp is planned with one or more sections of bright contrasting yarns, which are sometimes interlaced by the weft in plain weave, and sometimes left unwoven to float underneath. As the weft is drawn taut to make the surface warp-faced, the warps are squeezed in to fill the empty space, creating the meander. This is indicated in the pattern diagrams by the empty diamonds and the curved lines. It is quite easy to pick the desired warps from the standard two-heddle setup, by simply dropping warps of the color not needed for each row. To prepare the warp for Tube 2b, wind the warp yarns in the following order: 5 s-bouts B / 2 s-bouts D, 2 s-bouts L, 2 s-bouts M / 5 s-bouts B. Rearrange the warps and install the heddles as indicated in Draft 2. Attach it to the edge as described for Tube 1. Weave three shots with the M warps dropped, then three shots with the D warps dropped, and repeat (Figure 3).

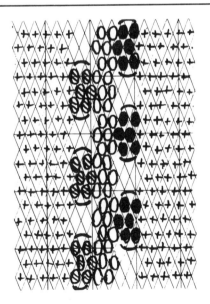

3. Motif for Tube 2b.

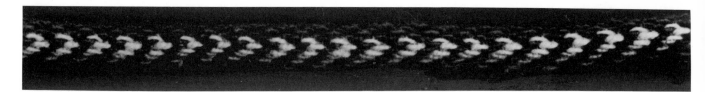

Tube 3. CWp even twill.

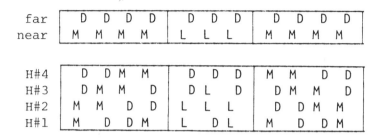

far	D D D D	D D D	D D D D
near	M M M M	L L L	M M M M

H#4	D D M M	D D D	M M D D
H#3	D M M D	D L D	D M M D
H#2	M M D D	L L L	D D M M
H#1	M D D M	L D L	M D D M

Draft 3.

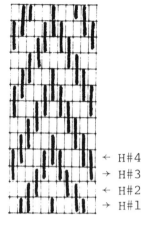

← H#4
→ H#3
← H#2
→ H#1

4. Motif for Tube 3.

Tube 3. CWp 2/2 Twill

This neat tube in vertical herringbone was reconstructed from one found on the edge of a plain brown poncho with red stripes. Chevrons of orange (M) with gold (L) points were lined up with brown (D) separating them. Wind the warp yarns in the following order: 2 d-bouts M and D / 1½ d-bouts L and D / 2 d-bouts M and D. Rearrange the warps into a working warp cross as shown in the top part of Draft 3. Install lease sticks, pushing them somewhat away from you.

Although it is possible to weave this tube by picking the pattern from two heddles, the pattern can also be completely heddle-controlled by using four heddles. Each warp is then included in two heddles, and a somewhat different method is used in selecting warps in preparation for installing the heddles. The warps for each heddle are selected separately from the working warp cross as shown in the lower part of Draft 3.

Start with the row for H 1. Place the warps from the near lease stick (the light warps) above the left index finger, with the dark warps under them on the middle finger. Stark picking the warps from the right as needed for the row, putting the opposite partner of each in turn *under* the left middle finger. Insert the heddle string from the right and make a multiloop heddle, watching the cross to be sure the warps are in order. When the heddle is completed, slide it toward the near end of the warp, and continue making H 2 and H 3 in the same way. H 4 may be a shed loop. Check the heddles.

Attach the band to the edge as described for Tube 1. To weave the pattern, merely lift the heddles in turn: H 1, H 2, H 3, and H 4, and repeat (Figure 4).

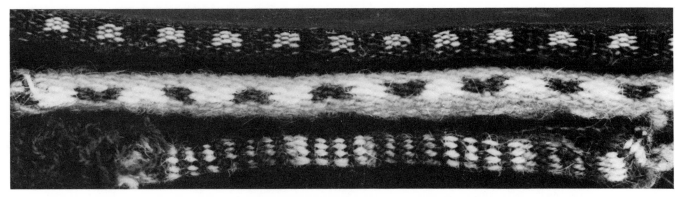

Tube 4. CWp plain weave.

far	B	M-D	M-D	B
near	B	L	L	B
	x3	x3	x3	

	far	B	M-D	M-D	
	near	B	L	L	
H#2		B		L	B
H#1		B	L		B
		x3	x3	x3	

	B				D	B
H#6	B				D	B
H#5	B			D		B
H#4	B				M	B
H#3	B		M			B
H#2	B			L		B
H#1	B	L				B
	x3		x3			x3

Draft 4.

Tube 4. CWp Patterning in Plain Weave

In Tube 4, complementary sets of warp interlace the weft for a surface of plain weave. Those warps that are not in use on the surface float on the back of the fabric, inside the tube. The sides of the tube resemble a border, having only one set of warps in plain weave, while the center section resembles warp-faced double cloth with the lower cloth left unwoven. Tubes 4a and 4c require the use of four heddles. Luckily, we were able to observe the weaving of Tube 4b, which was done with six heddles. The borders were orange, and the center blocks were wine and green, separated by blocks of white. The weaver used safety pins in place of lease sticks to hold the sets of warps after she had rearranged them for the heddles.

For Tube 4b, wind the warp yarns in the following order: 3 s-bouts B / 3 t-bouts L, M, and D / 3 s-bouts B. The first step in preparing the heddles is to rearrange the warps as shown in the top part of Draft 4. Install lease sticks. Next lift up the warps on the near side of the lease (the light warps) and rearrange them into two sheds, picking up the alternate border warps for the far finger, as shown in the middle part of the draft. Insert a safety pin to hold the cross. Rearrange the M and D warps in a similar manner, being sure to keep each warp in its proper order, as shown in the lower part of the draft. Install heddles 1 to 5 as multiloop heddles. H 6 may be a shed loop. Note that each border warp is included in three heddles.

Attach it to the edge as described for Tube 1. To weave the pattern, plan to have three shots of each color, separating them by three shots of white alternately: H 2, 1, 2; H 5, 6, 5; H 2, 1, 2; H 3, 4, 3; and repeat (Figure 5). Variations may be made if desired.

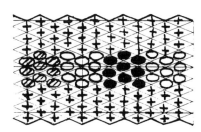

5. Motif for Tube 4b.

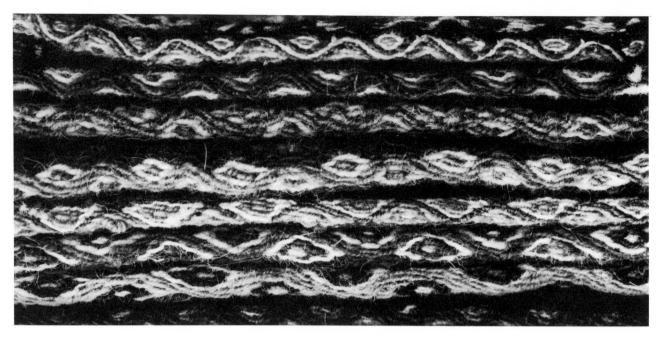

Tube 5. Crossed warp with diverted warps.

Tube 5. Crossed Warp with Diverted Warps

The structure of this tube is quite different from the others because of the crossing and recrossing of certain warps between the passages of the weft. The bright colors in the diamonds move from side to side and provide richness and sparkle. This also creates a snakelike effect, especially when the tube is secured to a fabric edge while it is being woven. It is sometimes also woven as a cord that is used as a tie for a belt or headband or attached to a tassel.

Thanks to a friend we were able to acquire an aksu with its ribete, or edge binding, only partly woven. It has four heddles, two of which are plain-weave heddles, and two are "doup" heddles that aid in the crossings. By careful unweaving, it was found that other manipulations had also been used to divert certain warps from side to side.

In the many ribetes and cords examined, considerable variation in the number of bouts and the number of colors was found. For the cords, there are usually only three or four colors in seven to ten s-bouts, while for the edge bindings, there are often five colors in nine to twelve s-bouts. Directions will be given for Tube 5a, which has nine bouts in five colors. To emphasize the movement of the colors, the initials of some actual colors will be used, instead of L, M, and D.

6. A doup heddle may be used to help cross the warps.

Wind the warp yarns as nine s-bouts in the following order: blue (B), red (R), white (W), red, green (G), yellow (Y), white, yellow, blue. Rearrange the warps as shown in Draft 5. First install H 3 as a multiloop heddle and H 4 as a shed loop, making each heddle around three fingers instead of two.

Heddles 1 and 2 are doup heddles, a special kind of heddle that facilitates crossing the warp yarns (Figure 6). To prepare H 2, reinsert the lease sticks at the near end of the warp, putting the near one in the shed of H 4 and the far one in the shed of H 3. You are now ready for crossing the warps as diagrammed in Figure 7. Note that for H 2 you will select and keep seven of the warps that are above the far lease stick, but that four of them need to be crossed under an adjacent warp. Also, the left two white warps are brought underneath for a greater distance, then picked up so one is at each side of the pair of white warps at the right. You may find it easier to make all the simpler crossings first, and then cross the white warps afterwards. Don't forget to pick up the warp at the far left that does not cross. Install H 2, making the loops larger by winding around four fingers to accommodate the crossing action. Push the three heddles somewhat away from you to make room to install H 1.

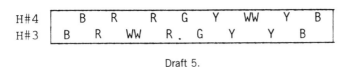

| H#4 | B | R | R | G | Y | WW | Y | B |
| H#3 | B | R | WW | R. | G | Y | Y | B |

Draft 5.

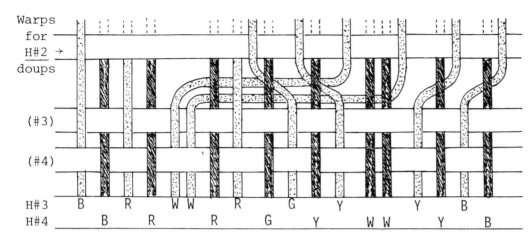

7. Insert the lease sticks as shown to prepare the warps for H 2, Tube 5.

After shifting the near lease stick to the far position, into the shed of H 4, proceed in the same way for H 1. This time the white pair is brought from the right, underneath, so one is on each side of the white warps on the left (Figure 8). Install H 1, making the loops around four fingers.

You may decide to weave this tube as a round cord instead of as an edge binding, although it is not as effective that way. This weave is basically heddle-controlled, but some extra manipulation is needed for each of the six steps in the sequence. Clearing the sheds is slightly more difficult because the loops of H 1 and H 2 tend to wrap around the warps. Beat down with your fingers after each new shed is ready, pull the weft firmly, then pass it in the shed from left to right. See Tube 1 for the method of attachment to a fabric edge.

Follow the steps below to produce the diamond design shown in Figure 9. In this figure, the tube is shown in a flattened version and also in a schematic one.

1. Lift H 3 and drop the two yellow warps near the right. Pass the weft to the right and leave the left index finger in the shed with the weft.

2. Lift H 1 and put the left middle finger behind the warp cross. Notice the four yellow warps that drop down below. Remove the left near finger and beat lightly with the far finger. Keeping a finger in the shed, reach down in the center of the white warps at both levels and bring up the four yellow warps. Pass the weft to the right.

3. Lift H 3 and drop the two yellow warps near the right. Pass the weft to the right.

4. Lift H 4 and drop the two red warps near the left. Pass the weft to the right, keeping a finger in the shed.

5. Lift H 2, locate the four red warps below, and bring them up in the center of the white warps at both levels. Pass the weft to the right.

6. Lift H 4 and drop the two red warps near the left. Pass the weft to the right. Then repeat the whole sequence.

After you have woven this tube with four heddles and understand what is happening, you may like to produce it using a *two-heddle method*. Wind the warps in the same order as for the four-heddle method and rearrange them in the same way, with H 3 becoming H 1, and H 4 (the shed loop) becoming H 2. Note that diamond shapes have been drawn around some of the warps in the draft, with the paired white warps for their centers. In weaving the tube, the diamonds become alternately aligned with the red diamonds to the left and the yellow ones to the right. For each diamond there are three shots of weft, with the second needing special manipulations for the crossings of the warps. These crossings are the same as those diagrammed for making the doup heddles in Figures 6 and 7, plus the additional step of adding the four colored warps from the other diamond between the white center warps. It should be noted that the crossings are more easily made on the right-hand side of the diamonds than on the left-hand side, where the direction of the crossing

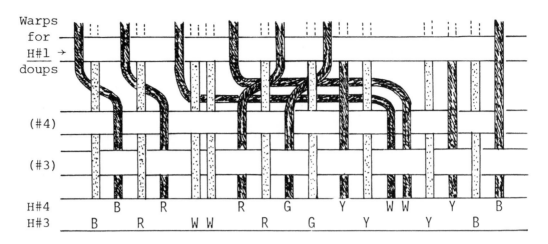

(#4)

(#3)

| H#4 | | B | R | | R | G | Y | W W | Y | | B |
| H#3 | B | R | | W W | R | G | Y | | Y | B | |

8. To prepare the warps for H 1, the order of the lease sticks is reversed.

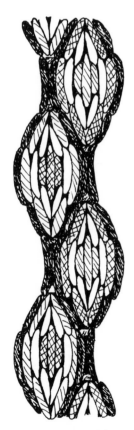

9A. Fabric sketch for Tube 5.

is reversed. Use the following steps to produce a yellow diamond:

1. Lift H 2 and drop the two R warps near the left. Pass the weft to the right, keeping the left index finger in the shed with the weft.

2. (While crossing the warps in this step, keep in mind that the warps above the far finger are the ones to be kept for this row. Collect the picked warps on your right middle finger to free other fingers for picking.) Lift H 1 to complete the cross. Drop the 2R and 2W near the left, keeping the blue warp at the left edge, and insert the left middle finger on the far side of the cross. To cross each of the first two warps on the far finger, reach under its partner to get it. Drop the partners off the near finger as you go. The WW pair should now be next on your near finger. Reach down below to get the four red warps you dropped and bring them up onto the far finger, inserting them between the two W warps that are on your near finger. You should have two crossed, picked warps on your right middle finger; add to them first one of the dropped W warps from below, then the four R warps from your far left finger, and then the other dropped W warp from below, putting it to the left of the near W W pair which should now be dropped. Now working beyond the left fingers, push the top Y warp down under its partner to its left to cross it, and pick it up; do the same with the green warp and its partner. The blue warp at the left edge is kept without crossing. Pass the weft to the right.

3. Lift H 2 and drop the two R warps near the left. Pass the weft to the right.

The steps are similar for the red diamond, with certain reversals for the heddles used and the warps dropped.

1. Lift H 1 and drop the two Y warps near the right. Pass the weft to the right, keeping the left index finger in the shed with the weft.

2. Lift H 2 and drop the 2Y and 2W warps near the right, keeping the blue warp at the right edge. Insert the left middle finger on the far side of the cross. Pick the right blue warp without crossing it. Then reach down under the partners of the G and R warps to cross and pick them. Bring up the four dropped Y warps and put them on the far left finger between the two W warps that are on the near finger. Bring up one dropped W warp from below, add the four Y warps and then bring up the other dropped W warp from below, to the left of the near W W pair which should now be dropped. Finish by crossing the R and B warps with their partners, by pushing each down and then picking it up to the left of its partner. Pass the weft to the right.

3. Lift H 1 and drop the two Y warps near the right. Pass the weft to the right.

Repeat, doing yellow and red diamonds alter-- nately. With some practice it will become quite rhythmic.

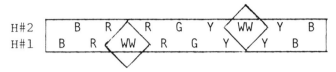

H#2   B   R   R   G   Y   WW   Y   B

H#1   B   R   WW   R   G   Y   Y   B

Draft 5. A two-heddle draft for Tube 5
with the diamonds drawn.

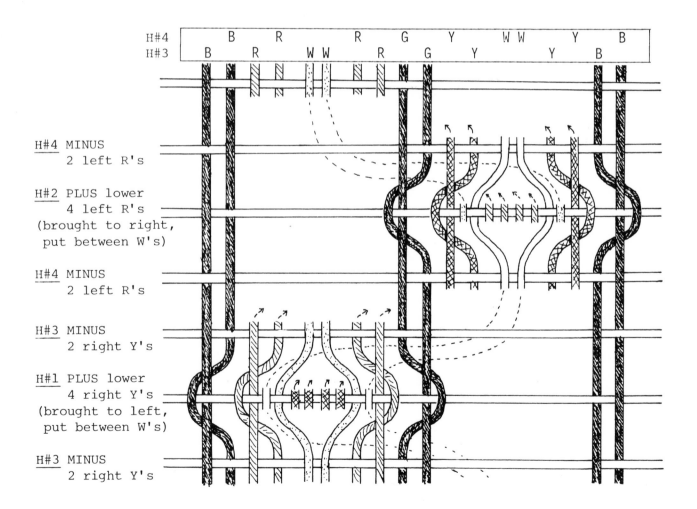

9B. Structure diagram for Tube 5.

NONWOVEN RIBETES

Two kinds of nonwoven edgings are also used—a cross-knit looping on chuspas, and crocheting on larger flat pieces. A color change is usually made every inch or two on the chuspa edge and every several inches on edges of larger pieces.

Cross-Knit Looping. This ribete, which resembles a knit frabic, is worked with a needle. Its varied colors accentuate the color scheme of the bag.

You may wish to practice this technique flat before working it around an edge. Begin with the first row shown in Figure 10, starting the needle from the wrong side and bringing it up through the fabric at the left. Then continue as shown. Each succeeding row is worked below the previous one in the same manner, except the loops are formed around those in the previous row instead of being attached to the fabric.

Crocheted Edgings. A crocheted shell stitch edging is used near Sucre to trim larger pieces. Near Lake Titicaca, the everyday brown ponchos have a crocheted edging that resembles saw-teeth. It goes all the way around the outer edge, and around the neck opening also. Its color matches the single narrow stripe of contrasting color that is traditionally placed near each outer vertical edge, often grass green or teal blue.

Before applying the crocheted edging, each of the four corners is turned back to form a small triangle, measuring about 4" / 10.61 cm along the selvedge edges. The triangular flap is stitched securely in place, and this is then considered the back or wrong side of the poncho (Figure 11).

To produce this edging, which is a variety of picot, single crochet on to the fabric,* chain 2, slipstitch in the base of the single crochet, single crochet on to the fabric*, repeat from * to *.

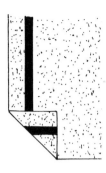

11. Before applying the crocheted edging to a poncho, the corners are folded back and tacked in place.

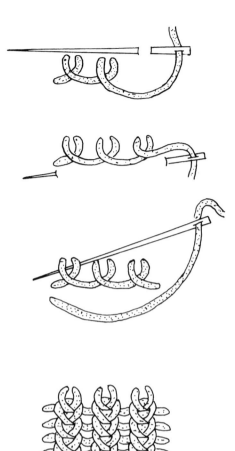

10. Cross-knit looping, a non-woven ribete in common use on chuspas, resembles a knit fabric.

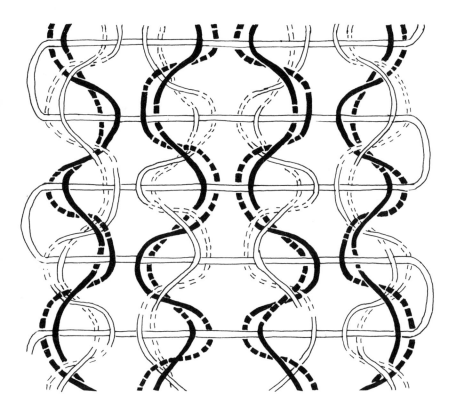

12. In this band, there are four groups of warps, each with four interworking warps that cross and recross.

Crossed Warp Band

At first glance, it seemed as if this little diamond-patterned band might be a four-bout pebble band without a selvedge. A trial soon proved that assumption wrong. We further observed that in this band the diamond is not located in the same place on the front and back, and that its surface is more in relief. Also, the color arrangement was the same on the front and back instead of being reversed.

Although examples were later found made of coarse yarns, the subject for analysis with the magnifying lens had been woven from unusually fine yarns, proving to be a real challenge. It eventually became evident that there were four groups of warps, each with four interworking warps that crossed and recrossed (Figure 12). On the basis of the unfinished Tube 5, which had four heddles (two of which were doup heddles) early trials for this band also made use of doup heddles. They worked but were later abandoned in favor of more finger manipulation. Unfortunately, we have not been able to observe how the Bolivians weave this band.

The Bolivians use this narrow band for ties on their headbands or straps on coca bags and capachos. However, it can also be done on a larger scale. It is effective when done with Aunt Lydia's rug yarn. Wind the warp yarns as eight s-bouts in the following order: 1M, 2L, 2D, 2L, 1M. If you start winding the bouts behind the left

post, the warp cross does not need to be rearranged. Install H 1 as a multiloop heddle and H 2 as a shed loop. Begin the weft in the end loops, with the tail to the right. Lift H 2 and pass the weft to the right, leaving a finger in the shed. Then lift H 1 to complete the picking cross.

This weave is produced by alternating picked design rows with heddle-controlled return shots. Heddle 2 is used for all the return shots. Two simple and two complex manipulations are required to complete each design row. These manipulations are used in certain orders, according to the pattern. For each design row a picking cross is formed with the H 2 warps on the near finger and the H 1 warps on the far finger. Starting at the right, you will work with two vertical pairs of warps, two ends each of two colors. Each *vertical pair* of warps consists of two warps of the same color, with one yarn of the pair on the near finger and the other on the far finger.

For the *simple type* of crossing, the manipulation is made *beyond* the far left finger, working with the two warps above and the two warps below the finger. Reach under the right vertical pair of warps and up to grasp the top warp of the left vertical pair. Bring it down under the right pair, and add it to the top right warp (Figure 13). Then collect these two warps on the right middle finger. Pull to the right so the group is free from the left fingers, and you are ready to start on the

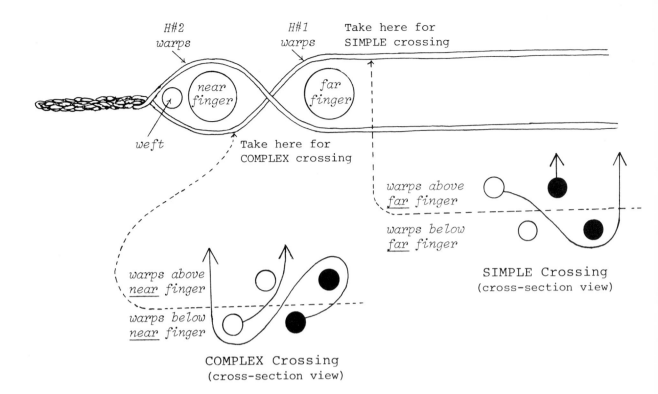

13. For each design row, the warps need to be crossed in either of two ways.

next group. Continue to use the middle finger to collect the warps that have been picked.

For the *complex type*, the manipulations are performed on the warps that are above and below the *near* finger. The warps are approached *under* the near finger. With the right index finger and thumb, grasp the warp of the right vertical pair under the near finger and pull it to the right, helping its partner to drop off and down. Temporarily park the grasped warp between the lower left fingers. Grasp the next warp under the near finger and pull it to the right, helping its partner to drop

off and down. Keep this grasped warp, and then get the warp that you parked below. It should be added at the left of the other warps of the group. Perhaps you can develop an easier method, since this was the result of experimentation rather than observation.

Two different design variations are produced by varying the order of the simple and complex manipulations, either connected large diamonds or small diamonds in a zigzag arrangement. Follow the directions in the schematic diagram in Figure 14 to produce these patterns.

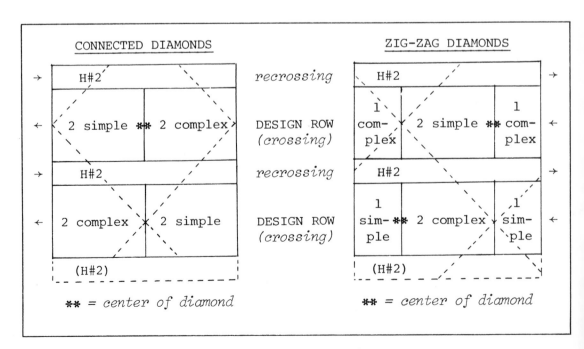

14. A schematic diagram of weaving sequence for crossed-warp bands.

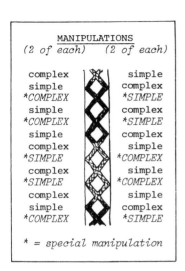

15. The weaving sequence for crossed-warp band with color changes.

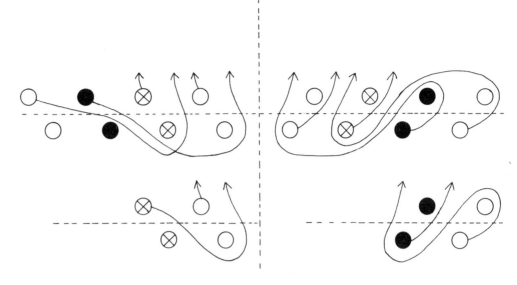

16. Special kinds of crossings are needed for a band with color changes. Diagrammed here are the simple special on the left and the complex special on the right.

Crossed-Warp Band with Color Shifts

In a few examples of the crossed warp band, a color shift was noted. Against an all-light background, the outline of the diamonds might be in the medium color for a while, then shift to the dark color for a while, with the colors in reverse on the back. Experimentation led to finding that some special manipulations are required.

Wind the warp yarns as eight s-bouts in the following order: 1L, 1D, 1M, 2L, 1M, 1D, 1L. The warp cross does not need to be rearranged if you start winding the bouts behind the left post. Install H 1 as a multiloopheddle and H 2 as a shed loop.

Design rows having manipulated crossings are alternated with return shots, controlled by H 2. If you make the crossings in the usual sequence for connected diamonds for this warp arrangement, there will be medium colored X's down the center, and the outer points of the diamonds will be dark. In order to change the line of the diamonds to be a single color, special manipulations are needed whenever the row is not like "home base." This adjustment sequence is charted in Figure 15, and all four types of manipulations are diagrammed in Figure 16.

The general procedure is the same as before, with the near finger in the H 2 shed with the weft for the picking cross; the picked warps are collected on the right middle finger. The special manipulations are also termed simple and complex, with the simple special crossings done

beyond the far finger and the complex special ones by the near finger.

1. Reach under two vertical pairs of warps (instead of the usual one) to get warp (a), keep it and pick up (b), but do not pull off to the right.

2. Reach under (x) and (y) only, to get (z) and bring it up to keep with (x), in the usual way. Collect the warps with the right middle finger.

The complex special crossing is made by the near finger, using the steps listed below:

1. With the right thumb and index finger, grasp (c) and pull it to the right, helping its partner to drop off and down.

2. Between the same fingers, also grasp (e) and pull it to the right, helping its partner to drop off and down. Temporarily park both warps between the lower left fingers, keeping (c) to the right of (e).

3. Now grasp (g) and pull it to the right, helping its partner to drop off and down. Keep (g) and add to it (c), the right-hand one parked below. Shift these two warps to the right middle finger.

4. Grasp (i), and pull it to the right, helping its partner drop off and down. Keep it and add to it (e), the other one parked down below. Shift these to the right middle finger.

FRINGES

Fringes are popular finishes for ponchos, uncus, and chuspas. The type used for ponchos and uncus is woven separately and then attached to the fabric with a joining stitch. For chuspas the fringe is applied directly.

For the woven fringe, the heading is a narrow warp-faced plain weave band that may have horizontal or vertical stripes. It is woven in the usual two-heddle manner, with the fringe yarn placed in the shed along with the weft (Figure 17). The fringe yarn, usually alpaca, is soft and loosely spun. The color of the fringe is changed every six to twelve shots. The loops may be either cut or uncut.

Two fringes may be woven at the same time if the warp is set up on a backstrap or a frame loom. The fringe yarn is carried from one heading to the other, and then cut in the center after the weaving is completed (Figure 18).

Just a simple fringe can make an elegant trim for the lower edge of a chuspa (Figure 19). After the fringe yarns are inserted near the bottom of the bag, twining, hand stitching, or even machine stitching is used to hold the strands in place.

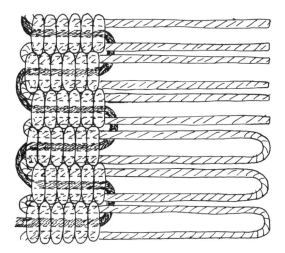

17. The heading for a woven fringe is a narrow warp-faced band.

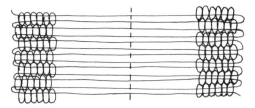

18. Two fringes may be woven at the same time.

19. A simple fringe can make a chuspa elegant. Collection of Lynn Meisch.

BRAIDS AND CORDS

Braids of various types are often used in finishing woven bands. Not only are the final end loops often braided, but braids are used for the end ties of belts (and sometimes winchas) and are often used for chuspa straps. Knitted items such as women's pouch bags also have braided ties. Plied cords are also used in finishing the ends of belts, either to gather the end loops of braids or to provide a means of attaching a tie.

Belts are not worn merely tied, with the ends hanging loose. Instead, they are worn wrapped around the waist with the ties continuing the encirclement, somewhat in the manner of a butcher's apron, but usually with the ties tucked under the decorative belt. In this way the belt can securely hold up the skirt or trousers.

The end ties are therefore functional, and need to be firmly anchored to the ends of the belt. They are attached in various ways. Probably the simplest way is to snitch a cord or braid into the end loops at each end of the belt (Figure 20). The five-loop braid is quite popular, though this is also done with three-strand (pigtail) braids, flat multistrand braids, or plied cords. For a woven beginning end, a heading cord is inserted in the end loops, and sometimes continues into the first woven row. This cord is composed of a number of strands of yarn, so it is thicker than the weft in the rest of the piece. Then the tie is snitched over the center of the heading cord and braided, often as a five-loop braid. At other times a plied cord is snitched in place.

In another example, the cord was first used to fasten the ends of the five-loop braids neatly side by side. It was inserted in the end loops of one of the edge braids and tied in a simple knot, inserted

in the next braid loop and tied in another simple knot, etc., continuing across the width of the band. The cord was then looped so each end was attached at the center, making a three-point attachment for the tie.

To spread the pull on the end of the belt, side attachments are sometimes made by first inserting a braid or plied cord in the end loops. These are later attached with a few stitches to the centrally attached tie, in a forked arrangement. To do the same thing at the final end of the belt, the end loops are braided into a series of five-loop braids that usually have a design in their color changes. Then the ends of the braids are needle-woven in plain weave for a final woven end, about an·inch in length. The same type of flat five-strand braid runs through the end loops and is tacked onto the main central tie, which is snitched or sewn on the center of the belt (Figure 21).

In one belt examined, two flat five-strand braids of different colors were interlocked and inserted in the end loops, woven into the first row, and then left hanging (Figure 22). Tassels were attached to the hanging ends. The central tie was especially interesting. Where it was snitched on, white warps were interlocked with colored ones. It starts out as a three-strand (pigtail) braid, then is woven into a snake-back cord (Tube 5) for the rest of the length. The other end of the belt has the same treatment, except that when the heddles were removed the weaver prepared a series of three-strand braids. These were made into a neat, solid end by sewing horizontally through their centers at intervals. At the end of the braids, the remaining loops are needle-woven into three or four rows of plain-weave horizontal stripes.

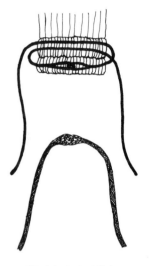

22. Interlocked flat braids are used to decorate the ends of this belt.

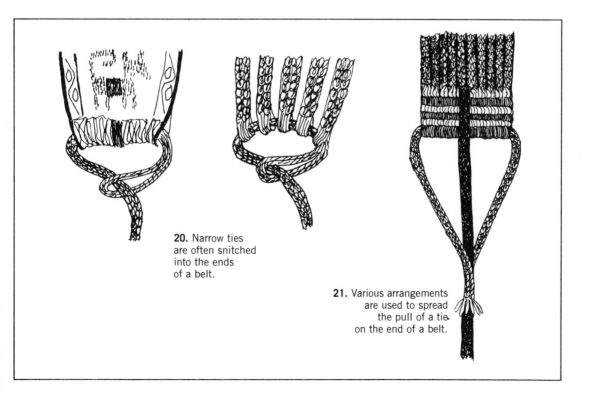

20. Narrow ties are often snitched into the ends of a belt.

21. Various arrangements are used to spread the pull of a tie on the end of a belt.

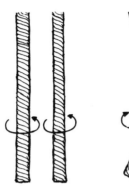

23. To make a cord, two yarns are twisted separately in the same direction and tied, then allowed to reverse together.

24. Yarns may have an S-twist or a Z-twist.

Cords

In preparing for weaving, the Indian woman often takes some of her yarn and makes it into a thick cord to use for a shed loop, for tying the end loops, or for a heading cord. Later, she may produce cords to be used for ties at the ends of belts.

To make a cord, first two yarns are twisted in one direction and held taut while their ends are tied in an overhand knot to hold the twist. Then the twisted yarns are allowed to reverse together in the opposite direction (Figure 23). This process must be coordinated with the twist of the yarn you are using. The direction you twist the yarns depends on whether you are using an *S-twist* yarn, such as carpet warp, or a *Z-twist* yarn, such as Knit-Cro-Sheen (Figure 24). Four simple methods follow.

A short piece of yarn may be held with one end in the left hand, while the other end is twisted with the right hand. Twist away from you for an S-twist and toward you for a Z-twist yarn. Bring the ends together, guiding the reversal. Knot the ends.

Another way is to put the midpoint of the yarn around a post. Then both ends are twisted at the same time. Twist clockwise for an S-twist and counterclockwise for a Z-twist yarn. Knot the ends and then allow the yarns to reverse before removing from the post.

If the pieces are somewhat longer, it is helpful to roll the yarns up or down your lap. With the yarn around a post or held in the left hand, the right hand holds the two ends parallel to each other, a short distance apart. Roll down the lap for an S-twist, up for a Z-twist yarn. The rolling works better if you dampen your hand slightly. Watch so the yarns don't slip away from you and untwist. It usually takes two or three rolls for a good cord. With practice you will discover how much to twist the strands. Knot the ends and guide the reversal.

If you want a thicker cord use four strands instead of two. You will need to start with a yarn that is much longer. Begin as above, with the yarns around a post and twist both ends. When the twist is quite tight, grasp the ends in the right hand and the bend behind the post in the left hand, holding the yarn taut. Then place the new midpoint around the post and bring the doubled ends together. Knot the ends. Guide the reverse twist before removing the cord from the post. It is fun to make cords in different colors to harmonize with your weaving.

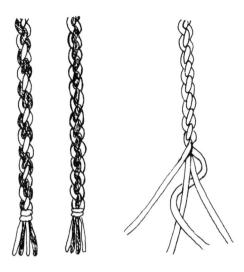

25. Near Lake Titicaca, four-strand braids are a popular finish for the ends of narrow belts.

Four-Strand Round Braid

Near Lake Titicaca, two narrow pebble-weave belts are attached to the pollera, one at each side of the waist opening. These are then wrapped around the waist in opposite directions and tied to hold up the skirt. Four-strand round braids are a popular finish for these belts. This braid is also commonly used as a small cord to which pompons are attached for trimming chuspas. It is commonly made by using two colors, with two strands, or groups of strands, of each color. The pattern can be varied by arranging the strands in different color sequences. A diagonal pattern is produced when they are placed in alternating or-der, LDLD. Vertical stripes result if the order is LDDL, or LLDD.

To make this braid, first cut the end loops and arrange the strands in the desired order. Then take one of the outside strands and move it under the two strands to the left or right of it. Next bring it up and move it back over one strand in the opposite direction (Figure 25). Repeat this same sequence of under two, back over one on the other side, then continue alternating sides. Work to within about an inch from the end of the strands. Take a single yarn, wrap it around the braid and fasten with a half hitch.

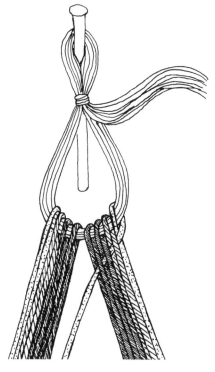

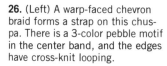

26. (Left) A warp-faced chevron braid forms a strap on this chuspa. There is a 3-color pebble motif in the center band, and the edges have cross-knit looping.

27. (Above) Weave from edge-to-center to produce a warp-faced chevron braid.

Flat Braids (Oblique Interlacing)

28. A more unusual braid has 2/2 twill braiding.

The simplest and most familiar braid is the three-strand "pigtail" braid. This is often used to finish the larger-scaled pieces having coarse yarns.

Other flat braids with four or more strands are also produced in the same manner as the three-strand one, only going over one, under one, for more strands. If the number of strands is odd, start alternately at each side. Braids with an even number of strands may be produced by either of two methods. One way is to start always on the same side. The other way is to alternate sides, beginning with under one on one side and over one on the other side. These flat braids may be woven as either a warp-faced or a balanced weave. Interesting variations are produced by using two or three colors, and by varying the number of ends of each color along with their order.

Sometimes a warp-faced braid with a chevron pattern is produced, like the chuspa strap in Figure 26. It has two separate parts attached to each other in the center; the warps for one half are interlocked with those for the other half (Figure 27). The warp ends were arranged in the following order for the first half: 2L, 2D, 8M, 2D, 2L; and for the second half: 2L, 2M, 8D, 2M, 2L. This braid is woven from edge to center, alternating sides. Since there is an even number of strands, begin with under one on one side and over one on the other side.

A braid at the end of a narrow double-cloth belt had 2/2 twill braiding, or oblique 2/2 twill interlacing (Figure 28). It was composed of 13 strands, 11 darks on the left and two lights on the right. To produce this braid, work always from the right edge to the left one, going over two, under two, all the way.

29. Five-loop braids may have more than one color. These diagrams show the front and back of two types: one has two or three colors with a programmed pattern (left), and the other is bi-color, with color shifts (right).

Five-Loop Braid

This braid, sometimes called five-finger braid, is attractive, useful, and fun to make. Similar braids are made in Europe, sometimes with more or fewer loops. In Bolivia, it is frequently used for ties, chuspa straps, and also to finish the ends of wide, patterned belts. It may be in one color, in two or three colors with a programmed pattern (Figure 29), or it may be bi-color. In the bicolor braid there is one color on the front of the braid and another on the back with the colors usually reversed at intervals.

To prepare for a one-color braid, cut five lengths of yarn each about a yard in length. Fold the yarn in half and tie the ends in an overhand knot. Attach the knotted end to a post, and straighten the yarn so you can insert a finger into each of the five loops. Each hand alternately has loops on three fingers and on two fingers. To describe the sequence, the fingers are numbered as shown in Figure 30: L1, L2, L3 and R1, R2, R3. The little fingers are not used. Start with the loops on L2 and 3, and R1, 2 and 3, one loop on each. Then follow the steps below:

1. The first step is illustrated in Figure 30. Since L1 does not have a loop, it proceeds to get one by reaching through its neighbor's loop (the one on L2), and takes the loop from R3 (right ring finger), bringing it back through the neighboring loop. Now the left hand has three loops.

2. The hands are stretched apart to tighten the braid. (At first this seems useless.)

3. The two loops remaining on the right hand are now shifted downward to provide loops for R3 and R2, and R1 is left without a loop.

The sequence is now repeated in the opposite way. R1 reaches through the loop of R2 to get the loop from L3 (left ring finger), the hands are stretched apart, the two loops remaining on the left hand are shifted downward onto L3 and L2, and L1 again has no loop. Repeat again from Step 1. After you learn the rhythm, you will be able to avoid an extra motion by not removing finger 1 from its neighboring loop during the shifting of the loops downward, and it will be ready to reach for its loop from the other hand.

For the braid with the programmed pattern, the method is the same except that two or three colors of yarn are used. For L2 and 3 and R1, 2, and 3, respectively, use colors in the following order: LL DDD for two colors, or LL MDM for three colors. Vary these color combinations as you wish.

The bicolor braid is used most frequently to finish the ends of double-cloth belts after the heddles are removed. For each finger loop, two end loops are intercrossed—one light, one dark—in such a way that a double-strand loop results that

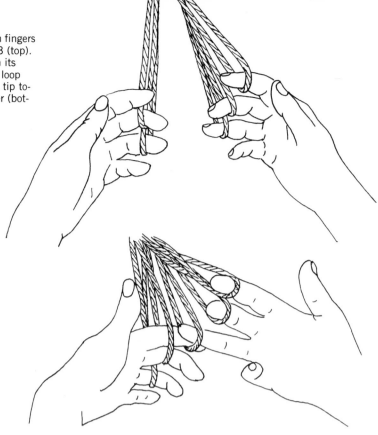

30. Start with five loops on fingers L2 and 3 and R1, 2 and 3 (top). Finger L1 reaches through its neighbor's loop to get the loop from R3, hooking from its tip toward the base of the finger (bottom).

31. Dark and light end-loops are intercrossed to form the five loops for the bi-color braid.

is half light, half dark (Figure 31). Start with the dark side up on each finger. If desired, cut ends may be used by knotting a light and dark end together for each loop.

Follow the same sequence as before, first with one hand, then with the other. The forefinger should take the loop off the opposite ring finger by sliding it along the ring finger from its tip toward its base, as shown in Figure 30. This will keep the loops so the same color is on the upper side of each finger, and the upper side of the braid will continue in the same color. The lower side, which resembles a three-strand braid, will continue with the opposite color.

To reverse the colors involves a different direction of taking the loop off the ring finger. The forefinger hooks the loop by sliding along the ring finger from its base toward its tip, as shown in Figure 32. That brings the opposite color to the top of each loop. The color shift is completed in five turns. It will not seem evident in the braid until almost the end of the five turns. Braiding should then continue as before, until another color shift is desired. It takes a little practice to stretch apart evenly to have an even braid, and sometimes a little adjustment of the yarns may be needed.

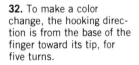

32. To make a color change, the hooking direction is from the base of the finger toward its tip, for five turns.

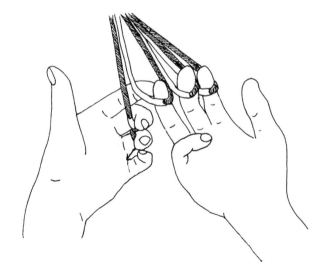

OTHER FINISHING TOUCHES

The depth of imagination possessed by the Bolivian craftsmen is revealed in the varied embellishments they use to finish their weavings. Soft, loosely spun yarn is favored for many of these techniques.

Joining Stitches. In joining the halves of a solid-colored poncho, or one patterned with just a few plain-weave stripes, the simplicity of design is not disturbed by a complicated joining. In this case, the weaver joins the two halves with the ancient stitch (also called ball or baseball stitch), using matching yarn (Figure 33). This stitch is also used to attach a woven fringe to the edge of a poncho or uncu.

A variation of the ancient stitch is perhaps the most widespread and most commonly used joining throughout Bolivia. To make this joining, three ancient-type stitches are made back and forth, right next to each other, all at the same slant. Then three more are made at the opposite slant (Figure 34). This stitch may also be done with the edges in a horizontal position. The color often is changed at regular intervals, and additional designs like flowers and stars are sometimes added at the side of this joining (Figure 35).

When the two halves to be joined are elaborately patterned, the overall composition may be accented by colorful triangles or diamonds worked in satin stitch. In one instance we observed a bar stitch that had been embroidered into a parade of llamas (Figure 35).

33. The ancient stitch is an unobtrusive joining.

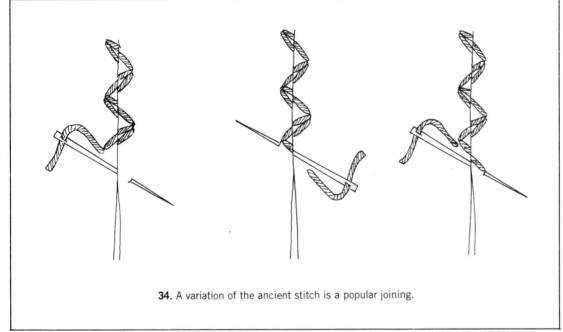

34. A variation of the ancient stitch is a popular joining.

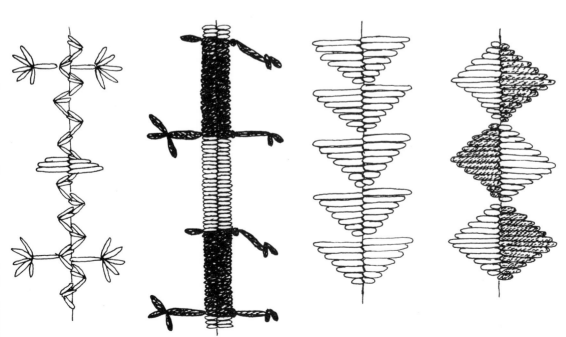

35. More elaborately patterned fabrics often have fancy joinings to provide additional interest and color.

145

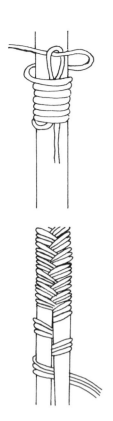

Wrapping. Wrapping is a favorite trim of Bolivian weavers that is used often for trimming chuspas, belts, and winchas. In one traditional arrangement on the lower edge of chuspas, there are three long, finely scaled wrapped cords embellished with tassels or pompons. Color changes in the wrappings are coordinated with the scheme of the bag. This is a simple process and the only thing to remember is that both ends of the wrapping yarn must be bound to secure them, which is easily accomplished as shown in Figure 36.

For winchas, a figure-8 type of wrapping is used to decorate the warp loops that remain after the heddles have been removed. Pleasing color patterns that enhance the design of the band are usually worked into this finish.

Tassels. Small tassels are used in a variety of ways as a soft delicate embellishment (Figure 37). They are often used in a series, especially on the bottom of chuspas, and in tulas. Sometimes they go in opposite directions, and at other times the top of the tassel has decorative stitching, such as two cross-stitches made back-to-back to form a diamond shape at the top of the tassel with an extra stitch added in the center.

Pompons. Pompons are also a favorite adornment, used particularly for decorating chuspas, the ends of bands, and hairbands. There are several varieties in common use, some of which are ingenious extensions of the wrapping technique.

Very compact pompons that resemble miniature pumpkins are composed of numerous vertical segments over a knotted and wrapped core. Each segment is made by wrapping yarn around a thick needle. This same wrapping technique is used to make a variegated finish along the bottom of chuspas (Figure 38).

Another type of pompon has horizontal segments. They are also produced by wrapping, but this time around something thicker like a smooth twig. The twig is notched with the weaver's pocketknife, and a needle is placed in the groove. These pompons are usually composed of two to five segments. Often the lower layer is white, while the upper layers are shades of a single hue with the darkest at the top.

A small bud-shaped pompon is sometimes used on the same piece with the horizontal segment type. This pompon has decorative stitching applied over two or three small horizontal segments. In a related embellishment, a double

36. Bolivians use two types of wrappings to decorate their weavings.

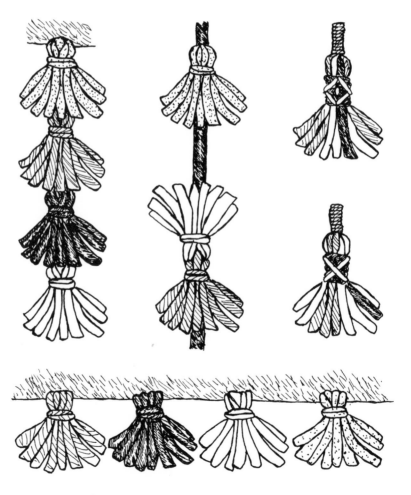

37. Tassels make a soft, delicate embellishment.

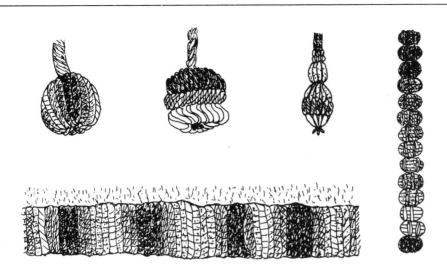

38. Pompons are a favorite adornment for chuspas.

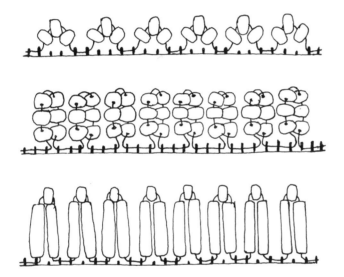

39. Winchas are traditionally finished with a beaded edging. The ends of the ties may also have beads and coins. Collection of Judy Conger.

40. Beads are attached to the edges of winchas in various arrangements.

strand of yarn is wrapped around a cord several times and then the same strand overcasts the group of strands together as a separate unit. This process is repeated many times over, to produce a dangle resembling a string of beads.

The familiar cut pompon is also popular though perhaps less common than the other types. It may be multicolored to coordinate with the wrapping or item to which it is attached.

Accessory Objects. Beads and coins are used as accessory objects in the area noted for fine double cloth (Figure 39). One author (Osborne) explains the curious custom of using coins in this manner, stating that the Indian regards coins as objects for preservation and decoration rather than as a medium of exchange.

The two items most often embellished with these objects are winchas and chuspas. Winchas are traditionally finished with a beaded edging (Figure 40). The beads are usually attached during the weaving of the band, although sometimes the string of beads is stitched on later as is done at the braid end.

The ends of the ties may also have beads and/or coins. In Figure 39, small beads are strung in loops at the bottom of a long tubular bead, below which a coin is hung. Sometimes a long string of beads is wrapped around a cord, instead of using the tubular bead above the coin. Although beading is not as common on chuspas, exquisite beaded dangles and coins sometimes enhance the lower edge.

1. The Bolivian weaver often produces a small backstrap loom with a minimum of effort and materials.

Chapter Five

Wider Weavings

The finger-tension method of weaving is very useful for making narrow belts and ties and for doing samples of pattern weaves. Most Bolivian fabrics, however, are woven with the warp stretched between two sticks. A backstrap may be used with these two sticks to provide flexible tension control. When the sticks are lashed to slanting poles or stakes in the ground, to form a Bolivian frame loom, the tension is stable yet adjustable. Bags and wider fabrics are customarily woven on a frame. Belts may be woven either on a frame or with a backstrap.

The string loop heddles used by Bolivians have some real advantages over the steel heddles in the harnesses of a standard modern loom. Because it is easy to install the heddles and to remove them, the end loops do not need to be cut, so one may either have a piece with four finished edges or have uncut loops suited to many interesting finishes. A single yarn may be operated by two or three different heddles. New ways to use heddles will be presented in this chapter for the weaves described in Chapter 3.

BACKSTRAP WEAVING

Once you have learned how to do a narrow band with finger tension you are ready to try doing a wider, longer band in the same technique. Such a band is easier to weave with the backstrap or the inkle loom, for then both hands are free for the manipulations. This is especially true if the yarns are a bit sticky or fragile, or if there are more heddles or more complicated manipulations.

EQUIPMENT

The Bolivian weaver often produces a small backstrap loom with a minimum of effort and materials by cutting some sticks from a nearby branch (Figure 1). She then anchors the far end to a spike in the ground. Try doing an additional sample band, but this time fastening it to your belt or backstrap so your hands are both free for the manipulations. As you begin doing bands with more bouts or problem yarns, you may want to add some simple pieces of equipment that are easily available and inexpensive.

For your first project it is easiest if you merely have a stick in the near end loops. If you plan on a fringed end, this should be followed by some rows of filler. If you are going to do a small hanging, select a suitable rod for later use at the top (perhaps a sanded and stained dowel, or a suitable piece of driftwood). If you have a firm leather belt, the rod can be securely tied to it at your waist, but it is usually better to fasten it to a longer rod attached to a strap that goes around your hips. A good rod is a ¾" (1.9 cm) dowel, 16" (40.64 cm) long, with a groove made about an inch from each end to keep the strap in place. Improvise with something for a temporary strap, then weave a strap as a first project (Figure 2).

As you begin doing bands that are wider, the control of warps at the far end becomes more important. Three ⅜" (.95 cm) dowels, each 7" (17.78 cm) long, with ⅛" (.32 cm) holes drilled near each end can be a big help. One would be put in the far end loops (Figure 3) and the other

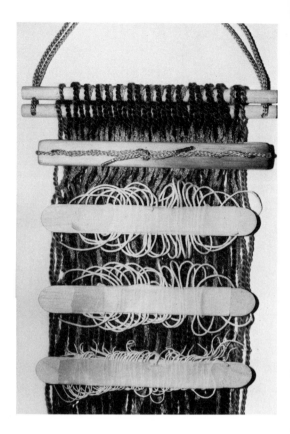

2. (Above) Weaving the strap for your loom makes a good beginning backstrap project. This was woven with Aunt Lydia's rug yarn by Karen Searle.

3. (Right) There are several ways to make it easier to handle wider bands or problem warps: a dowel inserted in the far end loops; a lease-type arrangement at the far end; a shed-clamp; and tongue-depressor heddles.

two used as lease sticks. Shoestrings may be run through the holes in the near lease stick, then both ends run together through the holes in the other two sticks. By tying each of the shoestrings at the ends, they may be fastened to a clamp on each side, or to some other stable object. The yarns are then held in a separated but firm position. For a shorter warp, the nearer lease stick may be omitted. A special way to install the lease stick(s) will be described later, in connection with suggestions for the far heddle.

In weaving longer warps, the fell soon becomes too far away to reach comfortably, and the weaving needs to be brought closer. After trying a variety of methods used by others, we developed a very simple friction-clamp method that seems ideal for bands several inches wide. All that is needed is a pencil or similar sized dowel, two 18″ (45.72 cm) shoestrings, and two 7″ (17.78 cm) pieces of screen molding, with a ⅛″ (.32 cm) hole near each end. The sticks are held with the flat sides together, then, at each end, the center of the shoestring is secured to the bottom edge of the sticks by threading the ends of the shoestring through the holes in opposite directions. Fold back part of your woven end and slide the fold down between the sticks, inserting the pencil or dowel in the fold to keep it from slipping out. Then tie the shoestring firmly at the top with a single knot and tie the ends very firmly around the rod of your backstrap (Figure 4). Some weavers like to use a similar friction clamp to shorten the far end of a long warp, while others shorten the warp by using a slipknot.

Heddles may be made in various ways. For narrower bands the bunched multiloop heddle may be quite satisfactory. Making two half-heddles in place of each whole one sometimes helps spread the warps. Another help is to put at least H 1 on a stick to space the warps; on wider or more sticky warps, more stick heddles are needed. The simplest method is to wind the loops on three fingers as for a multiloop heddle, then insert a stick to replace the fingers, tying the ends of the heddle string to the ends of the stick, and adding a tie across the top to keep them in place. Popsicle sticks or tongue depressors may be used, with masking tape to hold the heddle loops in place.

Another very satisfactory way of making heddles was described in Harriet Tidball's monograph on inkle weaving. She suggested using a heddle string with knotted loops at intervals of 6″ (15.24 cm) as shown in Figure 5. Wind the heddle string around a firm cardboard or a pair of warping clamps, with the outside edges measuring 6″ apart. The authors suggest marking the fold line with a felt pen, so when it is unwound you have guide marks 6″ apart (Figure 6). Fold at each mark in turn, tying an overhand knot so it leaves a loop to fit a fairly slender heddle stick. Make enough loops so you have one more than the number of warps for the heddle. Insert the heddle string in the shed under the selected warps and install the loops on the heddle stick as you lift up each small loop between the warps. These heddle loops are always even in length and the heddle string is reusable. If your loopy string is not long enough for a wider warp, just prepare an

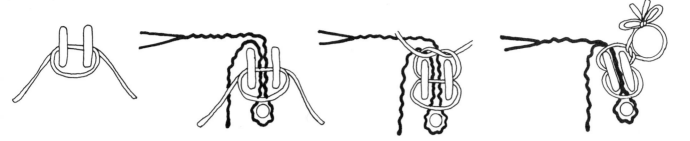

4. The friction clamp is simply constructed from two pieces of screen molding, a pencil, and a pair of shoestrings, as shown in this sequence.

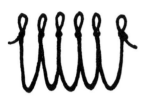

5. Knotting your heddle string keeps the heddle loops even in length.

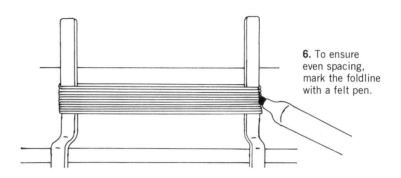

6. To ensure even spacing, mark the foldline with a felt pen.

addition. Tiny rubber bands wound over the loop at each end of the stick will keep the loops from sliding off.

For the far heddle, instead of using a shed loop or even a shed rod or stick, we developed a simple shed clamp (Figure 3). This holds the yarns neatly in place, and may be merely tilted back instead of lifted to operate as the far heddle. Two 7″ (17.78 cm) strips of screen molding with ⅛″ (.32 cm) holes drilled near each end are placed with the warps between them, then tied firmly together with one 18″ (45.72 cm) shoestring. However, before installing this heddle, a special operation should be performed to install the lease stick at the back. In Figure 3, it was a short warp so only one lease stick was used with the end rod. The weave was intermesh, and since the H 1 warps were the opposites of the H 4 warps, they were the ones that needed to be moved back to the lease stick. After the first three heddles were installed, the H 4 warps were lifted to make a

shed at the near end, and a temporary shed loop was tied to hold the warps. The H 1 warps were then lifted and its shed opened to the *back* of the other heddles, so the lease stick could be entered in the H 1 shed. It was then secured to the warp beam. Finally, the H 4 warps were lifted back through the heddles and the shed clamp installed with the warps spaced evenly. It was possible to use even as fragile a yarn as rayon chenille by properly spacing it and using techniques that avoid friction.

Shuttles. Although the fingers can manage the beating in a narrow band, they need help as the band gets wider. A flat stick shuttle may be used, but with more warps, an inkle shuttle with a sharp edge is better. Openings on the top tend to catch on the warps, so shuttles with end openings are preferred. Grooves along the side for winding the warp make the shuttle less bulky in the shed. (Grooves may be made with a router.)

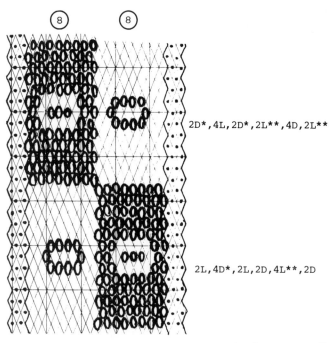

2D*,4L,2D*,2L**,4D,2L**

2L,4D*,2L,2D,4L**,2D

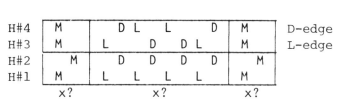

H#4	M			D	L	L			D		M	D-edge
H#3	M				L		D		D	L		M	L-edge
H#2		M			D		D	D		D			M
H#1	M			L		L		L		L		M	
	x?					x?					x?		

Draft 1. Four-heddle pebble weave, with alternating warp order.

7. The pattern diagram for a contemporary belt in double cloth.

* drop L partner   ** drop D partner *(order reversed)*

Pebble Weave on the Backstrap

One of the first projects you might like to try with your backstrap is a wider pebble-weave band woven with four heddles instead of two. Later, you might like to do this also on the inkle loom. Although we do not know whether Bolivians ever use four heddles for this weave, we have found it a helpful method, either with the alternate warp order (abab) of Band 1, or the irregular warp order (abba–baab) of Band 8. The method to be described here is for the alternate warp order, with all light warps on H 1, and all dark warps on H 2 (Draft 1). The pebble rows have some irregularity in spacing. Each warp is included in two heddles. Follow the draft closely in rearranging the warps for the heddles. To avoid confusion, it is best to prepare the heddles in steps as described below:

First, rearrange the original warp cross for H 1 and H 2 as usual and secure in place with lease sticks, but install each of them as multiloop heddles. Tie them together if desired with at least an inch between them. (Aunt Lydia's may be used.) If you wish to have a tab end, it is a good idea to insert the weft beside the pin in the end loops now, with the shorter tail to the left. Secure the weft by tying it temporarily into a loop. Remove the lease sticks and check the heddles.

Form a picking cross with the H 1 warps on the near finger and the H 2 warps on the far one. Taking the border warps from the near finger, pick in the usual manner for a D-edge pebble row. Lift the picked warps back through H 1 and H 2, and install a shed loop for H 4. Push it back toward the far end of the warp.

Form another picking cross as before, with H 1 near and H 2 far. Pick for an L-edge pebble row, again taking the borders from the near finger. Lift the picked warps back through H 1 and H 2, and install H 3 as a multiloop heddle. If desired, tie H 3 and H 4 together, leaving space between them. Check H 3 and H 4, and remove the warp from the posts. Untie the weft, lift H 2, and snug the warp end loops evenly in place. Pass the weft to the left, tucking in the tail.

Now you can use H 3 and H 4 alternately for the pebble rows, whenever you pass the weft from left to right. Form a picking cross for each design row (when the weft is at the right), placing the H 2 warps on the near finger and the H 1 warps on the far one. Pick according to the pattern, taking the borders from the near finger. Pass the weft to the left.

It is easier to avoid friction on the warps with this setup, but it is wise to try to improve your techniques as outlined at the end of Chapter 2. Tug at the heddles as needed to straighten them. After the H 2 warps have been lifted for the near side of the picking cross, hold them taut with the thumb. H 1 can then be easily lifted for the far side of the cross.

Either H 3 or H 4 may be lifted more easily if the warps in front of them are gently strummed, or fanned out to the left between the left forefinger and thumb, then gradually released

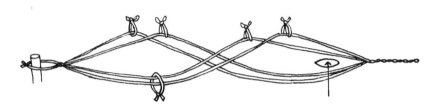

*H#5 M	MM	L–D	DᴸL'	MM
H#4	M	D	L'	M
H#3	M	L	D'	M
H#2	M	D	L'	M
H#1	M	L	D'	M
	×2	×8	×8	×2

Draft 2. A draft for a contemporary belt in double cloth.

8. A diagram of the sword and lower shed loop for needle-picking double cloth.

from your grasp. When the warp is wider or more sticky, the warps of the back heddles may need to be lifted through the other heddles by sections.

A Contemporary Double-Cloth Belt. It was noticed that in one Bolivian belt, an attractive, colorful pattern was achieved with very little picking, partly due to reversing the order of the L D warp pairs on one side of center. On one half, the light warps were polychrome, and on the other half the dark warps were polychrome also. Light and dark blocks alternate with a checkerboard effect (Figure 7). Only the small 0's in the center of the blocks need to be picked. Three pairs of units with the 0's are followed by two plain pairs of units without pickup, then repeated.

Wind the warp yarns in the following order: 2 d-bouts M / 8 d-bouts L' and D' / 8 d-bouts L" and D" / 2 d-bouts M. Install heddles according to Draft 2. Notice that the D" warps are at the left of the L" warps at the right of center. This reversal of the L D order to D L must be kept in mind during the picking too. The weaving sequence proceeds as described for Band 7, following the pattern diagram (Figure 7).

Needle-Picking: An Alternative for Double Cloth. Some Bolivian weavers do not form a picking cross while picking a double-cloth pattern. Instead, they separate the light and dark warps into layers, with the background warps in the upper layer and the pattern warps in the lower layer. Using a long needle, they slide the needle under the desired background warps until a pattern warp is called for. Then the pattern warp is picked up and the corresponding background warp is dropped. A sword inserted between the upper and lower sets of warps keeps them sepa-

rated during the picking. Also, a lower shed loop around the H 1 and H 2 warps positioned on the far side of the warp cross (under H 3 and H 4) is used to aid in separating the sets (Figure 8).

While there is a chance of accidentally picking the wrong pattern warp from the lower layer, with practice it is possible to observe which pattern warp corresponds to the background warp. An advantage of needle-picking is that it is very easy to see which pattern yarns need to be picked. Once mastered, this method is more rapid than the picking-cross method for some types of designs. Since both hands are necessary in this method, either a backstrap arrangement or an inkle loom must be used. Because of the simplicity of its design, the belt described above makes a good project for learning this technique.

Use the following steps to weave a left-slant row (assuming a dark motif on a light background):

1. Lift H 1 and H 2. (It helps to grasp the H 3 and H 4 warps with one hand while lifting H 1 and H 2 with the other hand.) Insert the sword and draw it to the fell.

2. Lift H 1 and place a left finger under the warps. With the needle in the other hand, beat lightly to separate the warps into two layers.

3. Pick the desired warps according to the pattern, using the left thumb to push off the unpicked background warps. Pass the weft to the left.

4. Lift H 3 and H 4, enlarge the lower shed, and pass the weft to the right.

A similar method is used for the right-slant rows. Pull down on the lower loop heddle to aid in lifting the H 3 and H 4.

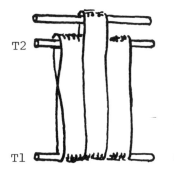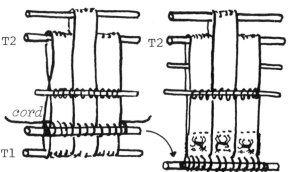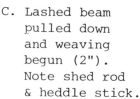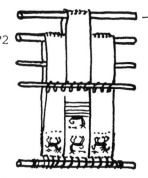

A. Warp wound as *figure-8*, and center section on extra beam to allow length for pocket.

B. Permanent lower beam lashed on to replace the temporary lower beam (T1).

C. Lashed beam pulled down and weaving begun (2"). Note shed rod & heddle stick.

D. Pocket section woven separately. Extra upper beam is then removed and used later for second lashed beam (see below).

9. Steps in weaving a chuspa: To weave a chuspa, the loom is rotated several times. To allow for a pocket, one section of the warp is longer than the rest.

Weaving a Chuspa

One of the highlights of our summer's research was observing the weaving of a small modified intermesh coca bag, from start to finish. It was woven by a young Indian mother named Maxima, in the courtyard of a once-elegant hacienda that has not been in operation since 1952 when, as a result of a revolution, large land holdings were broken up and given to the Indians. The steps used to produce the bag are shown in Figure 9.

Her Loom. Except that it is secured onto two long oblique poles, her loom is essentially like the ancient backstrap loom. It is portable so she can work in the sun or shade. It is adjustable so she can roll up the weaving, work from either end of the warp, and also raise and lower it as necessary.

Most of the loom parts (Figure 10) are rods or poles of varying sizes. In addition to the usual two horizontal beams, there is an extra one lashed to the poles above the upper beam. This holds taut the center section of warps, which are wound longer than the rest to provide for the pocket flap of the bag. The shed rod is as long as the beams, so that it too can rest against the poles. A thinner stick is used for the heddle rod. From a nearby tree, she cut three thin sticks, peeled them, and sharpened them. One she prepared to use as a shuttle. The second one was used to hold the far shed of the picking cross, and the third one was used to hold picked sections until she was ready to put in the sword. Other pieces included her

sword and the small accessories shown in the illustration.

The upper beams are lashed firmly in place, while the lower one is used for tension control. It is held in place by a 1″ (2.54 cm) leather strap or a special rope made of llama hair. There is a secure loop at one end of the thong that is brought up the front through a notch in the bottom of the poles. Behind the pole, the thong is brought up from the back over the lower beam, beside the inner edge of the pole. It is then threaded down through the loop and brought over the end of the beam by the outer side of the pole. Last it is pulled taut, wrapped around the pole above the beam, and the end secured. An additional notch on the front of the pole helps keep the thong in place.

In assembling the loom, measurements are not made with items we might feel a necessity, such as a tapemeasure or a ruler. Instead, the weaver improvises with what is available. Most often she will use a hand's width. For example, the pocket beam is a hand's width above the upper beam. A cord with a loop knotted at each end is used to insure that the beams are parallel.

Preparing the Warp. With the temporary upper and lower beams lashed in place, warping is done on the loom in a figure-8 fashion (Figure 9). When a color change occurs in the warp, the new color is not tied on, but held in place by the

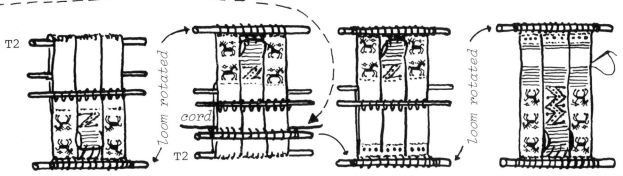

E. Pocket folded & lashed to beam, eliminating extra length of warps.

F. Loom rotated & extra beam lashed on to replace the other temporary beam (T2). Shed rod moved to other side of heddles.

G. Lashed beam pulled down and weaving begun at other end (1").

H. Loom rotated, shed rod moved. Pattern finished, & stripes woven with heddles. Heddles removed, & terminal weaving begun with needle.

tension of the previously wound warps (Figure 11). A safety pin is used as a marker to enclose counted warps for the various pattern sections. The warp yarns were wound in the following order. Left section: 2 s-bouts orange / 26 d-bouts white and wine. Center pocket section (wound around both upper beams): 2 s-bouts white / 11 d-bouts orange and white, 2 d-bouts fuchsia and white, 11 d-bouts orange and white / 2 s-bouts white. Right section: 26 d-bouts white and wine / 2 s-bouts orange.

Rearranging Warps and Installing the Heddle Stick. The warps were rearranged for an alternating warp order, one section at a time, working from right to left across the warp. The plain-weave areas needed no rearranging. The darks were put on the far finger for the shed rod and the lights on the near finger for the heddle.

An ingenious method of combining the llama bone and the heddle rod is used to install the string heddle. The heddle string is inserted from right to left under the upper warp layer on the near (lower) side of the warp cross. A slip knot at the left end of the string is passed over the "knob" at the end of the bone. The heddle rod is inserted in the hole at the pointed end of the bone (Figure 12). The heddle loops are made around the bone, next to the knob. When the bone is full of loops, they are pushed off onto the heddle rod. This is repeated as necessary, and the right end of the heddle string is finished with a slip knot.

Lashing on the Permanent Lower Beam. To have a four-selvedge piece, the warps need to be lashed to another beam so the loops at both ends of the warp are not enclosing thick beams. The lower one is done before the weaving begins.

To lash the lower beam, first a heading cord (a quadruple strand of warp) is inserted in the end loops next to the lower beam. Then the cord is raised a few inches and each of its ends are tied to the nearby poles to keep it taut. With the lashing cord rolled into a small ball, three half-hitches are made at the left end of the permanent lower beam. Then another half-hitch is made around both the beam and the heading cord, which is held parallel to it. Working from left to right, the ball of lashing cord is pushed through the upper warp layer after every third L D warp pair, passing it around the beam and the cord (Figure 13). The cord is temporarily held in place at the right end of the beam with a half-hitch (Figure 14). The heading cord is unfastened from the poles and temporarily tied across the tops of the lashings on the permanent beam, and the beam is pulled down to the ends of the loops. Hand measure is used to assure an even width at the top and bottom of the warp. The bone is used to tighten the lashing cord, and then the right end is tied securely. Last the tension straps are tightened.

She adjusted the height of her loom on the poles so it was at a convenient height as the situation changed. With her knees between the poles, she half-knelt, half-sat, with her feet out to the right. A folded blanket was her only cushion.

The shuttle was wound in preparation for the first shot. First the yarn was wound a couple times around one end of the stick, then, while the shuttle was rotated a single turn, the yarn was brought to the other end where it was wound

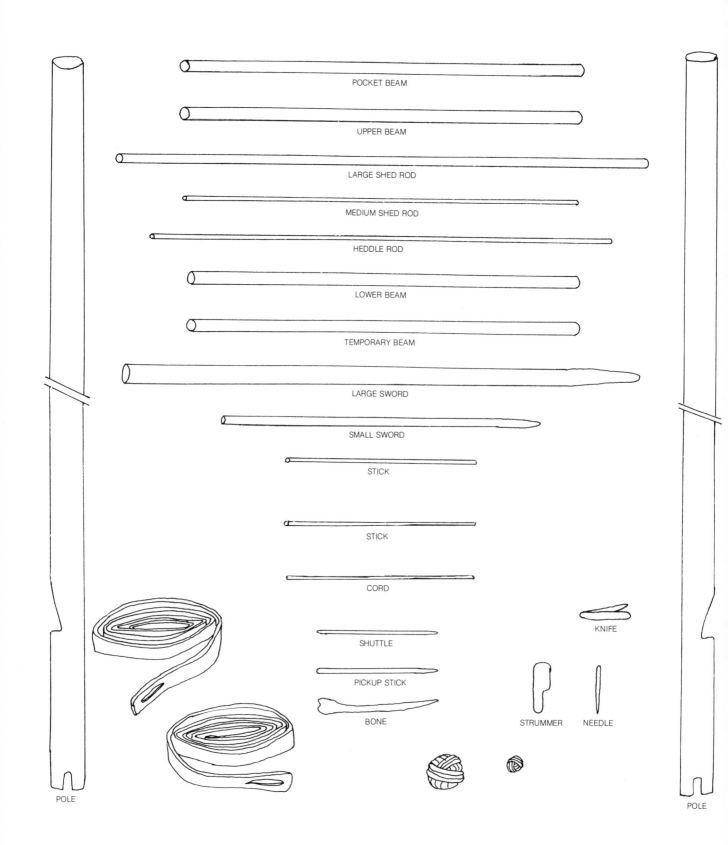

POCKET BEAM

UPPER BEAM

LARGE SHED ROD

MEDIUM SHED ROD

HEDDLE ROD

LOWER BEAM

TEMPORARY BEAM

LARGE SWORD

SMALL SWORD

STICK

STICK

CORD

KNIFE

SHUTTLE

PICKUP STICK

STRUMMER   NEEDLE

BONE

POLE

POLE

10. Most of the loom parts are rods or poles of varying sizes.

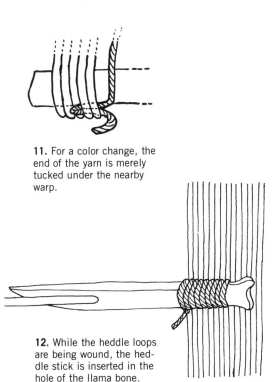

11. For a color change, the end of the yarn is merely tucked under the nearby warp.

12. While the heddle loops are being wound, the heddle stick is inserted in the hole of the llama bone.

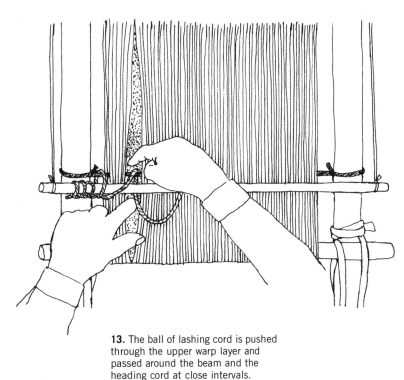

13. The ball of lashing cord is pushed through the upper warp layer and passed around the beam and the heading cord at close intervals.

around the end a few times. Then the stick was twirled as the yarn was brought back to the first end, and this process was continued until there seemed to be enough, about a dozen or two twirls. Some of the overspin of the yarn was allowed to untwist while winding the shuttle.

Opening the Sheds. The first four weft shots are plain weave (D, L, D, L), which affords a little practice in using the heddles but allows checking for errors. A quadruple strand of weft is used for the first three shots, and a double one for the fourth.

Because the warps are so close together, special methods are needed to open the shed. For the first shot the dark warps need to be lifted. First the tip of the bone is strummed across the warps between the heddle and shed rod, and then the shed rod is moved down next to the heddle. With the bone held in the left hand, the weaver reaches under the dark warps and pushes down on the light ones with the tip of the bone, working from left to right across the warp. When the warp layers have been completely separated, the sword is inserted in front of the heddle. Then the heddle is moved up in preparation for beating.

Using the llama bone, the warps are lifted as small sections over the sword and down to the fell in rapid beats. After about twelve strokes, the sword is pulled down to within 1½" (3.81 cm) of the fell, and the beating is repeated with rapid strokes back and forth across the width, about 60 strokes.

She then passed the weft by inserting her shuttle. With her fingers she pressed the weft in place

at one selvedge, and tacked the free end under the end of the beam at the pole. With the tip of her bone, she beat down the new weft lightly with about six strokes near the middle.

To lift the white warps, the shed rod is pushed up, and while the left hand lifts the heddle stick, the right fist is thumped against the warps on the far side of the heddles to allow the light warps to be freed and lifted. The sword is then inserted with a rocking, sawing motion as the heddle rod is lifted from right to left.

Picking the Pattern. Because of the width of the piece, a cord is put in the near shed of the picking cross instead of inserting the near finger. A thin stick holds the warps on the far side of the cross. The left fingers lift the warps of the far shed from the shed stick, in sections. The right hand holds the pickup stick, and the warps are selected with the help of the left middle finger and right thumb tip. She picked across the row by sections, inserting a thin stick to hold the picked warps as she worked toward the left. For the narrow plain weave stripes and the selvedges, she took the warps from the far side of the cross. After each row was picked, she removed the cord from the near shed and inserted the sword in place of the stick. Then she moved the heddle up to prepare for beating and passing the weft. Next she put her sword in the near shed of the new picking cross.

To form the new picking cross for the next row, she inserted her left index finger along the sword and cleared the shed for one third the width. The cord was inserted for this third, and

14. One half-hitch

15. (Right) The weaving is continued in the center section for the pocket only.

16. (Far right) The loom has been rotated and the weaving begun at the other end.

then the process was repeated for the other two sections. The far shed was then opened according to whether it involved lifting the light or the dark warps.

Her timing was recorded, from weft shot to weft shot, in the pattern area. On the average, each shot took five minutes. One fourth of the time was spent in changing the shed, one half in picking the pattern, and the remaining fourth in beating down the previous weft and cleaning the shed.

Weaving the Pocket. After she finished one motif in each of the sections, she began to weave the center section only using the warps of the plain-weave stripes as selvedges (Figure 15). She prepared a butterfly for her weft. Since her center warps extended a hand's width above the side warps, she planned on a pocket motif about a two-finger width in length. This was followed by some heddle-controlled horizontal stripes for the back of the pocket.

She untied the bottom beam, then removed the extra top beam. Then she pulled down the pocket section and folded it, bringing the center warps into place on the upper beam. With a double strand on her needle, she lashed the fold of the pocket to the bottom beam, then retied the bottom beam. Since the center section was a little lower than the side ones, she continued the center stripes for a while, then resumed picking all the way across until she had finished another motif in each section.

Beginning the Other End. She untied the beams of the loom and rotated them (so the lower beam became the upper one) and then relashed

the beams. Then she transferred the shed rod to the other side of the heddles and inserted a heading cord next to the beam now at the bottom. Picking up the extra "pocket" beam, she lashed it to the heading cord, repeating the technique described above. She removed the temporary beam and lashed the new permanent beam to the poles.

She began by weaving three plain weave stripes, (L, D, L), using a double yarn for the weft. On the fourth row, which she picked, she cut off the extra strand and shot the weft as a single yarn. After weaving about an inch, she ended with an all-light row, and lashed the weft in place with several spirals around the lower beam (Figure 16). The shed rod was then transferred to the other side of the heddles.

Continuing the Front of the Bag. She again untied the beams and rotated the loom. This time it was lashed on at a lower level because of the height of the fell. She continued weaving the pattern, making a third motif, which brought her a little past the center of her warp (Figure 17). Then she wove heddle-controlled stripes until she could no longer operate the heddles. The stripes would become part of the back of the bag.

Terminal Weaving. When there were three or four fingers width of warp length left, she took out the heddle string and rolled it up. With her bone, she brought the dark warps down, put in the sword, and beat down hard in small sections with her bone.

She unlashed the weft at the top, and with the pickup stick made a special rearrangement of the warps (Figure 18) one section at a time. She started at the right of each, but did the left section

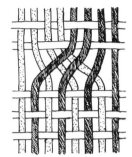

17. (Far left) After an inch of pattern had been woven on the back edge of the bag, the loom was rotated, and the weaving continued on the front.

18. (Above) A special rearrangement of the warps makes it possible to weave vertical stripes in the terminal area.

19. (Left) The heddles and shed rod have been removed for the terminal weaving.

first. One of the thin sticks was used to collect the rearranged warps. The rearrangement makes it possible to weave alternating light and dark vertical stripes in the terminal area, providing a nice contrast to the horizontal stripes below (Figure 19).

Working at the top of the terminal area, she reached to the right of and under the light warps to rearrange the first four dark ones. The first and second darks were left under the pickup stick, and the third and fourth were picked. Next she worked with the first four light warps. The first and second lights were pushed down below the pickup stick, and the third and fourth were picked. This pattern was repeated across the width of each section, working first with a group of four dark warps then with four light ones, clearing the shed above and below. When the warps were completely arranged, she inserted the sword and beat both at the top and the bottom of the opening. Both wefts were passed in the same direction, the upper one on a needle and the lower one on the shuttle.

The next row had, from the right, 2D up, 2D down, 2W up, 2W down, etc., continuing as a plain weave with paired warps. The wefts were again passed going both in the same direction, and then the upper one was secured around the end of a beam to keep it taut.

When the space got very small, a needle was used instead of the shuttle, and only a third to a half of a section could be done at a time. It became tighter and tighter until the last row was just barely squeezed in. She then untied the loom, unlashed the fabric from the beams, and folded the web in half. With large stitches, she basted the

20. Applying the ribete is the first step in trimming the bag.

side of the bag together near the outer edges.

Additional Observations. She occasionally had some little problems. When her warp broke, she pulled it and slipped the end under the neighboring warps. Another time she tied it to a neighboring warp. When her selvedge broke, she tied it with a knot. When she came upon a knot in the warp, she untied it and slipped the end under the neighboring warps. When her weft broke, or she ran out and needed to add a new piece, she unwound the ply a bit and sewed the new one into the end of the old one.

BEAM

LARGE SHED ROD

HEDDLE ROD

BEAM

TEMPORARY BEAM

21. Most of the *awayo* loom parts are nearly identical to those of the chuspa loom, except they are larger in scale.

Weaving an Awayo

Near Lake Titicaca, where pebble weave is the preferred patterning method, wider pieces are woven on a horizontal loom. Two pairs of iron or wood stakes in the ground are used to keep the beams in position. During warping, the beams are held against the stakes by the tension of the warps. Later, during weaving, the near set of stakes is moved in back of the weaver and the tension can then be adjusted by the ropes that tie each end of the near beam to a stake. Rocks are used to hold the beams up from the ground. Other loom parts are nearly identical to those of the chuspa loom, except that they are larger in scale (Figure 21).

Preparing the Warp. Awayos are woven as two separate four-selvedge pieces that are later joined to form a square. In each half, the Aymaras use relatively large areas of plain weave in graduated shades of colors, accented by an asymmetric arrangement of several narrow stripes of various pattern weaves, such as pebble, doubled pebble, intermesh, and layered three-color.

The length of the warp makes it practically impossible for one person to prepare alone, so it is done cooperatively. With the beams temporarily lashed to the outside of the stakes, one person sits by each beam. A cloth is stretched on the ground between them to keep the yarns clean. The ball of yarn is rolled from one end to the other, passing under the beam each time, to form the figure-8 bouts.

Each pattern band has its own set of two to four string heddles. The warps are rearranged in each band and the heddles installed as multiloop heddles, so it will be possible to form the sheds when the loom is rotated. If the pattern stripe is wide, the heddle loops may be spaced on a small twig.

The sheds for the plain-weave sections are controlled by using the shed rod and a loom-wide heddle stick. With a figure-8 warp, there is no need to rearrange the warp cross in these sections. The warps above the back beam provide a natural shed to insert the shed rod for H 2, while the warps above the near beam can provide the countershed when they are installed in the heddle-stick loops for H 1. To prepare this heddle, the heddle string is passed in the shed, but brought up over the pattern stripes as it is inserted from right to left. If one of the pattern bands is wider than about an inch, the heddle is either made in two separate sections on the stick or secured at each side of the band, with the string carried across the top of the rod.

After the heddles are set up, the permanent cloth beam is lashed on and pulled toward the near end of the warp. The temporary cords on the stakes are removed, and large rocks are placed under the ends of the beams to keep the warp a

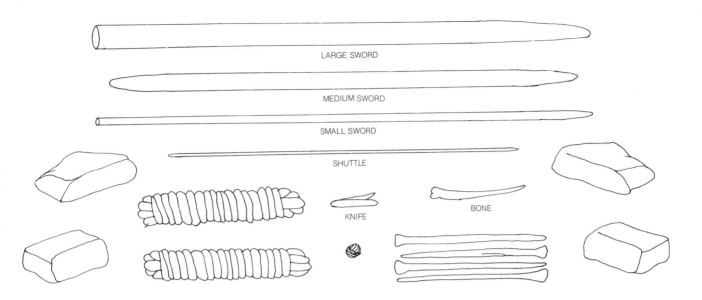

LARGE SWORD

MEDIUM SWORD

SMALL SWORD

SHUTTLE

KNIFE

BONE

comfortable distance above the ground. The near stakes are driven in about a foot away from the cloth beam, to which they are tied with llama rope to provide an adjustable tension on the warp.

Weaving Sequence. The weaving is begun with a few shots of plain weave using a doubled weft. The same techniques used for obtaining the sheds on the oblique loom are also used on the horizontal loom. However, because of the pattern stripes, the shed cannot be opened all the way across as it was for the chuspa. Instead, each section must be cleared separately, stopping to pick the warps for the pattern stripes along the way. A sword is slid into the shed to hold the picked warps as each section is finished. The far shed is the easier to open because the plain-weave warps can be lifted and held on the picking finger without being cleared, while picking the pattern warps in the following section (Figure 22). Then both sections are cleared together. The hand positions for lifting the heddle rod and inserting the sword to open the near shed are shown in Figure 23.

The point at which the loom is rotated depends upon personal preference. In many instances the weaver will work to within about a foot of the end of the warp before rotating the loom. She then weaves as far as possible in plain weave and removes the heddles. The terminal area continues the previous plain weave without rearranging the warps, so it is not possible to tell at which point the heddles were removed.

22. The plain weave warps are easily picked off the shed rod. Photo by Elizabeth Barnard.

23. To open the near shed, the sword is worked in as the heddles are lifted. Photo by Elizabeth Barnard.

ADAPTING THE LOOM FOR INDOOR USE

Because of climate and convenience, it is impractical for many weavers to work outdoors as the Indians do, but the simplicity of their loom makes it possible to improvise indoors easily. In an early trial, we used the top of a packing crate, with large metal screw-eyes added to hold the beams in place (Figure 24), but there were some tension problems with this arrangement. For medium-width pieces it was later found satisfactory to tie the warp beams to the rotating beams of a frame loom, such as the Kircher model (Figure 25). Another possibility is to build a simple, inexpensive frame loom with a tension adjustment. For wide pieces, it is possible to lash the beams to those of a floor loom.

24. A frame from a packing crate was adapted for weaving a wedding gift. Photo by Robert Burningham.

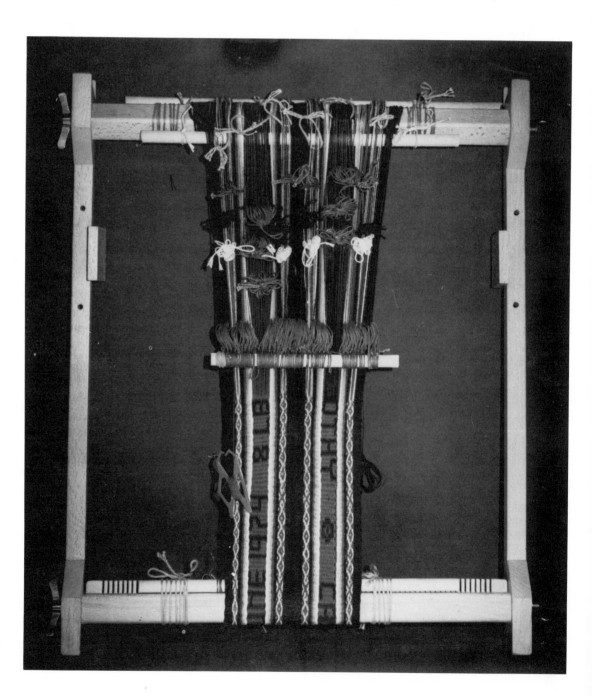

25. The tension of the warp is controlled by tying the end rods to the rotating beams of a frame loom. Extra heddles were added to avoid picking, in some of the pattern areas, in this hanging woven to commemorate the birth of Margie's son.

27. The inkle loom is very useful for Bolivian three-color weaves. A cord is used in the near shed of the picking cross, in place of the near finger. A "Nisbet" stick has been inserted here to hold the far shed of the picking cross, which is to be held by the left hand. The L warps are in the inkle heddles and the other two colors are controlled by multiloop H 2 and the shed-stick (H 3). An extra loop was added to easily separate the warps in the center, to check the pick-up.

Inkle Loom Weaving

Although Bolivian Indians do not use an inkle loom, it has proven to be very satisfactory for producing their pattern weaves. An inkle is similar to their frame looms in that it has a tension that is stable, yet adjustable. However, it is ordinarily not as wide, it is more expensive, and four-selvedge pieces are not possible because of its heddle arrangement. Books with instructions for inkle looms may be found in the Bibliography. The suggestions included here are based chiefly on our own experiences adapting Bolivian methods to the inkle loom.

Equipment. The inkle loom has been found useful not only for the two-heddle pickup weaves, but also for multiheddle weaves such as intermesh, warp-faced double cloth, and three-color weaves. Since these weaves require more manipulations, it is important that the loom be one with ample open space between the front bar and the inkle heddle area, and that it have a deep shed. Good tension control is also important. An open-sided loom is easier to warp, but it must be sturdy enough not to bow in under the tension of the yarns, with hard beating. The Leclerc Cendrel is a floor model that is especially satisfactory. It can be braced against the chair on which the weaver sits, which permits firm beating.

With an open-sided loom, you have an option of using either of two very desirable types of hed-dles. They can be installed during the winding of the warp or afterwards. The first type is the kind described for the backstrap (Figure 5). A little experimentation may be needed to determine the correct size for your loom. The size of the heddles should be such that when they are installed, they will pull the heddle warps down to the same level as the open warps. In this case, the overhand knot should be tied so the loop it forms will be large enough to slide on to the heddle bar.

The other type of heddle is made up of circles of heddle string (Knit-Cro-Sheen), each pretied individually around properly spaced posts. The circle is folded so double strands go over the warp yarn and the two end loops are slipped onto the heddle bar (Figure 26). Both types are reusable and easily removed. By tying a partly woven warp and its heddles in a few strategic spots, it may be safely removed from the loom, to be later returned. This is sometimes a real advantage.

Suitable tools make a big difference in the ease of inkle weaving, the resulting product, and your sense of satisfaction. The tension is considerably tighter and less flexible than either finger-tension weaving or backstrap, so more work is done with the help of tools than with the hands.

The inkle shuttle should have unbroken lines on the two long edges, and the bottom edge should be tapered to almost a knife edge. Grooves along the flatter sides for winding the warp make

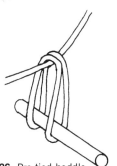

26. Pre-tied heddle circles are folded over the inkle warp, and the ends looped around the heddle post.

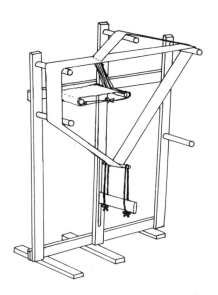

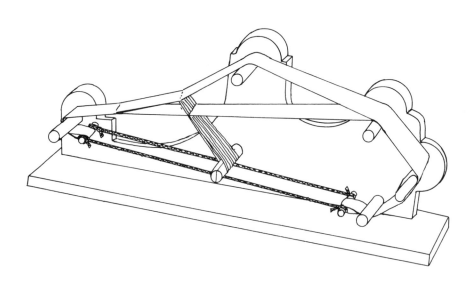

28. The Leclerc "Cendrel" loom is well-suited to Bolivian weaving. Notice the simple shelf added between the bars keeps tools conveniently at hand. For a short circular warp, the tension may be adjusted by remote control.

29. The end-bars of a modified figure-8 warp may be connected with cords so that a more Bolivian-type warp may be woven on an inkle loom, either a floor or table model.

it less bulky in the shed.

It is desirable to have two or three flat pickup sticks of the type designed by Jacquetta Nisbet (see Appendix A). They are easily made from 8″ (20.32 cm) pieces of screen molding. It should be tapered down to a flat point at each end and well sanded. With heavier yarns it can serve as a pickup stick. With finer yarns, it may be slipped in beside a more slender pickup stick, then turned to open the shed for the shuttle. You should also have a more slender pickup stick that works well for you. Some possibilities are a knitting needle; a ¼″ (.64 cm) dowel that is sharpened in a pencil sharpener and well sanded; or a clay modeling tool.

For some weaves, a shed stick is used in back of the inkle heddles (Figure 27). A flat stick, a flat shuttle, or piece of yardstick can be used. Drill a hole near each end to thread with a cord so it can be tied to the top bar. A rubber band at the end of the bar prevents the cord from slipping off.

To keep the tools conveniently at hand, we designed a simple shelf for the loom using a terry washcloth (Figure 28). It was folded in half and the ends sewn almost to the fold, so a small dowel could be inserted at each end. These were tied with connecting cords under two of the inkle bars. A third dowel was tacked in place inside the fold line to provide an edge on which to rest the tools. This is particularly valuable when using a floor model loom for a weave that requires more tools.

Warping Considerations. If you want a shorter warp than is standard for your inkle loom, try

either of two methods the authors have used. For the first method, the warp was wound without going around the tension bar. A rod was then inserted in the circular warp, and a cord attached at each end of it to draw it snugly toward the tension bar (Figure 28). The tension was then adjusted by remote control.

The other method is suited for even shorter warps. The warp is not a continuous circle, but is wound around end-sticks that in turn are attached to each other by cords which go around the tension bar (Figure 29). The warp may be wound temporarily around some of the inkle posts, then the end loops are transferred to the end sticks if the loom is open-sided. If it is not, the end sticks need to be temporarily but securely tied between certain bars of the loom (then later attached to the connecting cords that go around the tension bar.) The warp is wound as a modified figure-8, but the yarns that are to be in the inkle heddles must be run over the top bar. If the loom is open-sided, it is easier to put the heddles on after the warp is wound.

This method permits a more Bolivian treatment of the ends, although the final end is quite long and of two lengths due to the type of heddle set-up. The beginning end may be a finished selvedge by lashing the warp end loops to the end bar in the manner described for the Bolivian frame loom. If the weaving is to be a hanging, a suitable hanger-rod may be inserted in the near warp end loops and lashed firmly to the end stick.

Preparing the Warp. If you are warping the loom in the usual manner, you will have a con-

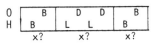

```
        B       D   D       B
0     
H   B           L   L       B
      x?        x?          x?
```
Draft 1. Two-heddle weave with alternating warp order.

```
        B     D L   L D     B
0
H   B   L D         D L     B
      x?        x?          x?
```
Draft 2. Two-heddle pebble weave with irregular warp order.

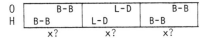

```
         B-B        L-D        B-B
0*
H    B-B        L-D        B-B
       x?        x?          x?
```

```
         B-B        L-D        B-B
0
H    B-B        L-D        B-B
H#2      B   B      D   D      B   B
H#1  B   B      L   L      B   B
       x?        x?          x?
```
Draft 3. Intermesh.

```
         B-B        L-D        B-B
0
H    B-B        L-D        B-B
       x?        x?          x?
```

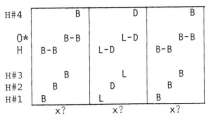

```
H#4          B           D           B
0*       B-B        L-D        B-B
H    B-B        L-D        B-B
H#3      B           L           B
H#2  B           D           B
H#1  B           L           B
       x?        x?          x?
```
Draft 4. One-weft double cloth.

```
         B    M-D M-D      B
0
H    B   L    L            B
       x?      x?          x?
```

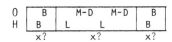

```
H#3                 D     D
0            B    M-D M-D      B
(H#1) H  B   L    L            B
H#2               M     M
         x?       x?          x?
```
Draft 5. Three-color-warp weave.

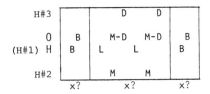

```
         B    D  D  D  D      B
0
H    B   L  L  L  L        B
       x?       x?          x?
```

```
         M    D  D  D  D      M
0
H    M   L  L  L  L        M
H#2  M        D L    L D     M    D-edge
H#1  M   L    D   D L     M       L-edge
       x?       x?          x?
```
Draft 6. Pebble weave with four heddles.

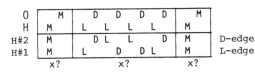

```
         B    D D  L L    L L  D D     B
0
H    B   L L  D D      D D  L L      B
       x?        x?          x?
```
Draft 7. Doubled pebble, irregular warp order.

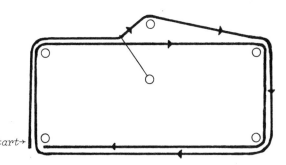

30. For the circular inkle warp, two circles of warp are needed for each s-bout.

start→

tinuous, circular warp, with each yarn in the circle counting as one warp end. Since one s-bout has two warp ends, you need to wind two circles for each s-bout; one for the heddle (and top bar) and one for the open position (Figure 30). Since each d-bout has four warp ends, usually 2L and 2D, you need to have *four* circles for each d-bout. For two-heddle weaves with alternating warp order, a d-bout is wound as LDLD, in heddle (H), open (O), H, O (Draft 1). In that way, each L warp is to the left of its D partner, in the H position for H 1, and each D warp is in the O position for H 2. Since the warping on an inkle loom proceeds from left to right, the draft should be read from left to right, and consequently, the warping of the border and pattern areas should begin with a heddle warp and end with an open warp. To continue the consistency, for Band 8 (pebble weave with irregular warp order) the L-edge tie-down row should be on H for H 1, and the D-edge tie-down row should be on O for H 2. It is important to follow Draft 2, which is basically the same as for the sample band. Other two-heddle weaves, such as those with supplementary warp, can be adapted for the inkle loom in a similar way.

Multiheddle Weaves. After some experimentation, we discovered that adding extra Bolivian-type string heddles to the inkle loom greatly expanded its capabilities. This was done first for a three-color warp, then for intermesh, and finally for warp-faced one-weft double cloth, with real success. The warping is done in steps according to the drafts for each weave.

For the four-heddle weaves, intermesh (Draft 3) and double cloth (Draft 4), there is an L D warp pair in each H and in each O position. This means that for each d-bout, there are two double-yarn circles. The first one should be in the H position to correspond with the draft. For three-color weaves, the common color is wound first on H, then the other two colors on O, as shown in Draft 5.

Up to three multiloop heddles are installed on the near side of the inkle heddles, and often a shed stick is used beyond them for lifting some of the warps in the open position. Pebble weave, basically a two-heddle weave, can be woven more easily as a four-heddle weave as shown for the backstrap loom. Two multi-loop heddles are used in addition to the inkle heddles (Draft 6). For narrow repetitive patterns, picking can sometimes be avoided by installing heddles for the design-row pattern, as will be shown later.

Techniques in General. Try to avoid friction of the warps and heddles. The warp will change sheds more easily if you spread the inkle heddles a little rather than bunching them. With a wool warp it is helpful to bring through only a few warps at a time. If you are using supplementary heddles, tug at them as often as necessary to straighten their loops. In lifting these extra heddles, do not push them back and forth, but fan the warps out to the side with the left fingers while your right hand is lifting the heddle.

For the picking cross, it is very helpful to replace the near finger with a cord, such as a laundered piece of old cable clothesline (Figure 31).

The far shed can then be easily held in the left hand. In picking up dark warps, it is often easier to see and to count the light partners and push them toward the right to identify the dark warps to pick.

The weaves that involve more of the special sheds are done more easily with the help of the various tools listed earlier. When the Nisbet stick is in the picked shed, turn it on its edge to widen the shed for the shuttle. Slide the shuttle in against the stick. If you still have trouble snagging warps, meet the open end of the shuttle with a finger to seal its gap. To ensure having picked up all the right warps, rotate the two tools around each other.

When you weave a shot of weft, leave a one-inch loop at the edge of the weaving. Pull it firm after pressing open the next shed. This corrects the weft tension, making it easier to obtain the proper warp-faced effect and a good selvedge. For some weaves you need two loops, one on each side.

Advance the weaving as needed by pushing back the heddles and pulling on the shuttle in the shed. Reduce the tension slightly when it gets too tight.

SUGGESTED PROJECTS

To become familiar with using the inkle for the pickup weaves, you may want a first project to be a belt or bag strap woven in one of the two-heddle weaves with alternating warp order. Next you might try doing pebble weave with a four-heddle setup as shown in Draft 6. Two extra multiloop

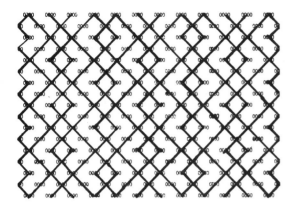

32. Pattern diagram.

33. One-weft double cloth is more easily woven on the inkle loom. A cord is used for the near side of the picking cross, and the lower shed is easily made with the help of the Nisbet stick and a good inkle shuttle. The L–D warp pairs of H 1 and H 2 are in H; the L–D warp pairs of H 3 and H 4 are in O. In addition, multiloop heddles are used for H 1, H 2, and H 3, and a shed stick used behind the inkle heddles for H 4.

heddles are installed in front of the inkle heddles so the pebble rows can be heddle-controlled. Other suggestions follow.

Bookmarks in Intermesh. It is fun to weave the names of your friends into little bookmarks. Prepare your warp according to Draft 3, with an L D warp pair in each H and O position. Then install two multiloop heddles in front of the inkle heddles, H 1 for the L warps, and H 2 for the D warps. It might be easier for you if you think of the dark-warp heddle as H 4. Then the H warps would be H 2 and the O warps H 3, to resemble the tie-down heddles of Band 6. Refer to Band 6 for directions and to the Appendix for the alphabet. You may omit the serifs if you prefer.

Man's Tie in Doubled Pebble. This tie may be worn with its light side or its dark side out. Weave the front with the pattern (Figure 32). Then start to taper in the width for the neck, weaving in the plain color of your background. Pull the weft evenly tight as you shape the tie for the neck, then taper it wider for the back end of the tie, but not quite as wide as for the front of the tie. A six-bout selvedge, picked like the one-bout selvedge of Band 8, is a good edge finish for this project.

Wind the warp yarns in the following order: 6 s-bouts M, 48 d-bouts L and D / 6 s-bouts M. Follow Draft 7. The irregular warp order requires concentration during warping to get the proper sequence of colors in the H and O positions. The pattern and its 48 d-bouts may be too wide for your tie. The width can easily be reduced. The tie

shown in Chapter 6 was woven from one-ply weaving wool.

In picking the pattern, because this is done in doubled pebble, each diagonal line equals 4 dark warps to be picked, each diagonal space equals 4 light warps. Refer to Band 9 for instructions.

Belt in One-Weft Double Cloth. The contemporary belt that was suggested for a backstrap project can also be done on the inkle loom. You may prefer to design another one using patterns from the Appendix. Plan the number of bouts you need and warp the loom, following Draft 4. There is an L D warp pair in each H and O position. This is a big help in forming the lower shed. Heddle 1, H 2 and H 3 are installed as multiloop heddles in front of the inkle heddles, and H 4 needs merely a shed stick behind the inkle heddles.

Follow the sequence for Band 7, adapting it to the inkle setup. Make use of the tools (Figure 33) and develop a rhythm.

Necklace in 3-color CWp 2/1 Twill. You may not want to exactly copy the necklace described here, but if you understand how it was done you can then improvise with designs of your own choosing.

Wind a very short figure-8 warp on the inkle loom, about a yard long or a bit longer. It was done with cottolin yarns in the following order: 1 s-bout D, 5 s-bouts M / 3 d-bouts L and D / 2 s-bouts M, 3 s-bouts L / 9 d-bouts L, M and D, 2 d-bouts L', M', and D', 9 s-bouts L", M" and D" / 3 s-bouts, L, 2 s-bouts M / 3 d-bouts L

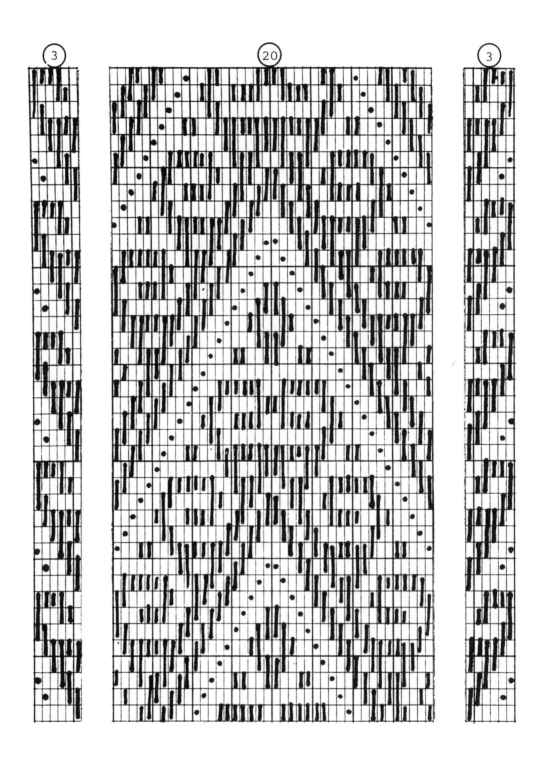

34. Pattern diagram for CWp uneven twill, used for the cottolin necklace. The center band has a three-color warp.

	row	selvedge	pebble	pw	PICK FIRST intermesh	pw	pebble	selvedge	
ALL UP →	1	X ↓	↓	↓	↓	↓	↓	↓ —	PEBBLE ROW
←	2	— (pick)	A OR B	↑	PICK	↑	A OR B	(pick) X	DESIGN ROW
ALL DOWN → except pw	3	X ↑	↑	↓	↑	↓	↑	↑ —	PEBBLE ROW
←	4	— (pick)	A OR B	↑	PICK	↑	A OR B	(pick) X	DESIGN ROW

35. With a little extra manipulation, one may weave a combination of weaves on the inkle loom. In this band, pebble weave and plain weave were combined with lettering in intermesh. Multiloop heddles were added in front of the inkle heddles for the pattern bands, after the manner in which the awayo is woven.

	(edge)	(pebble weave)							(warp stripe)				(intermesh) (center)		
0	G	B W Y R R Y W B							G Y G R				L-D		0
H	G	W B R Y Y R B W							G Y G R				L-D		H
									x2 x2						
H#A		B B Y Y Y Y B B											D D		H#2
H#B		W W R R R R W W											L L		H#1
													x12		

Draft 8. This extended draft illustrates the threading used for the band in Figure 35.

36. A four step sequence was used for the combination weave in Figure 35. Three different colored warps were woven on the loom, and the sequence did not seem as complicated as it appears.

and D / 5 s-bouts M, 1 s-bout D. Use the basic 3-color Draft 5 and the pattern shown in Figure 34. Refer to Band 18 for the method, adapting it to use on the inkle loom. Five-loop braiding was used at the upper end of the necklace and the lower ends were twisted.

Combination of Plain Weave with Intermesh and Pebble. The plan for the bookmark in Band 6 can be expanded by adding a strip of plain weave and a multicolor pebble border (Figure 35), in the manner of the awayo weaving. Badges for the Midwest Weavers Conference were made in this way for hostesses, officers, and other officials. Set up the warp as shown in Draft 8, then refer to the weaving sequence charted in Figure 36. It looks complicated, but is not as difficult as it appears.

Side loops can be added so the center pattern band in intermesh can be found quickly to be picked first. It needs only a little tug on the loop. The pebble border in this case has heddles for the design pickup. Warp in the irregular warp order.

37. Dress with Handwoven Band Trimming by Stana Coleman. Five yards of yarn was wound in one section of a sectional beam and woven on a floor loom, using the heddles but not the reed. Pebble weave, Bergå tapestry yarn, floor loom. Photo by Byron Bennett.

H#4	M		L		L		M
H#3	M		D			D	M
H#2	M			L	L		M
H#1	M			D	D		M
	x?			x?			x?

Draft 9. Floor loom draft for pebble weave.

				H/4				
O	O			4	O		O	
		O	O	3		O		O
	O		O	2	O			O
O	O			1		O	O	
1	2	3	4		1	2	3	4

39. Two choices of tie-up for pebble weave on the floor loom.

Floor Loom Weaving

Since neither of us had used the floor loom for our Bolivian-inspired weaving, we are indebted to some of our pupil-friends for the information in this section. Three projects were woven as combinations of pebble and plain weave, but in very different ways, and of three different fibers: a wool band to trim a dress (Figure 37), a silk blouse with an allover pattern in the front (Figure 38), and a cotton hanging with tucked bands beginning and ending at various levels.

Warping the Loom. The reed was not used for either the dress trim nor the hanging, which were both woven as warp-faced fabrics, but it was used for the blouse, for which the warps were spaced somewhat further apart. All three had warps in alternating order, with the same threading draft (Draft 9), except that for the blouse a third-color warp was used in two sections where the pattern colors overlapped in the design.

Since each yarn can be threaded in only one steel heddle on one of the four harnesses, the draft is somewhat different from the pebble drafts previously given. The tie-up takes care of the combinations from various harnesses, and the treadle numbers correspond to the heddle numbers of the draft as it was used for the backstrap. The tie-up is a matter of choice. Two of the weavers used tie-up A (Figure 39), with plain weave on treadles 1 and 4, while the third weaver used

tie-up B, with plain weave on treadles 1 and 2, for the hanging.

Some Details of the Methods Used. Because the three items woven differed so much from each other, each weaver faced some different considerations.

For the dress trimming, five yards of wool tapestry yarn were wound in one section of a sectional beam. There was enough length when woven to trim a matching bag. Because the fiber used was wool, it was possible to tack the band around the curve of the neck and then steam-shrink it in place.

Silk yarns were used for the blouse, one to a dent in the plain-weave sections at the sides, two to a dent for the two-color pebble, and three to a dent for the sections that were woven as 3-color nonreversible pebble (Band 15). As the garment was woven, it was shaped on the loom at the sides and at the neckline. The third-color warps were dropped at the shoulders by cutting them off about an inch from the fabric. Weaving was continued and the back was shaped in plain weave.

After learning how the Indians make the flap pocket on their chuspas, the third weaver designed a hanging with a number of similar flaps, but left them open at the sides. She also planned for fringes and some open spaces. She used carpet warp, inserting a heavy wire into the unknotted

38. Blouse (left) by Marie Nodland. In coral, with a pebble weave pattern in avocado and lime, this blouse was woven and shaped on the floor loom, using both the heddles and the reed.

40. (Above) A hanging, by Sue Baizerman combines sections of plain weave and of pebble weave, and is woven on the floor loom.

end loops, which she lashed on to the apron rod of her cloth beam (tie-up B). She temporarily rolled some of her fairly short warp on to the cloth beam a little, then threaded her heddles from her lease sticks. Dividing her warp into the band-sections of the design, she tied the warp on to the rod of the warp beam in sections, leaving ample length to release later, when she had woven any of the flaps in her design.

Her method follows in detail. She inserted flat shuttles as sticks for the picking cross, planning it so she consistently took warps from the far stick for the plain-weave sections. In the pick-up, she worked across the row with her hands until her fingers became full, then transferred the picked yarns to an extra shed stick (Figure 40). She continued in this manner, and when she had finished the row, she turned the stick on edge to insert the weft after some extensive beating. (It is often helpful to beat in sections with a bonelike tool, Bolivian-style. The pattern tends to elongate if the weft is not beaten enough, or if the warps are too close together. The closer the warps are together, the harder it is to lift the harnesses to make the shed, and the harder it is to do the beat-

ing. The type of yarn makes a big difference too.)

Her design combined pattern bands and plain-weave bands, sometimes joined, sometimes separate. With more selvedges than usual, she developed a method for them. She always left a weft loop at the edge of the pattern bands. Prior to inserting the next weft, she pulled the weft taut, holding the selvedge warps out a bit to the side as a control. For the wider sections it did not seem necessary to leave the weft loop. She developed a rhythm, keeping her sticks in the same positions, as she worked in the following sequence:

Picked Design Rows
1. Treadle 1, insert near stick; treadle 2, insert far stick.
2. Pick pattern from both sticks; pick plain weave sections only from *far* stick.

Tie-down Rows
1. Treadle 3 (or 4), insert near stick; treadle 1, insert far stick.
2. Take pattern from near, and plain weave from far stick.

Bag by Stana Coleman. This bag is made from the extra woven band material that was used to trim the dress in Chapter 5.

Chapter Six

Planning Your Own Projects

Some classes we taught inspired a small study group of weavers to learn more of the Bolivian techniques and to share ideas on how to make use of them in different ways. Many projects have been planned, and some have barely been begun. We are indebted to the members of this group for their contributions to this chapter. The projects suggested are only the beginning of what can be achieved.

Experimenting with Different Yarns. In using carpet warp for your sample bands, you have perhaps become more familiar with some of its virtues and possibilities. It can even be used for some larger projects, such as the contemporary hanging shown in the color gallery. The other cotton yarns are also worth trying, in different weights—crochet cotton, pearl cotton, and others. Jute can work out well for a project larger in scale and the weaving seems to proceed quickly.

As you improve in the techniques of avoiding friction, you can be successful with many more kinds of yarn, especially if you weave with the spacing and tension of a backstrap or inkle loom, or some other kind of a frame. Experiment with other yarns, selecting a scale and texture suited to your purpose. It is wise to try a very small sample band before winding a new warp for a large project. Some synthetics stick so fiercely that it is impossible to open a shed, even in a band only an inch wide, but a yarn as fragile as rayon chenille can be used if handled well.

Some of the blends are good. Cotton-rayon rug yarns such as Aunt Lydia's and Woolco are fine if spaced and under good tension. Cottolin, a combination of cotton and line , comes in a beautiful range of colors in a finer scale, and results in a product with a very good 'feel.' Nordica (linen and rayon) may be used as a complementary warp with wool yarns. Linen yarns form a good ground weave for supplementary wool yarns, or may be used as the finer light yarn with wool in intermesh or modified intermesh.

The wool yarns perhaps offer the largest field for experimentation. If you spin, try overtwisting some yarns like the Bolivians do. This makes the yarn so kinky that it almost appears unusable, but under tension it is easy to handle. Otherwise, there are many kinds of wool yarns that have been used successfully, such as rya yarns, hard-twist rug yarns, tapestry yarns, weaving wools, and many others. Since there are variations within each type, try them out with sample bands before you attempt a large project.

Silk has been used in thicker yarns and in very fine ones, with gold threads. On the other extreme, clothesline rope has been dyed for working on a very large scale. Use your imagination and experiment!

Sketching Designs. While there is no denying the charm of the numerous Bolivian motifs, it is also very fulfilling to create your own. The Bolivian weaver draws upon her physical and social environment to create animal, plant, and human motifs. She also makes use of traditional geometric designs. Over hundreds of years the Bolivians have developed designs that were functional for their uses. While their designs are not always directly usable for our projects, we can follow their

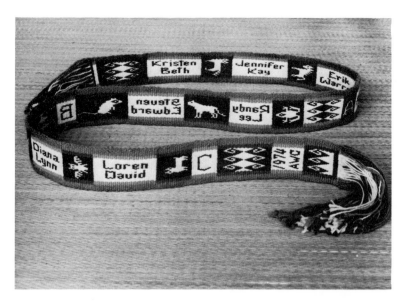

1. (Above) It's fun to create your own designs. It is perhaps easiest to do this with one-weft double cloth. Carpet warp, inkle loom.

2. (Right) Wall hanging by Helen van den Berg. The juggler at the circus is surrounded by many happy faces. Pebble weave, carpet warp, frame loom.

example and turn to our environment and culture for inspiration to create new motifs or to adapt some of theirs.

With this in mind, Adele created her "granny" belt, weaving in the names of each of her grandchildren and creating motifs appropriate to the special interests of each child (Figure 1). The wall hanging in Figure 2 was created around a circus theme. If you don't feel comfortable creating your own designs, you might enjoy making several variations of a Bolivian motif (Figure 3). Even a narrow four-bout band can be used in a variety of ways (Figure 4).

In the Appendix you will find empty grids for the different patterning versions. Some of these grids we designed especially for the weaves. They are available from a supplier listed in the Appendix, or they may be copied by a copy machine. If you prefer, there are some other alternatives, although in some cases, the proportions are not as good:

1. Pebble Weave: Type staggered pairs of O's with an elite typewriter, double-spaced, OR draw the O's on squared graph paper (6 sq./in.) with two O's/sq. in alternate rows, staggered. The O's may also be drawn on Engineer's rectangular grid, such as K+E 46-3290 (Kueffel and Esser).

2. Other Complementary-Warp Double-Faced Weaves (intermesh, 2/1 twill, etc.): Engineer's rectangular grid, K+E 46-2290 (larger scale). Engineer's rectangular grid, K+E 46-3010 (small scale).

3. Double Weave and Other Plain Weave Surfaces: Engineer's isometric grid, K+E 47-4030 (11 x 16½"), 46-4110 (8½ x 11").

Planning Color and Design. Visual interest in warp-faced fabrics is created by making maximum use of subtle or bold color schemes. Some areas are noted for using a series of related shades instead of a single light color in the pattern area. In other places the darks are varied, using contrasting colors instead of related shades. Sometimes both the lights and darks are varied. Beautiful color combinations occur in narrow border stripes. While the principle of interest through contrast is the keynote of the pattern bands, using closely related shades on either side of the pattern stripes brings unity and restfulness.

In a small traditional type of bag, both the lights and darks are varied in the center band. The variation in color is indicated by the warp order used (repeated in reverse order for the other half of the warp):

3 s-bouts medium blue
3 s-bouts fuchsia
3 d-bouts maroon & white
3 s-bouts fuchsia
3 s-bouts dark green
3 d-bouts fuchsia & medium yellow
3 s-bouts dark green
2 s-bouts natural white
3 d-bouts orange & medium green
3 s-bouts natural white
3 s-bouts maroon
2 s-bouts fuchsia
2 s-bouts medium blue
8 d-bouts dark green & medium yellow
2 d-bouts fuchsia & white

Most wider pieces combine solid plain weave areas with pattern stripes. Even very narrow pat-

3. (Left) Even dividers between motifs can be variations on a theme. These were mostly adapted from parts of the llama. Pebble weave, Troy one-ply weaving wool, inkle loom.

4. (Above) The same narrow pebble pattern was used in these three bands, with the opposite side showing in the center band. Cotton yarns, woven on finger tension, inkle, and backstrap loom.

tern stripes, like the 4-bout pebble pattern shown in Figure 4, can effectively be combined with plain or pattern areas to produce an attractive band.

In planning the solid and pattern areas, it is helpful to make a yarn winding (Figure 5). Experiment with different color combinations and varying widths of stripes as you proceed. To approximate the visual effect of the pattern area, you can crisscross the motif color over the background color.

Individuals vary in their approach to the overall plan of the design in a pattern stripe. Some weavers prefer to finalize the sequence of motifs before beginning to weave. Others prefer to make these decisions as the weaving progresses. In either case, it is important to consider how the individual motifs relate to each other and to the whole piece.

Options for the Edges. Among the options to consider before a weaving is begun is the treatment of its edges—the beginning edge, side edges, and final edge. Many factors enter into the choices.

A fringed end is the easiest for a beginner. Rag stripping or other fillers should be woven for several inches at the beginning end to save space for the fringe. The tail of the weft should be tucked into the second shed at the beginning end. The same finish may be done in reverse at the final end by inserting a long needle into the next-to-the-last row with the weft. Before beating down the final row of weft, thread the needle with the weft and pull it through the width of the band Open the shed that is opposite to the last row of

weft, adjust the weft snugly in place, and beat well. Insert some filler for the desired number of rows.

Depending on the intended use of the weaving, additional means may be needed to anchor the weft. If the piece must withstand wear, as in a belt, the ends may be overcast, hemstitched, or otherwise suitably finished. For a wall hanging the last shot may be tacked with glue.

Fringes are often finished as a series of small braids. The most frequently used kinds are the four-strand round braid, the three-strand "pigtail" braid, and the five-loop braid, described in Chapter 4. Flat braids may be tacked together and a tie run through the end loops across the width of the band.

The method for producing a four-selvedge piece is described in Chapter 5. Until one is more experienced, it might be advisable to plan on just three finished edges, since the fourth can be a real challenge. For a narrow finger-woven band, a finished end may be woven at the beginning by inserting a safety pin in the end loops. For a belt you may wish to insert a cord, suitable for later use as a tie-cord. Insert the cord in the end loops, alongside a doubled weft. Weave two plain-weave rows with the doubled weft, and then continue with the usual weft arrangement.

A buckle may also be installed at the beginning end of a belt, but it requires a bit of extra manipulation. Cut the warps at the knotted (left) end, and thread the warps through the buckle, lining them up in order on the cross bar. Tie the loose ends together and attach a hanger loop. Rearrange the warps near the buckle and insert lease sticks, in preparation for the heddles.

5. To visualize the interaction between colors, it is a good practice to make a yarn winding.

Another way to finish a belt is to enclose the ends with pieces of leather, which may be equipped with a fastening device. Also, the ends may be hemmed onto a pair of belt fasteners, such as a special two-piece buckle.

For a wall hanging you may wish to insert a suitable rod in the end loops. This rod may then be attached to a backstrap if it is long enough, or lashed to a longer rod if it is too short. It could also be lashed to the breast beam of a frame or floor loom.

Different types of side-edge treatments were introduced in Chapters 2 and 3. The type you choose for your project is somewhat limited by the patterning version you will be using. You may wish to refer back to the bands for which the different types were explained, as listed below:

Plain weave border—Band 1

Intermesh border—Band 6

Tubular double cloth border—Band 7

One-bout, chain-link selvedge, irregular warp order—Band 8

Four-bout, double chain-link, irregular warp order—Band 9

One-bout, chain-link selvedge, alternating warp order—Band 15

Warp Calculations. To weave a design of your own or a motif in a fabric or a photograph, you need to know how many warp ends the pattern requires. Remember that in a double-yarn bout (d-bout) there are two light and two dark warp ends. Each d-bout occupies two vertical lanes on the diagram. In examining a fabric, you can count

the light *or* dark warps, either in a horizontal stripe, or along a diagonal line, to find the number of ends. Divide this by two for the number of bouts. If you are going to weave a pebble design, try to find a light-edge pebble row (assuming a dark motif on a light background) and count the dark pebbles (OO's). Multiply by two for the number of bouts. A similar method can be used to determine the number of bouts for a pattern drawn on the pebble grid.

The yarn winding can be used as an approximate guide to determine the number of bouts needed for plain weave areas. To achieve the width of a given stripe, use slightly less than the number of ends on the winding, because it will spread out during the weaving.

It is difficult to give very reliable guidelines in calculating take-up during weaving, because of the difference in yarns. As you experiment with different yarns, if you make a record of the take-up in relationship to the unwoven length you will begin to become more accurate in your calculations. A good general rule to follow is to allow for 10–15% take-up.

Weaving for Special Occasions. One of the more delightful reasons for designing a fabric is to celebrate a special occasion. The project need not be complicated, but may be as simple as a card such as one created with golden rayon chenille yarn to celebrate a fiftieth wedding anniversary. Small hangings can serve many purposes, such as the logo and the bar mitzvah gift in Figure 6. Weddings have been a favorite inspiration for the creation of wall hangings, like the one in Figure 7. The wall hanging shown in Figure

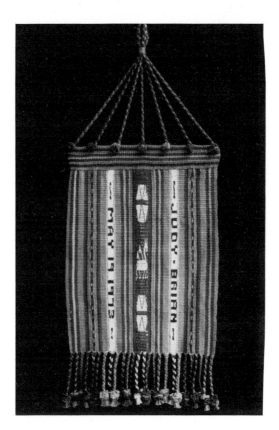

25, Chapter 5, was woven as a birth announcement for the arrival of Margie's first child.

Possible Uses of Bands. From students, books, and other sources, the following list was compiled to suggest some of the many ways that pattern bands may be used:

The Band Alone
belts, that tie, buckle or have ties
suspenders (pants, skirt)
neckties
hat-band, headband
shoestrings, boot-laces
straps for clogs, sandals
necklace, choker, bracelet
watchband
drawstrings (traditional)
small bags, pouches
napkin ring
curtain ties
upholstery webbing
luggage rack
camp stool
yardstick sheath
swinging holder (plant)
small hanging for wall or door
bell pull
bird warner at window
wind chimes
scissors cord
dog leash
gift ribbons
guitar straps
bag straps

pin cushion
case for glasses
small bags and cases
badges (ex. hostess)
backstrap for loom
holder for trays, magazines

Bands Sewn Together
vest or tunic
purse, bags
pillow or floor cushion
recorder case
wall hanging (may may also be unjoined, hanging in
    series)

Bands Sewn on Something
blouse, dress, skirt
vest, jacket, coat
poncho, sweater
cap, hat
jeans, slacks
placemat, table runner
upholstery trim
bedspread, quilt
small tablecloth
canvas log carrier
larger bag
length or width additions to clothing

Band Woven on to Something
flat edge-band, using warp-fringe for weft of band
    as on bottom of vest
tubular edge-bindings (weft spirals through edge)
    on bag, garment, hanging, etc.

Appendix

COMPLEMENTARY-WARP Weave Structures - Patterning Versions

		DESIGN CHARACTERISTICS					
The patterning versions are listed below, according to features of the _plain ground_	heddles control tie-downs	tie-downs are in: alternate rows	every* row	smooth natural horizontals	may have 2-span floats	diagonal lines are reversible	reversible 3-color version
3-span warp floats in alternate alignment							
Band 3: Modified Intermesh	–	–	yes*	yes	yes	yes	Band 20
Band 6: Intermesh	yes	yes	–	no	yes	no	–
3-span warp floats, alternating by pairs							
Band 1: Pebble (alternate warp order)	–	yes	–	yes	yes	yes	Band 17
Band 8: Pebble (irregular warp order)	yes	yes	–	no	yes	yes	–
Band 4: Stepped Diagonals	–	–	yes*	yes	no	yes	Band 19
2-span warp floats in diagonal alignment, 2/2							
(used for areas of patterning in Bands 1, 3, 8 and 17)	–	–	–	–	yes	yes	(Band 17)
2-span warp floats in diagonal alignment, 2/1							
Band 2: Complementary-Warp Uneven Twill	–	–	–	yes	yes	yes	Band 18
Plain weave in horizontal stripes							
Band 5: Complementary-Warp Floats on Plain Weave	–	–	–	yes	no	yes	–

* Background has tie-downs in odd rows; pattern has them in even rows.

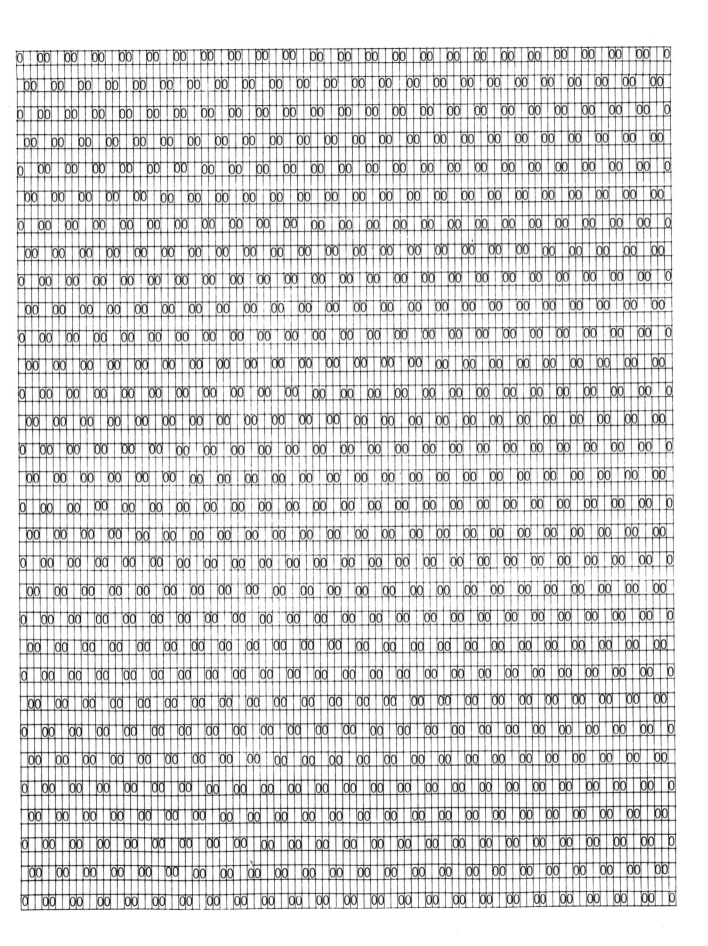

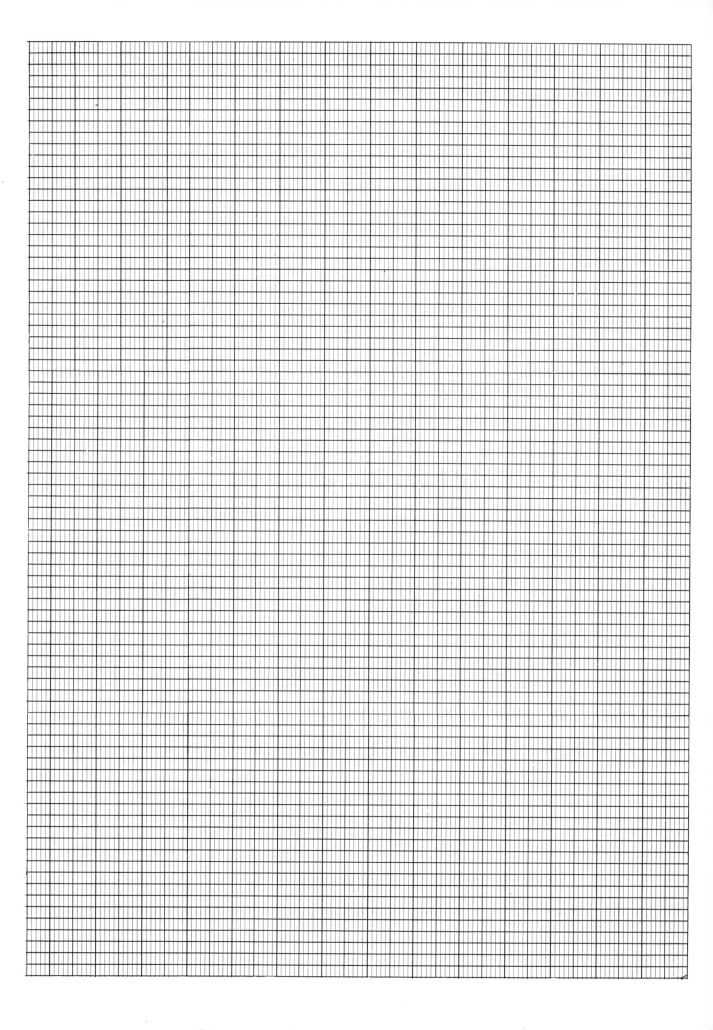

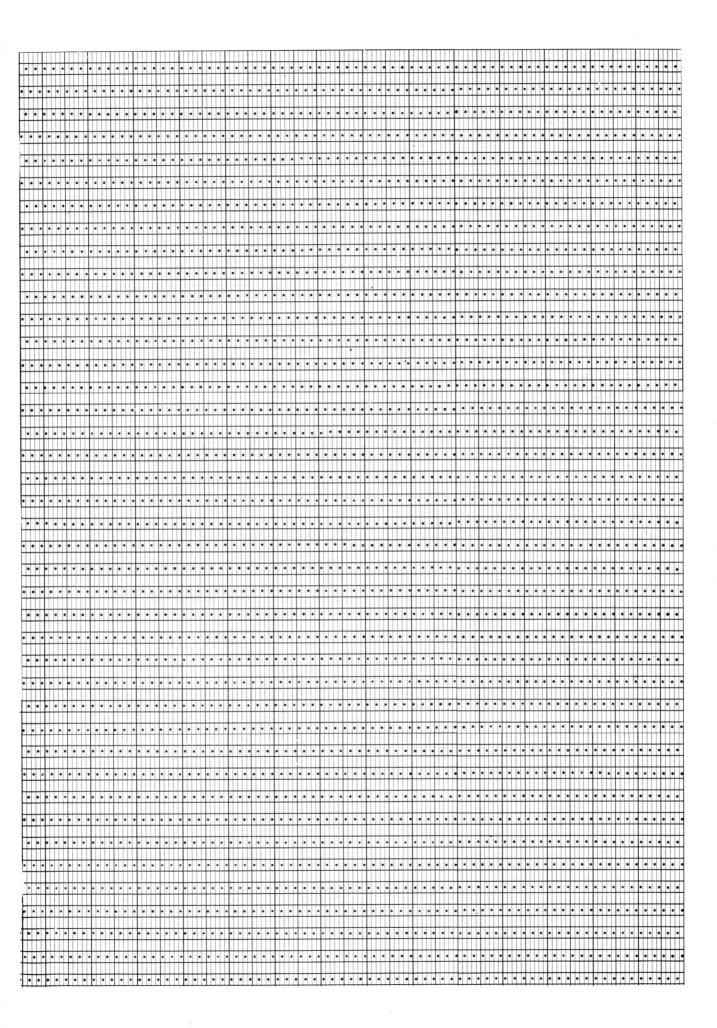

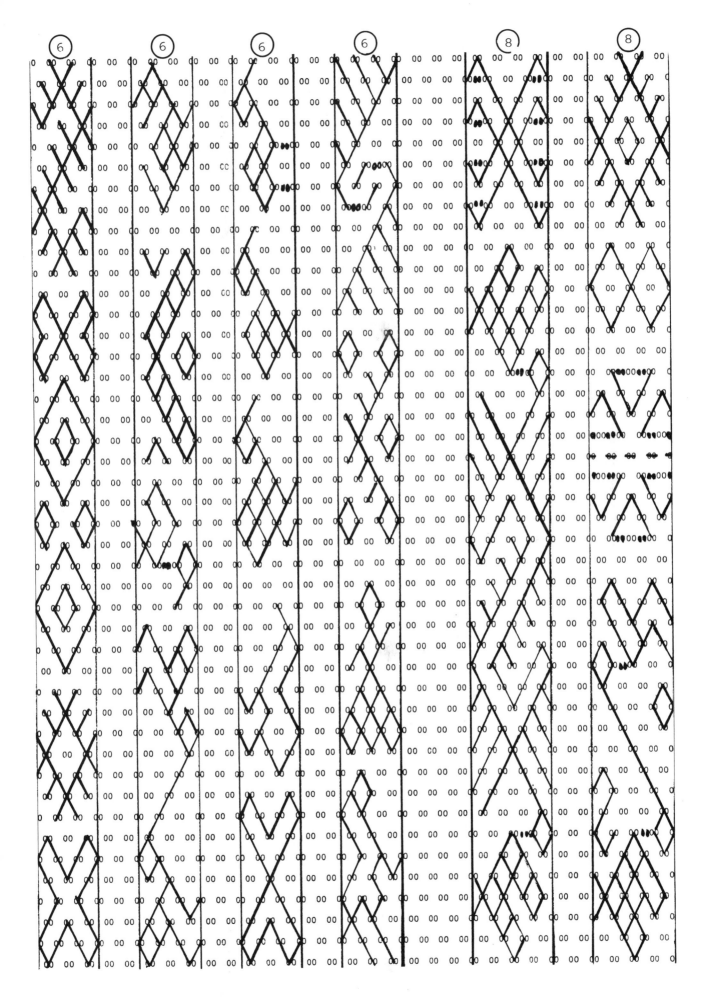

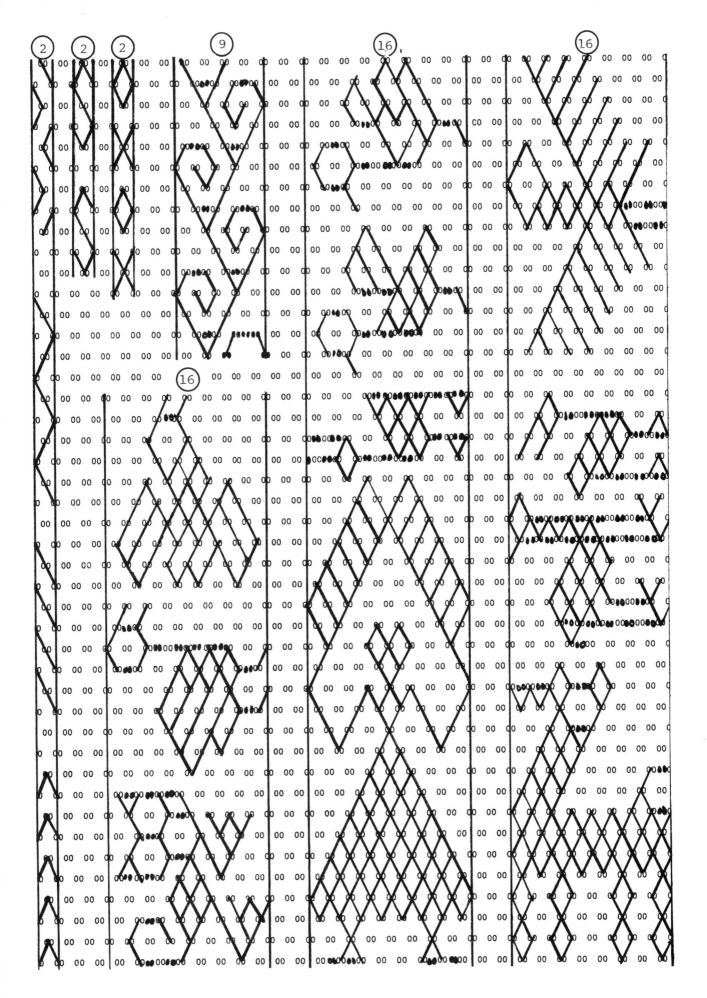

187

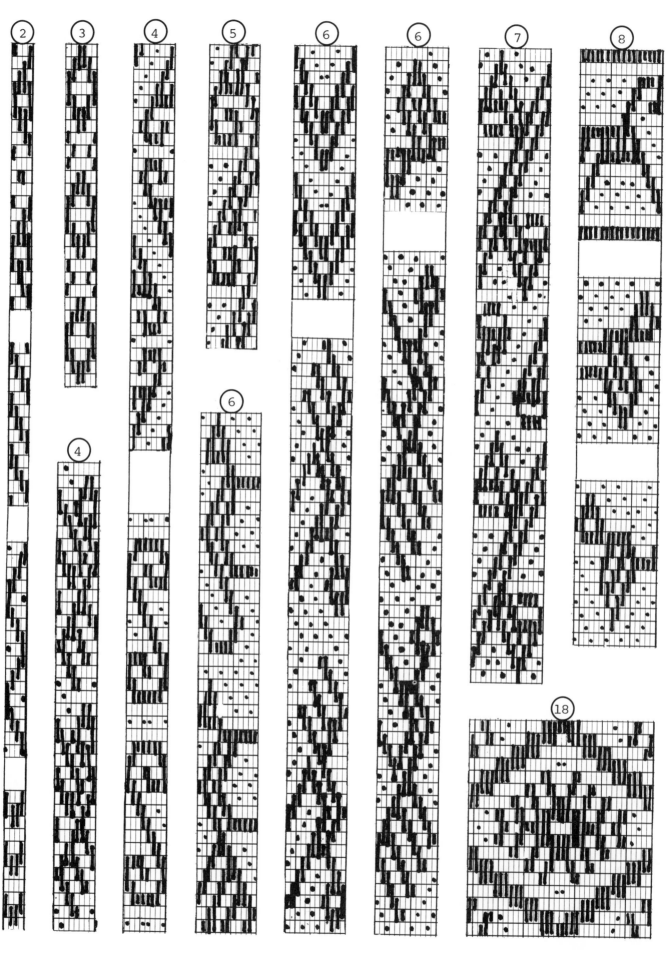

10

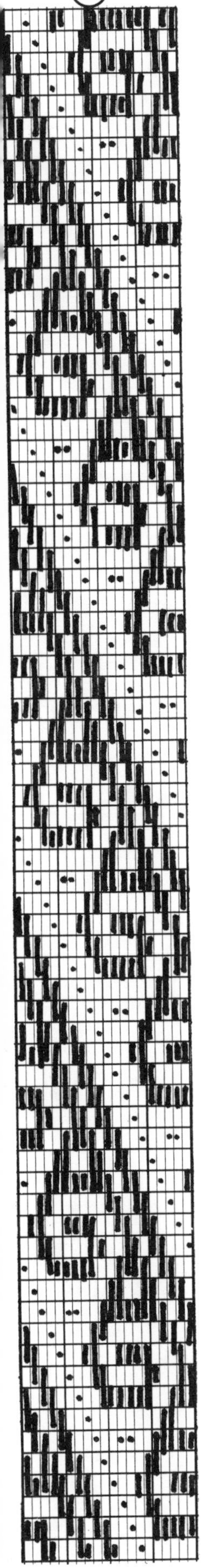

20

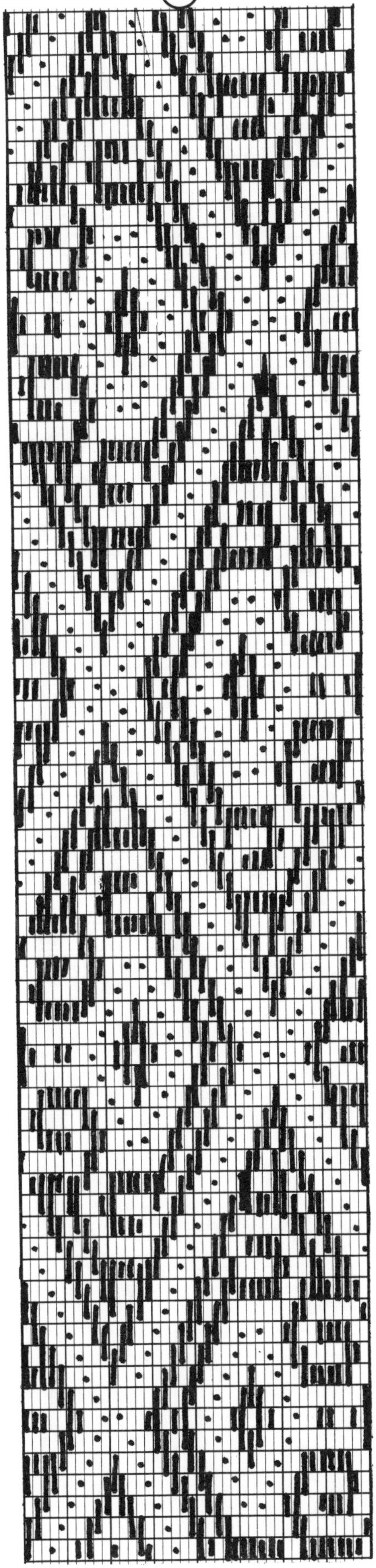

26

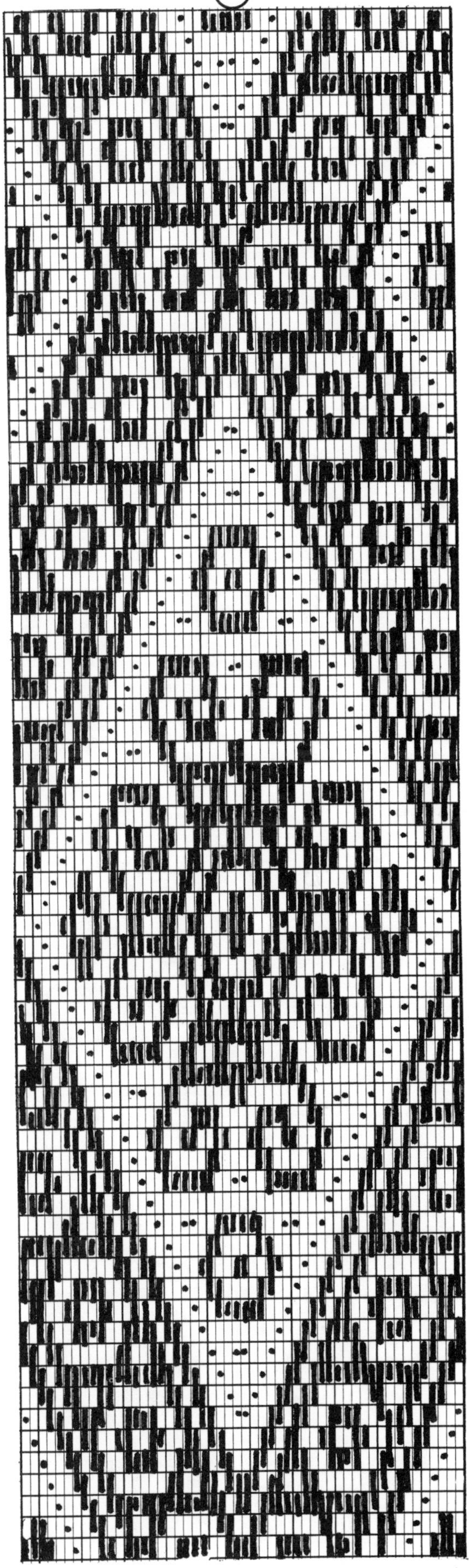

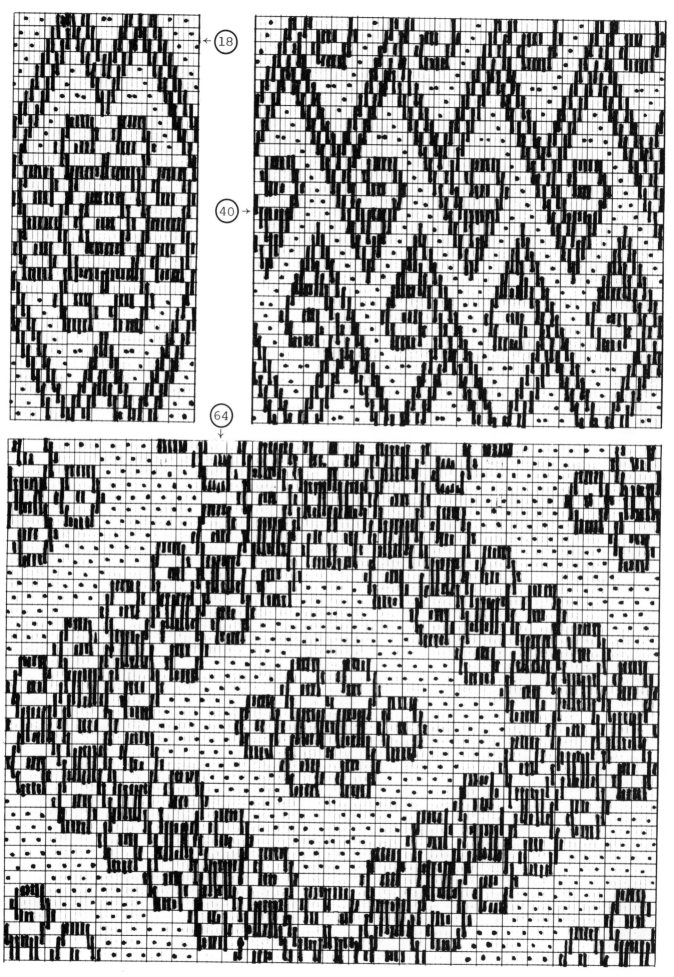

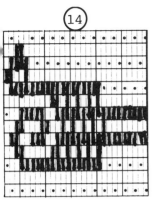

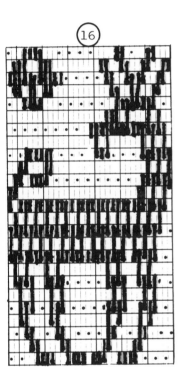

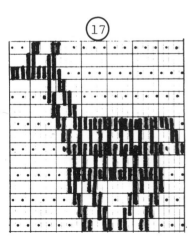

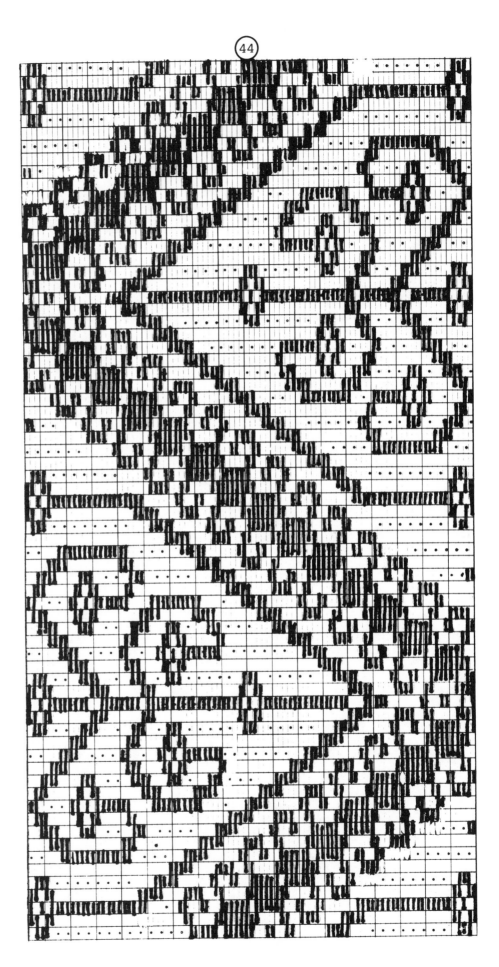

30

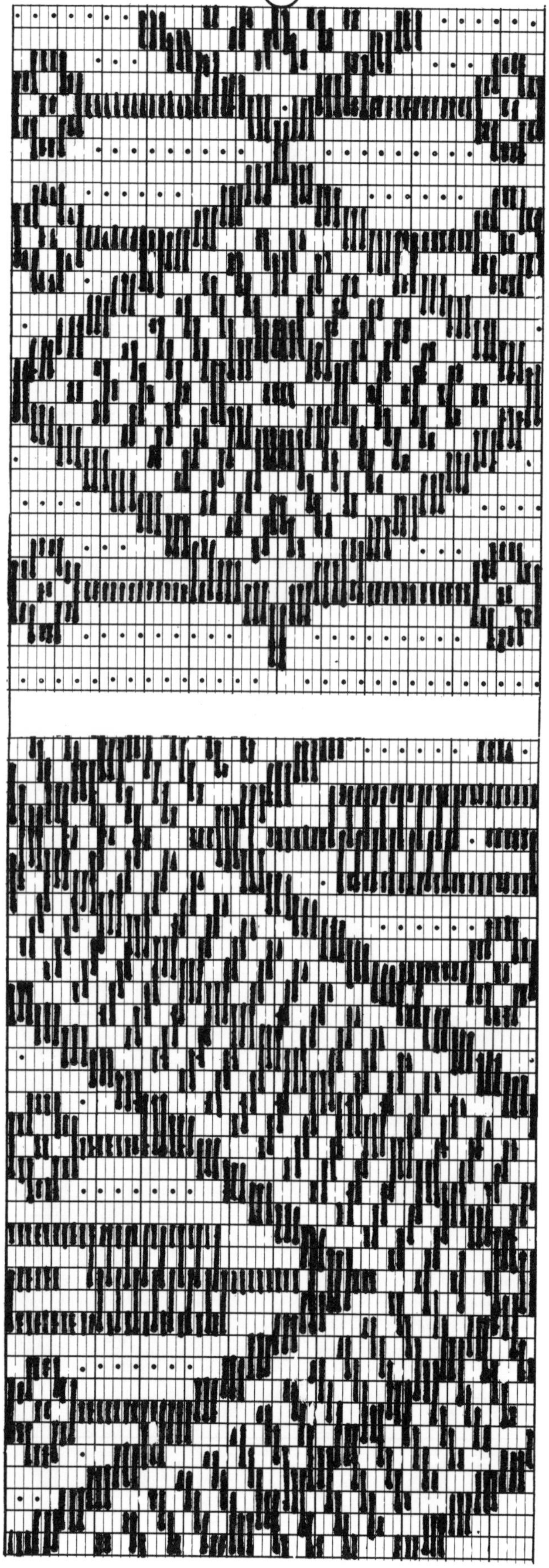

33

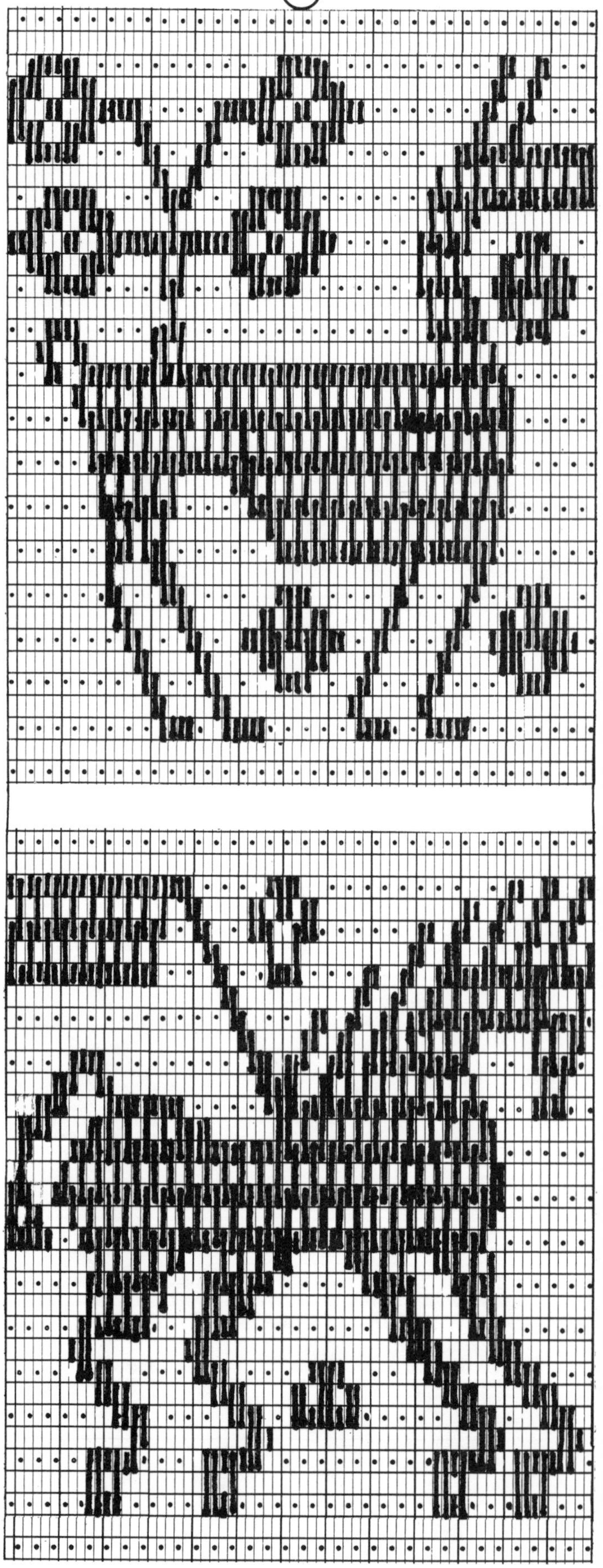

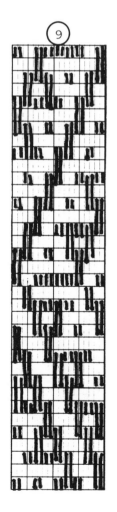

8

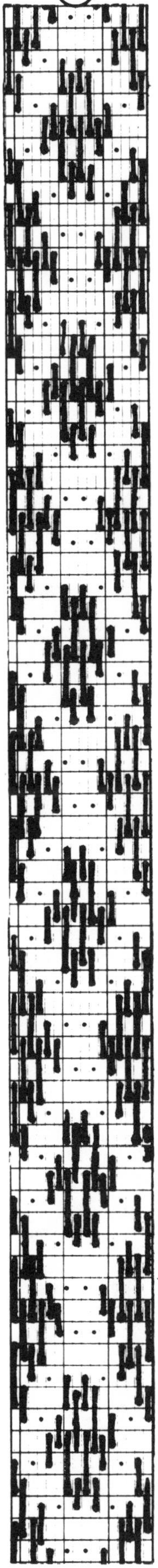

18

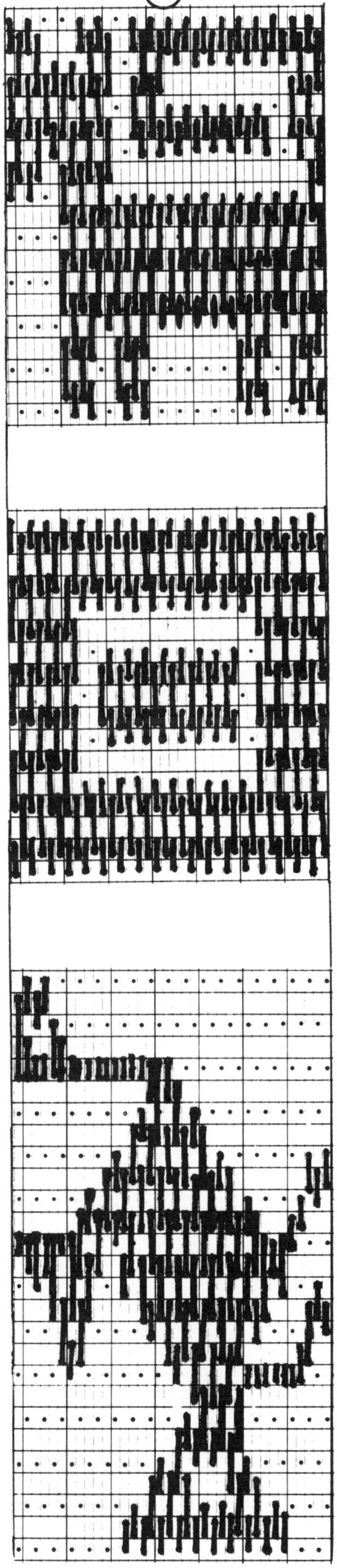

30

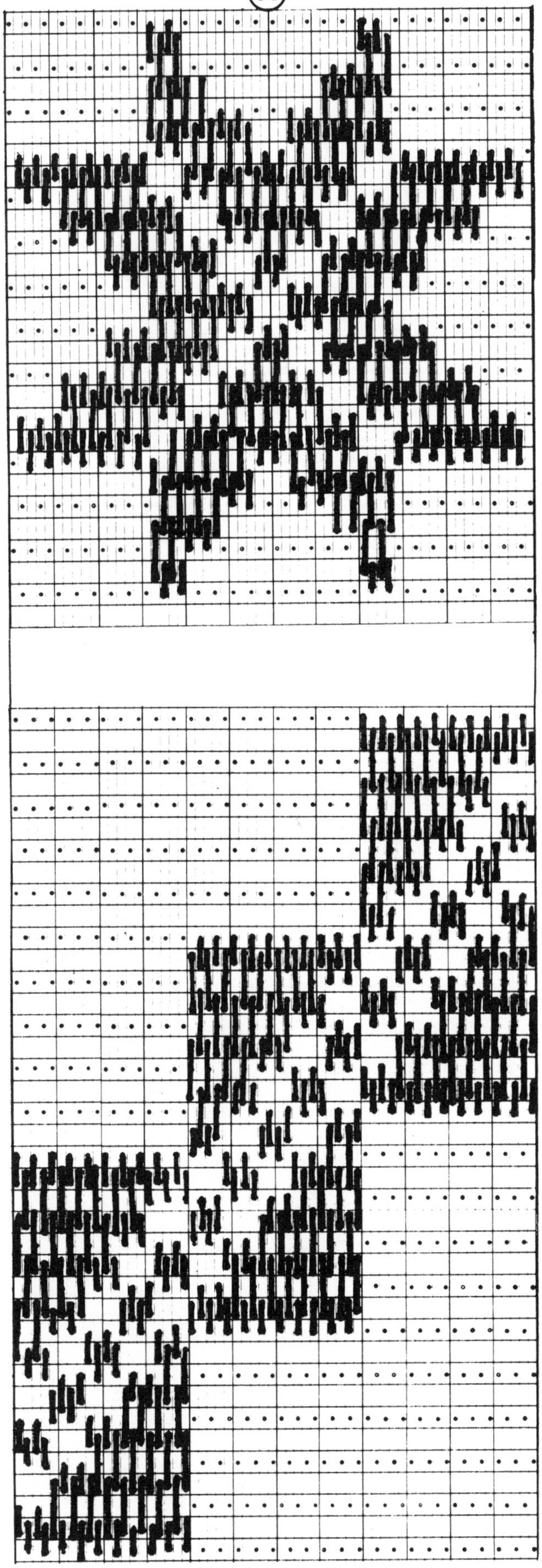

29

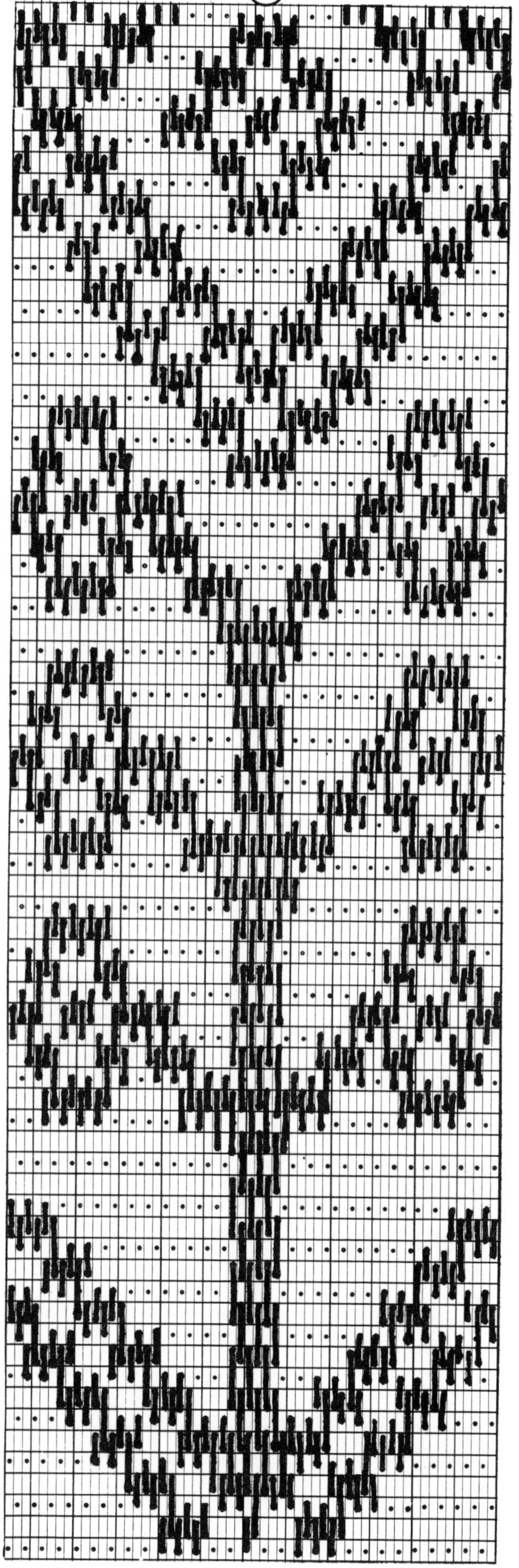

8

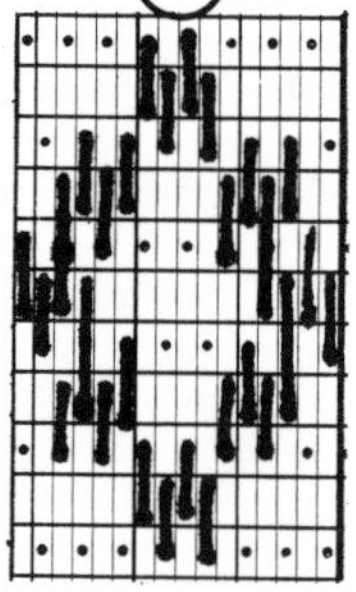

8

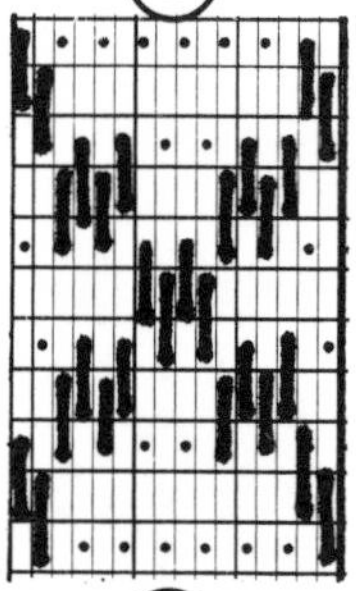

8

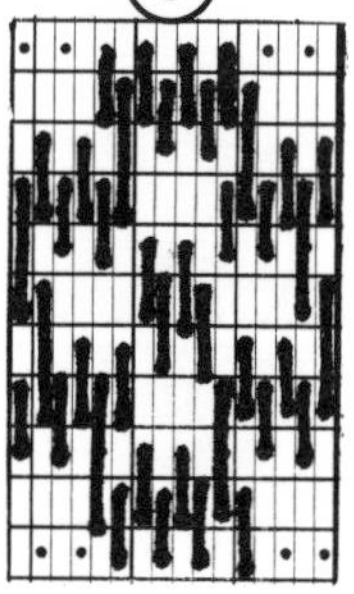

28

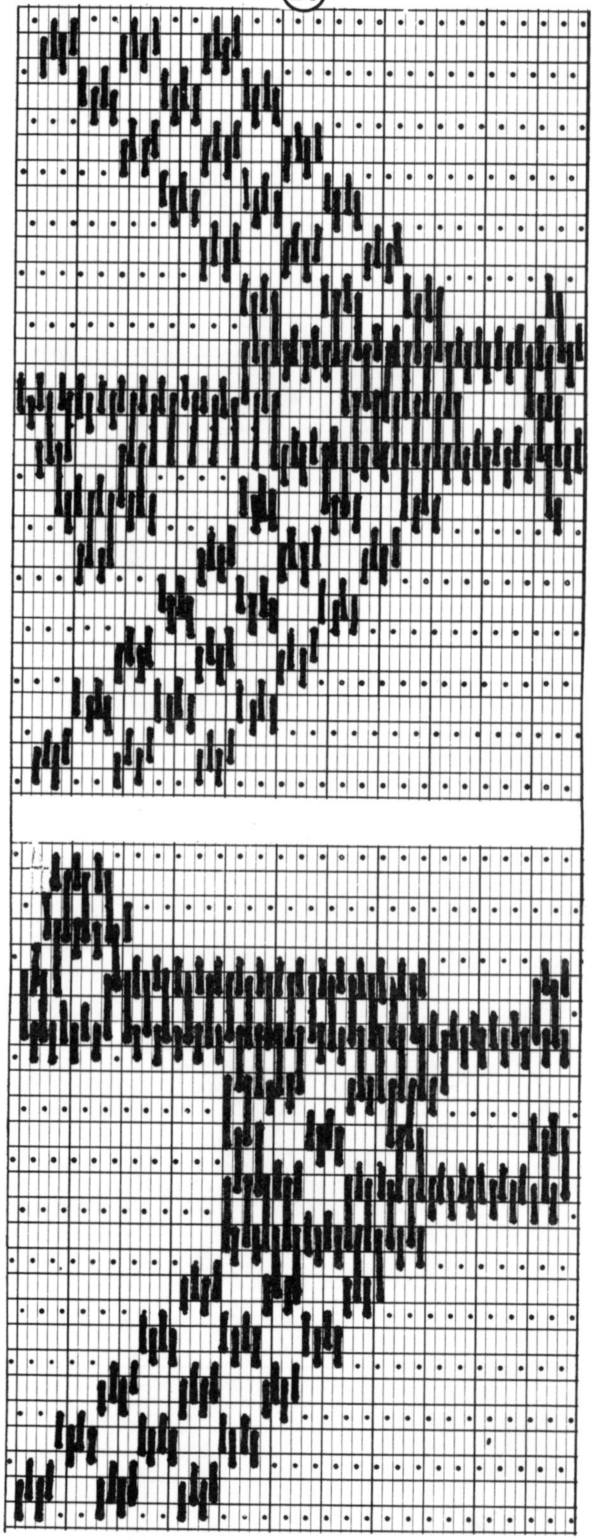

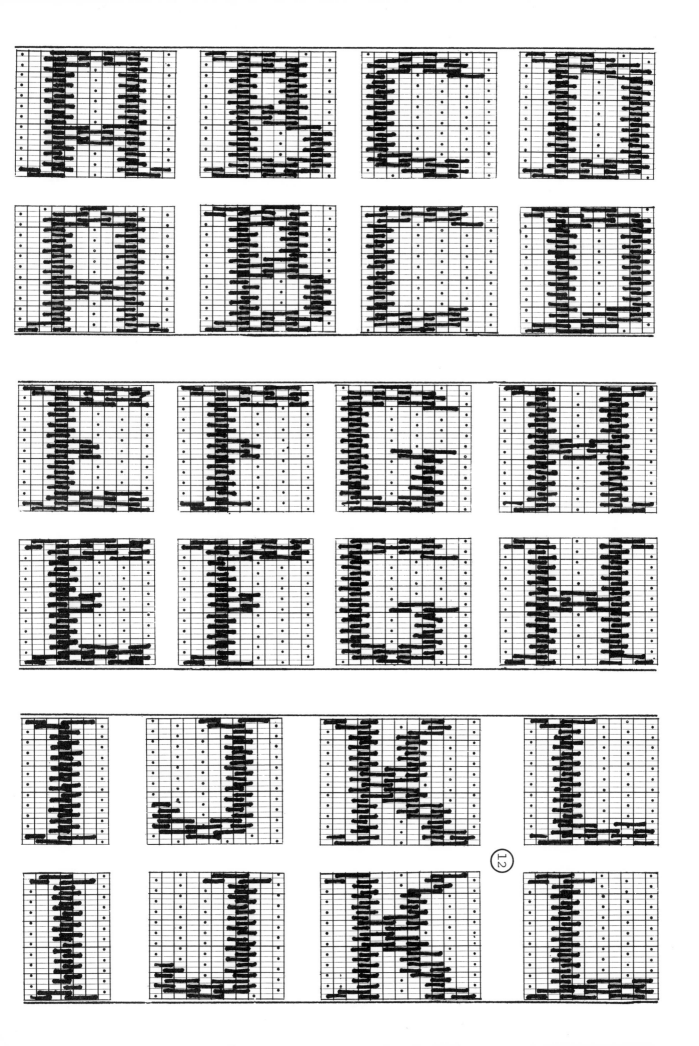

12

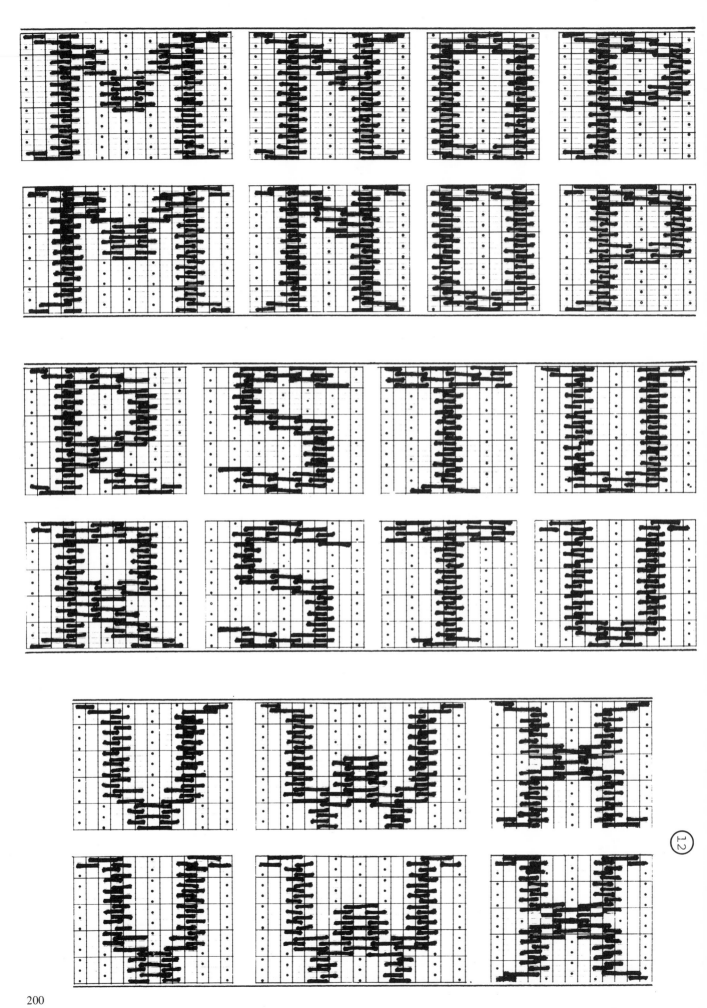

200

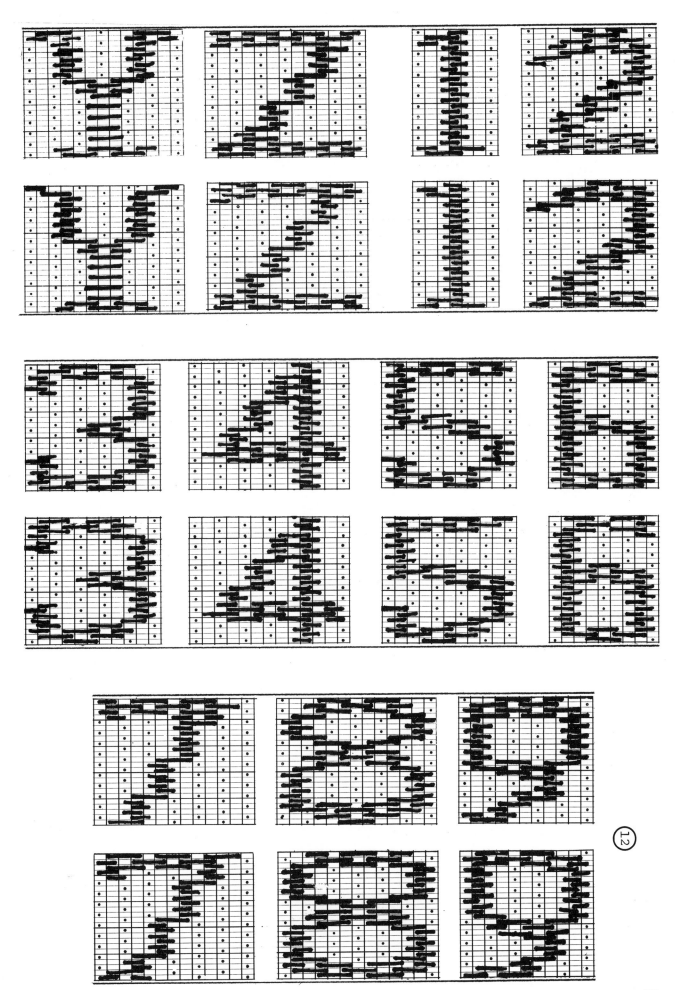

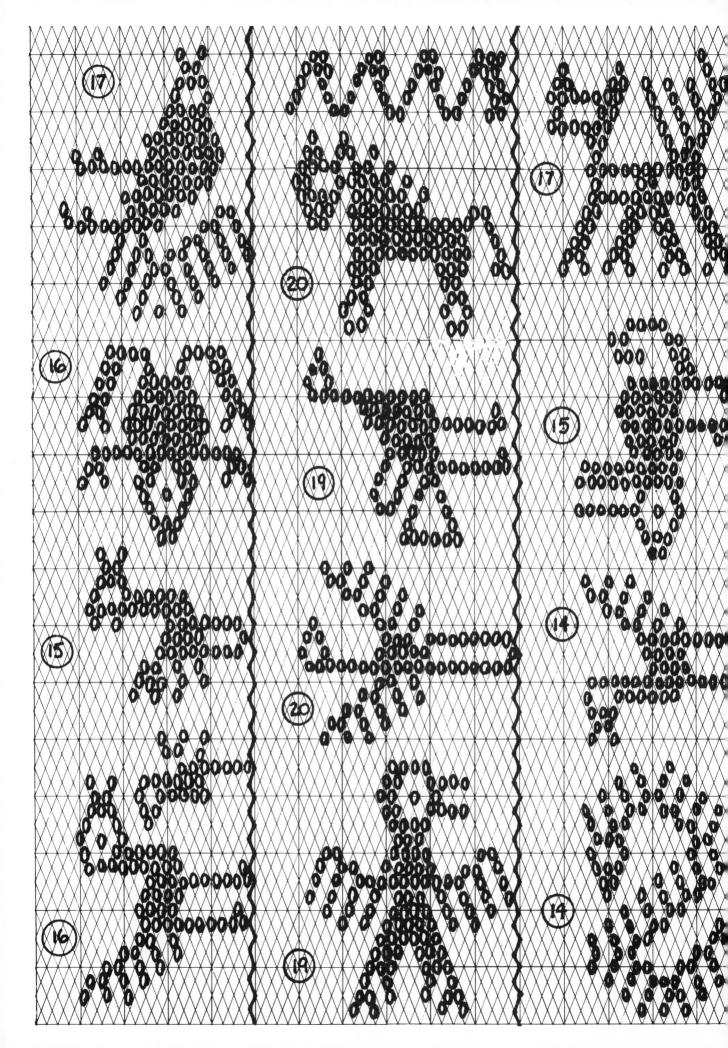

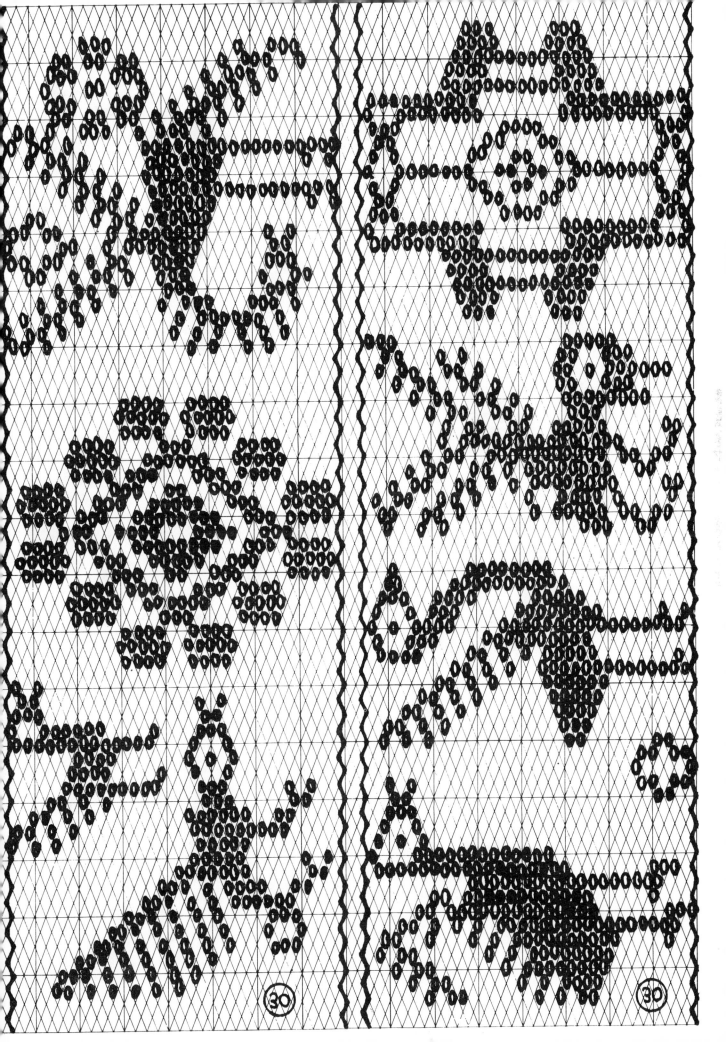

30 30

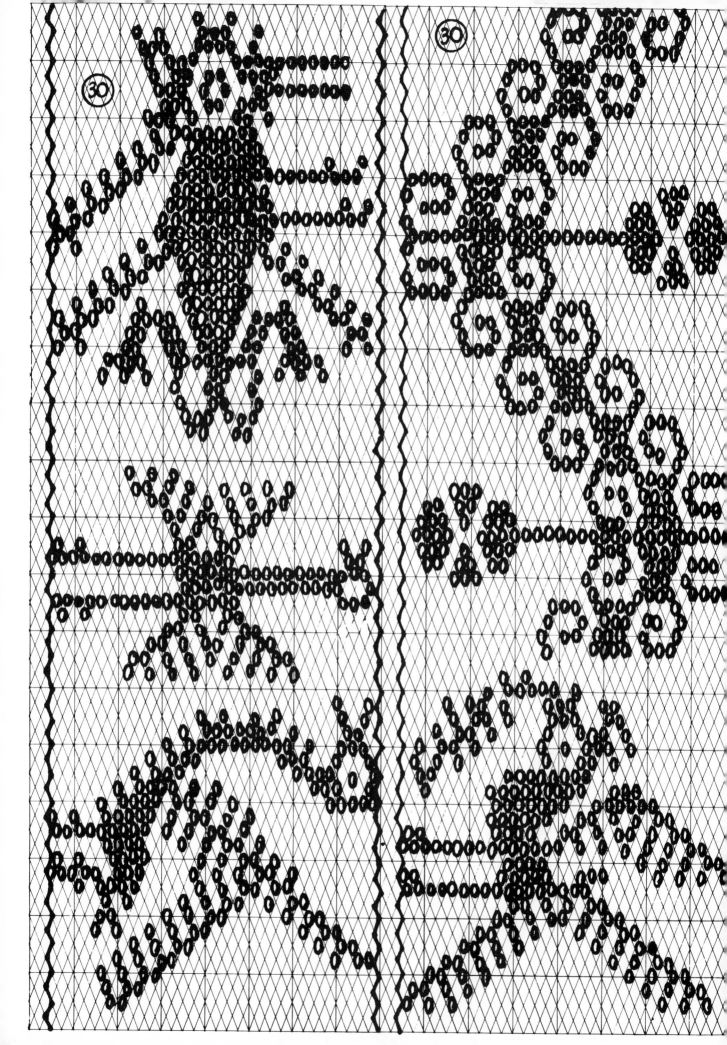

Glossary

Alpaca. The hair from an animal related to the llama.

Alternating warp order. The color sequence of the warp yarns is alternately light and dark: LDLD, etc. Also, the yarns are arranged alternately in the heddles, so on each heddle the yarns in the pattern band are monochrome.

Backstrap. A strap worn around the back of the weaver, usually at the hips, that is attached to the cloth beam.

Backstrap loom. A simple loom consisting of two parallel rods or beams between which the warp yarns are stretched. The far end is attached to a stationary object, and the near end is attached to the backstrap so tension may be maintained by the body of the weaver.

Back beam. The beam furthest from the weaver in a horizontal loom. *See* Warp beam.

Beams. Bars at each end of a loom between which the warp yarns are stretched. According to the type of loom, they may be: (a) top and bottom beams, or (b) back and front beams functioning as warp and cloth beams.

Beat. The movement of forcibly pressing the last-inserted row of weft into position before passing the weft in a newly-formed shed. The beating may be done with a strong finger in a narrow band, with the side of the hand, with the beveled edge of a sword or belt shuttle, or, in a wider piece, it may be done beside the shed rod

in narrow sections with the help of a llama bone or suitably pointed stick.

Binding weft. A weft that functions to bind (or tie-down) the warp floats.

Bottom beam. A beam at the bottom of the oblique loom, around which the yarn is passed during warping; later this may be replaced by a second or permanent bottom beam, to which the warps or heading cord are lashed. *See* Cloth beam.

Bout. One complete circuit of yarn around the warping posts (or beams) in a figure-8 pattern. The warp is counted in bouts. It may be wound in single yarns as s-bouts, with double yarns as d-bouts, or with triple yarns as t-bouts.

Braid. A narrow fabric band or cord.

Braiding. Process and the structure of oblique interlacing.

Cloth beam. The beam nearest the weaver where the weaving is begun, and on which the finished weaving may be wound as the weaving progresses. In the horizontal loom or the backstrap, this may be called the front beam; in the oblique loom, the bottom beam.

Complementary-warp pair. In this book, the term refers to two adjacent warp yarns—one light, one dark—that are treated as opposite partners in picking the pattern for a complementary-warp structure.

Complementary-warp structure. A compound fabric structure with at least

two sets of warps (interlacing with the weft) that are complementary to each other and co-equal in the fabric structure.

Compound weave. A fabric structure having more than two basic sets of elements (warp, weft) as compared with a simple weave having only two sets of elements (one set each of warp and weft elements).

Continuous warp (or circular warp). The warp is wound as a continuous circle with no end loops or selvedges. It is moved around as the weaving progresses, as with the standard inkle loom warp.

Design rows. The rows in which the pick-up causes the weft to separate the color layers and thereby determines the design, as contrasted with the tie-down rows, in the sequence for weaving certain complementary-warp structures (pebble, intermesh).

Diverted warp. A warp that follows a zigzag course. It is held in each successive position by moving to the opposite face of the fabric, and is kept there by the weft.

Double cloth. A compound fabric structure composed of two complete and correlative weave structures that are separate but interconnected.

Double-faced. Term to describe a compound weave whose two faces are structurally identical. Often the design is the same on both faces with the colors reversed.

Doup. A special string heddle loop that causes a crossing of warp yarns when it is lifted. It is made longer than the standard heddle loop so when it encircles a warp yarn it can pass under a neighboring yarn also.

Doup heddle. A special type of heddle with a series of doups; it causes some warps to cross under others as it is lifted.

Draft. A chart that shows the arrangement of yarns in a warp. It shows not only the warp order, but also the heddles by which the warps in a repeat unit may be lifted.

End. An individual warp yarn.

End selvedge. The finished edge woven in the end-loops of a warp wound as a figure-8.

Fell. The point at which the last row of weft meets the unwoven warp yarns.

Figure-8 warp. The warp is wound as a continuous yarn in a figure-8, without cut ends. Where the yarns criss-cross, the original warp cross is formed.

Finger-tension. In a narrow band, the warps can be held taut during weaving by tension of a finger in the shed.

Float. *See* Warp float.

Friction clamp. A clamp used to shorten either end of the warp on a backstrap loom. By this means it is possible to position the fell at a comfortable distance from the weaver; it also permits shortening the far end so the weaver may work in a relatively small area.

Front beam. The beam nearest the weaver on a horizontal or backstrap loom. *See* Cloth beam.

Heading. A few rows of plain weave at the beginning of the weaving.

Heading cord. A cord inserted in the end-loops of the warp, used for lashing on the permanent beam. Sometimes the weft is doubled for the first couple of rows for this purpose. On the end of a belt, a braided tie may be used.

Heddle. A means of lifting a selected group of warp yarns. It may be a multiloop heddle with a series of heddle loops either on a heddle stick or tied in a bunch, or it may be a shed loop, shed rod, or shed stick.

Heddle loop. A single loop which encircles one or two warps, and is usually part of a series of loops called a heddle.

Heddle stick or **rod.** The stick inserted within the heddle loops when the heddle is so wide that the loops cannot be merely bound together with a cord. It is most often used for the backstrap, horizontal and oblique looms, although occasionally for finger-tension bands.

Horizontal loom. A primitive loom simi-

lar to the backstrap loom that is anchored to stakes in the ground.

Inkle loom. A loom used for weaving narrow, beltlike warp-faced fabrics. It often consists of a frame with pegs and string heddles and the warp is usually wound as a continuous circle.

Inner weft. An extra weft used in an unusual example of reinforced double cloth that serves to lock the plain weave surfaces together. Also, a term used to describe the function of a row of weft that separates the warp color layers in a complementary-warp structure.

Intermesh. Term devised by the authors to identify a standard complementary-warp structure with 3-span warp floats in alternate alignment. There is a unit of four interlacing warps *abcd* (LDLD) in a regular four-row sequence. Odd-numbered rows one and three are heddle-controlled tie-down rows, which alternate regularly: in Row 1, warps *a* and *b* are lifted together for the width of the band; in Row 3, warps *c* and *d* are lifted together. The color layers are separated in the even-numbered Rows 2 and 4, the design rows. There these L and D warps act as opposite partners, with only one of *a* or *b* lifted, and one of *c* or *d*. Two span floats occur at points of color change. Where the change is in a horizontal line, there is an intermeshed effect; where it is on the diagonal, a "feathering" occurs on one side or the other of the fabric.

Irregular warp order. The color sequence of the warp yarns is irregular (i.e. they are not alternately light and dark). Because these yarns are taken alternately for each heddle, the yarns in each heddle are not monochromatic as for the alternating warp order, but relate to a specific type of pattern weave, such as pebble weave or supplementary-warp weave.

Lease. A crossing of the warps formed while warping that keeps the individual warp ends in proper order. Also called original warp cross.

Lease sticks. Sticks placed on either side of the lease and tied together to secure the lease. They may also be used to secure other warp crosses.

Loom. Any device used for weaving that performs the minimum function of holding the warp yarns taut and in their proper positions.

Modified intermesh. Term devised by the authors to identify a Bolivian type of opposites patterning, which usually combines complementary-warp even twill with areas of an intermesh variation in a complementary-warp structure. It is a 2-heddle, hand-picked patterning version in which the L and D warps are consistently treated as opposite partners in every row for the entire width of the band. In

the areas of the intermesh variation, the tie-downs are used in the odd-numbered rows for the light background, and in the even-numbered rows for the dark pattern areas. This results in neat straight lines at the horizontal color changes. Sometimes most or all of the patterning may be composed of complementary-warp even twill and other variations, such as interlocking scrolls. Traditionally, a thin white cotton yarn is used for the light warp.

Oblique loom. A primitive loom similar to the backstrap loom, in which the beams are lashed to long poles that lean against a wall, doorway or roof.

Opposites patterning. The type of patterning that results when light and dark warps are woven on opposites, in a complementary-warp structure. The design is the same on both sides of the fabric, but the colors are reversed. (Term could also be used for complementary-weft patterns.)

Pattern diagram. A motif or pattern drawn on a pattern grid.

Pattern grid. A special grid for recording motifs or patterns.

Patterning version. A variation of a complementary-warp structure in which the style of the design affects the basic structure.

Pebble row. Term adopted to refer to the tie-down row in pebble weave, where it is used regularly in odd-numbered rows across the width of the pattern band. The rows are alternately light-edge or dark-edge.

Pebble weave. This term was adopted by the authors to identify a complementary-warp patterning version. In its "pure" form, 3-span warp floats alternate in pairs, with a *pebbled* effect in the regularly alternating tie-down rows (the odd-numbered rows). In this book, these are called pebble rows. Patterning is determined by the warps picked up in the design rows (even-numbered) where the weft separates the color layers. The lines of color change may be horizontal, but most are on diagonal lines with 2-span floats. In this book, the term pebble weave is expanded to include all the opposites patterning based on the regular system of pebble tie-downs, including all the resulting combinations with twill in varying proportions. Designs on both sides appear the same with the colors reversed.

Pick-up. Use of the fingers or a pick-up stick to select warps for a pattern from more than one heddle or from only part of a heddle, before the weft is shot.

Pick-up stick. A small stick used to aid in picking up warp yarns in pattern weaving.

Plain weave. The simplest possible interlacing of warp and weft in unvarying alternation, over and under. It may be balanced, warp-faced or weft-faced. In most Bolivian hand-woven textiles, the plain weave is warp-faced.

Re-plying. Twisting together two or more plied yarns.

Ribete. A narrow edging used for decoration and to prevent fraying.

Secondary weft. A weft used to aid in separating the color-layers of warp in three-color pattern weaves. It is also used for one surface of a warp-faced double cloth band when it is juxtaposed with plain weave in a larger piece.

Selvedge. The edge of the fabric that is locked in place by the continuity of warp and weft, thereby preventing it from raveling. Although customarily at the sides of the fabric, there may also be end-selvedges in fabrics woven on a simple loom with uncut warps. *See* End-selvedge.

Shed. A temporary horizontal v-shaped opening between two planes of yarns, formed by raising a group of the warps, either by raising up a heddle, or by the hand-controlled pick-up of warps. *Also see* Shed rod.

Shed clamp. A device made of two short flat sticks held firmly together. It is used in place of a shed loop, having the advantage of keeping the warps in order and spread out.

Shed loop. A heddle in which all the warps for that heddle are enclosed in a single loop.

Shed rod. A rod placed behind the warp cross to hold up certain warps, usually the alternate warp yarns. When the original warp cross is used, as in plain weave, it controls the natural shed, while the heddle controls the countershed.

Shed stick. A stick used to temporarily hold open a shed. Also, in this book, a flat stick used in place of a shed loop. On the inkle loom, it is behind the inkle heddles and divides the open warps.

Shephed's check. A tiny check in plain weave, woven by alternating 2 dark and 2 light yarns both in the warp and in the weft.

Shot. One passage of weft through the shed.

Shuttle. A device to hold the weft and carry it through the shed.

Simple weave. An interlacing with only two sets of elements, one set of warp and one set of weft.

Stepped diagonals. Term devised for a complementary-warp patterning version with 3-span warp floats that alternate in pairs. In contrast to pebble weave, these 3-span warp floats in pairs are retained along the diagonal lines of color change, providing the characteristic "stepped diagonal" effect, instead of smooth twill lines. Consequently, the tie-downs do *not* occur regularly in alternate rows for the width of the band as they do in pebble weave. The floats are sometimes 5-span, but never 2-span.

Structure weft. The weft used for the ground weave in a supplementary-weft structure.

Supplementary warp. The extra warp used for adding supplementary pattern to a ground weave in a compound structure.

Supplementary-warp structure. A compound weave structure with supplementary warps adding pattern to a ground weave.

Supplementary weft. The extra weft used for adding supplementary pattern to a ground weave in a compound structure.

Sword. A stick used in weaving to separate layers of warp yarns, and to press the weft into place. Usually it is flat with a beveled edge, and is turned on its edge to open and widen a shed.

Take-up. The contraction of the length of the yarns caused by the interlacing of warp and weft. It is more evident after the warp tension is released.

Tension. Tightness or looseness of warp yarns.

Tie-down. The point where the weft binds the warp float. Also, the row in which the binding points occur.

Top beam. Beam at the top of an oblique loom. *See* Warp beam.

Two-faced. Term to describe a compound weave whose two faces are structurally dissimilar.

Vicuña. The fine soft hair of a South American wild cameloid, now almost extinct.

Warp. The yarns stretched lengthwise (usually between beams), and across which the weft is woven. Also, the same yarns in the finished fabric.

Warp beam. The beam at the far end (or upper end) of a loom, on which warp is wound or around which the warps turn.

Warp cross. *See* Lease. (Also, crosses formed by rearranging the warp order.)

Warp end. *See* End.

Warp-faced. Description of a fabric in which the warps are so closely spaced that the weft does not show.

Warp float. Any portion of a warp yarn that extends unbound over two or more shots of weft on either face of the fabric.

Warping posts. Devices that can be used as a means for winding the warp. Some are in the form of clamps.

Weave. A particular pattern or order of interlacement for warp and weft yarns.

Web. The woven part of the warp.

Weft. The crosswise yarns of a fabric that interlace the warp yarns.

Suppliers List

Beginnings,
3449 Mission Avenue,
Carmichael, California 95608
Hansen inkle loom with 8" pegs

Bergå-Ullman, Inc.,
P.O. Box 918,
North Adams, Massachusetts 01247
Bergå tapestry yarn - sample card $1

Earthworks Yarn,
407 Cedar Avenue,
Minneapolis, Minnesota 55404
*Leclerc Cendrel inkle loom,
cottolin yarn, large wooden tapestry
bobbin to use like a bone beater ($3)*

HGA Slide Library,
Handweavers Guild of America, Inc.,
998 Farmington Avenue,
West Hartford, Connecticut 06107
HGA Slide Kit A-4, Modern Textiles
of Bolivia and Peru, *rental fee $16,
165 slides (Ann Houston 99 slides,
Cason & Cahlander 66 slides) & commentary*

HGA Textile Kit, Bolivian Pattern Bands,
*woven examples of every sample band in
Chapter 3, to supplement the book.*

Hardware store and lumber yard
*dowels, screen molding, materials for
inkle & frame looms in Appendix A*

Minnesota Blue Printing,
2121 N. West River Road,
Minneapolis, Minnesota 55411

*Keuffel & Esser graph sheets
(numbers listed in chapter 6)*

Oriental Rug Company,
214 S. Central, Lima,
Ohio 45802
8/4 boilproof cotton carpet warp

Schacht Spindle Company,
1708 Walnut Street,
Boulder, Colorado 80302
inkle loom, belt shuttles

Someplace,
2990 Adeline Street,
Berkeley, California 94703
*large wooden tapestry bobbin
to use like a bone beater ($3)*

Spin It - Weave It Studio,
840 Leland Place,
El Cajon, California 92020
Gillan belt shuttles, belt clamp

Threadbenders,
2260 Como Avenue,
St. Paul, Minnesota 55108
*Kircher warping clamps, Kircher
frame looms, Schacht inkle looms*

Woolworth's or other variety store
*crochet cotton, cotton-rayon rug yarn,
18" shoestrings (Chino, taslanized nylon)*

Yarnery,
1648 Grand Avenue,
St. Paul, Minnesota 55105
*special pattern grid paper,
Beka frame looms, cottolin,*

Bibliography

Atwater, Mary Meigs. *Byways in Handweaving.* New York: Macmillan Co., 1954.

Bird, Junius B. "Handspun Yarn Production Rates in the Cusco Region of Peru." *Washington, D.C. Textile Museum Journal,* December 1968, pp. 9–16.

Birrell, Verla. *The Textile Arts.* New York: Harper & Row, 1959; Schocken Books, 1973.

Bolivia, Ministry of Education and Culture. "Trajes Regionales del Departamento de La Paz," in *Archivos del Folklore Boliviano, No. 2.* La Paz, Bolivia: Los Talleres de Empresa Editora "Novedades," 1966, pp. 51–97.

Burgos, Fausto. "Incan Weavings: I. The Incan Loom." *Bulletin of the Pan American Union* 61:353–356. United States Government Printing Office, April 1927.

Carter, William. *Bolivia: A Profile.* New York: Praeger Publishers, 1971.

Cason, Marjorie and Cahlander, Adele. "Bolivian Highland Weaving." *Shuttle, Spindle & Dyepot,* I. Spring 1975; II. Summer 1975.

Club de Escritores en Quechua. *Diccionario Trilingüe: Quechua - Castellano - Ingles.* vol. 1. Cochabamba, Bolivia: Imprenta Visión 1972.

Costas Arguedas, José Felipe. *Diccionario del Folklore Boliviano.* vol. 1–2. Sucre, Bolivia: Universidad Mayor de San Francisco Xavier de Chuquisaca, 1961.

Drum, Jim. "Andean Weaving Draws on the Past." *El Palacio.* Santa Fe, N.M.: Museum of New Mexico, vol. 81, no. 4, Winter 1975, pp. 35–45.

Emery, Irene. *The Primary Structures of Fabrics: An Illustrated Classification.* Washington, D.C.: The Textile Museum, 1966.

Fisher, Nora. *1500 Years of Andean Weaving.* Santa Fe, N.M.: Museum of New Mexico and the International Folk Art Foundation, 1972.

Girault, Louis. *Textiles Boliviens: Région de Charazani.* Catalogues du Musée de l'Homme, series H: Amérique IV. Paris: Musée National d'Histoire Naturelle, 1969.

Goodell, Grace. "A Study of Andean Spinning in the Cusco Region." *Washington D.C. Textile Museum Journal,* December 1968, pp. 2–8.

Harcourt, Raoul d'. "Note Technologique sur des Tissus Indiens Modernes de Bolivie." *Journal de la Société des Américanistes* 59:171–175, Paris: 1970. (ed. Louis Girault.)

———. *Textiles of Ancient Peru and Their Techniques.* Edited by Grace G. Denny and Carolyn M. Osborne. Translated by Sadie Brown. Seattle, Wash.: The University of Washington Press, 1962; paperback, 1974.

Held, Shirley E. *Weaving: A Handbook for Fiber Craftsmen.* New York: Holt, Rinehart and Winston, 1973.

Holland, Nina. *Inkle Loom Weaving.* New York: Watson-Guptill Publications, 1973.

La Barre, Weston. "The Aymara Indians of the Lake Titicaca Plateau, Bolivia." *American Anthropologist, Memoir 68.* Menasha, Wisc.: American Anthropological Assn., 1948.

Leonard, Olen. *Bolivia.* Washington, D.C.: Washington Scarecrow Press, 1952.

Lester, Kip, and McKeel, Jane. *Discover Bolivia: The First English Guidebook of Bolivia.* La Paz, Bolivia: Los Amigos del Libro, 1972.

Looser, Gualterio. "Araucanian Textiles." *Bulletin of the Pan American Union.* Vol. 61. U.S. Government Printing Office, April 1927.

Luquet, G.-H. "Decor de Ceintures Boliviennes." *IPEK.* 1930:93–108. Berlin: Klinkhardt & Biermann Verlag, 1930.

Marden, Luis, and Schulke, Flip. "Titicaca, Abode of the Sun." *National Geographic,* February 1971, pp. 272–294.

McIntyre, Loren. "Flamboyant is the Word for Bolivia." *National Geographic,* February 1966, pp. 153–195.

_____. "Lost Empire of the Incas." *National Geographic,* December 1973, pp. 729–786.

Mead, Charles W. *Peruvian Art.* Guide Leaflet #6, American Museum of Natural History, 1917.

Meisch, Lynn. *A Traveler's Guide to El Dorado and the Inca Empire.* New York: Simon and Schuster, forthcoming, January 1977.

Mullens, Barbara. *Recetas de Tintes Naturales.* Lima, Peru: Instituto Centro de Arte, 1973.

Osborne, Harold. *Indians of the Andes: Aymaras and Quechuas.* Cambridge, Mass., Harvard University Press, 1952.

Rowe, Ann Pollard. "Weaving Processes in the Cusco Area of Peru." *Washington, D.C. Textile Museum Journal,* vol. IV, no. 2, 1975, pp. 30–46.

Smets, A. Dorsinfang. "Sacs a Coca du Chile." *Bulletin de Musée Royaux d'Art et Histoire.* 1951:101–105.

Stevenson, I. Neil. *Andean Village Technology.* Oxford, England: Pitt Rivers Museum and Department of Ethnology and Prehistory, Oxford University, 1974.

Steward, Julian H., ed. "The Andean Civilizations," in *Handbook of South American Indians.* vol. 2. New York: Cooper Square Publications, 1963.

Tacker, Harold and Sylvia. *Band Weaving: Techniques, Looms, and Uses for Woven Bands.* New York: Van Nostrand Reinhold, 1974.

Tidball, Harriet. *The Double Weave: Plain and Patterned.* Shuttle Craft Guild Monograph One. Santa Ana, Cal.: HTH Publishers, 1960.

_____. *Peru: Textiles Unlimited.* Parts I and II, Shuttle Craft Guild Monographs #25 and #26. Santa Ana, Cal.: HTH Publishers, 1969.

_____. *Weaving Inkle Bands.* Shuttle Craft Guild Monograph #27. Santa Ana, Cal.: HTH Publishers, 1969.

Torrico Prado, Benjamin. *Indígenas en el Corazon de America.* La Paz, Bolivia: Los Amigos del Libro, 1971.

Zéndegui, Guillermo de. *Folk Arts of the Americas.* Washington, D.C.: General Secretariat, Organization of the American States, November–December 1973.

_____. *Image of Bolivia.* Washington, D.C.: General Secretariat, Organization of the American States, October 1973.

Index

Edited by Jennifer Place
Designed by Bob Fillie
Set in Times Roman by Gerard Associates/Graphic Arts Inc.
Printed and bound by Interstate Book Manufacturers
Color printed by Lehigh Press Lithographers